Future Directions for Inclusive Teacher Education

Are teachers ready for inclusion? What is appropriate teacher education?

Traditional approaches to inclusive education focused on learners with disabilities. Modern approaches, however, conceptualize inclusion in terms of providing educational equity and equality of access for all students within the same regular school system.

Future Directions for Inclusive Teacher Education provides a wealth of ideas about how to support teachers to become inclusive through applying positive training approaches. Written by some of the most influential internationally acknowledged experts in teacher education for inclusion and highly experienced researchers, together the authors provide a plethora of ideas for teacher educators to ensure that their training is pertinent, accessible, and futures-orientated.

This up-to-date and accessible book combines three key areas related to teacher education for inclusion, which provide:

*   A review of what is happening across the globe by offering examples from different regions;
*   Preparation for teachers to support learners with a range of diverse needs including disability, poverty, ethnicity, gender, cultural diversity, learning disabilities, autism spectrum disorder, sensory impairments, and those who are considered gifted and talented;
*   A consideration of systemic approaches, policy, and partnerships, and how these can be better employed in the future.

This highly topical text will support all teaching professionals, educational systems, and schools in their transformation of inclusive teacher education.

Chris Forlin is Professor of Special and Inclusive Education, Hong Kong Institute of Education.

Future Directions for Inclusive Teacher Education

An international perspective

Edited by Chris Forlin

Routledge
Taylor & Francis Group

LONDON AND NEW YORK

First published 2012
by Routledge
2 Park Square, Milton Park, Abingdon, Oxon OX14 4RN

Simultaneously published in the USA and Canada
by Routledge
711 Third Avenue, New York, NY 10017

Routledge is an imprint of the Taylor & Francis Group, an informa business

British Library Cataloguing in Publication Data
A catalogue record for this book is available from the British Library

Library of Congress Cataloging in Publication Data
    Future directions for inclusive teacher education : an international perspective /
    edited by Chris Forlin.
    p. cm.
    Includes index.
    1. Teachers—Training of. 2. Inclusive education. I. Forlin, Chris.
    LB1707.F88 2012
    370.71'1—dc23
    2011051369

ISBN: 978-0-415-51899-4 (hbk)
ISBN: 978-0-415-51900-7 (pbk)
ISBN: 978-0-203-11358-5 (ebk)

Typeset in Bembo & GillSans
by Swales & Willis Ltd, Exeter, Devon, UK

MIX
Paper from
responsible sources
FSC® C004839

Printed and bound in Great Britain by
CPI Group (UK) Ltd, Croydon, CR0 4YY

Contents

Figures

Tables

Contributors

Gilada Avissar is a Senior Lecturer and Researcher at the Beit Berl Academic Teacher Training College in Israel. Her areas of interest and research include curriculum with regard to inclusive education, teacher education for inclusion and professional development of teacher educators. She has published in Israeli as well as international journals and is co-editor of an Israeli professional journal. Email: gavisar@beitberl.ac.il.

Jayne Brady is a Research Fellow of the Capacity-Building Programme at UNESCO IBE, Geneva. She holds an LLB from Edinburgh University, and a master's degree in international studies and international law from the Graduate Institute of International and Development Studies, Geneva. She has taught in Europe, North Africa and Asia. Her research explores the legal right to education, educational policy and curriculum issues. Email: jayne_brady@hotmail.com.

Verity Donnelly is Project Manager with the European Agency for Development in Special Needs Education. She holds a PhD in Education, a BEd in Special Education, and a diploma in management. She is currently working on the Agency Teacher Education for Inclusion project and the Inclusive Education in Action project with UNESCO. Email: verity@european-agency.org.

Leana Duncombe is a Consultant for the Capacity-Building Programme at UNESCO IBE, Geneva. She holds a BA (Hons) in international development from McGill University, and a master's degree in international affairs from the Graduate Institute of International and Development Studies, Geneva. Her research has focused on girls' and women's right to education, as well as educational policy. She has taught in both early childhood education and adult education settings. Email: leana.duncombe@graduateinstitute.ch.

David Evans is Associate Professor of Special Education at the University of Sydney. He teaches and researches in the area of quality inclusive education programs for students with special needs. Email: david.evans@sydney.edu.au.

Lani Florian is Professor of Social and Educational Inclusion at the University of Aberdeen (UK) working with colleagues on the reform of initial teacher education programmes for inclusion. She is Scotland's national expert on the European Agency for Development of Special Needs Education multinational study, "Teacher Education for Inclusion". Recently, she co-authored "Preparing general educators to improve outcomes for students with disabilities", a White Paper commissioned by the American Association of Colleges of Teacher Education and National Council for Learning Disabilities. Email: l.florian@abdn.ac.uk.

Chris Forlin is Professor of Special and Inclusive Education at the Hong Kong Institute of Education. She has published extensively on research in this area, particularly in reference to preparing teachers for inclusion. She consults internationally on curriculum and pedagogy for inclusive practice. Email: cforlin@ied.edu.hk.

Becky Francis is Professor of Education and Social Justice at King's College London, and is currently seconded part-time to Pearson where she directs their UK centre for education policy. Becky's academic expertise and extensive publications center on social identities (gender, "race" and social class) in educational contexts, social identity and educational achievement, and feminist theory. Email: Becky.Francis@rsa.org.uk.

Michael M. Gerber is Professor of Education in the Education Department of the Gevirtz Graduate School of Education, University of California, Santa Barbara. He is a member of the faculty for the Special Education, Disabilities, and Risk Studies Emphasis and immediate past president of the Division for Learning Disabilities, Council for Exceptional Children. Email: mgerber@education.ucsb.edu.

Wayne Hammond is President of Resiliency Initiatives and holds an adjunct status with the School of Medicine at the University of Calgary, Alberta Canada. He has published on the development of a resiliency framework and strengths-based model of evaluation. He is an active lecturer with regard to the implications of strength-based practice for mental health concerns and intervention practice. Email: wh@resil.ca.

Nur Aishah Hanun is Manager of the Childcare and Education Centre at the National Child Development Research Centre (NCDRC) in Sultan Idris Education University (UPSI). She has extensive experience in early childhood care and education and is an active advocate of resiliency for children within a wide spectrum of development. Email: nuraishah@upsi.edu.my or nuraishahhanun@yahoo.com.

Fuk-chuen Ho is Assistant Professor of Special and Inclusive Education at the Hong Kong Institute of Education. His research interests are reading and writing problems, autism spectrum disorders, and professional development for teachers of students with special needs. Email: fcho@ied.edu.hk.

Ming-tak Hue is Associate Professor in the Department of Special Education and Counselling at the Hong Kong Institute of Education. He teaches graduate courses in school guidance and inclusive education. He is interested in pastoral care, ethnic minority education, and the development of school-based guidance and discipline programmes. Email: mthue@ied.edu.hk.

Haniz Ibrahim is an Associate Professor in Special Education teaching at Sultan Idris Education University in Malaysia. He was attached to the Malaysian Ministry of Education Special Education Department before joining the university and was involved in formulating national policies in Special Education. Email: haniz@fppm.upsi.edu.my.

Kamarulzaman Kamaruddin is Professor of Educational Psychology and Child Development at the Sultan Idris Education University (UPSI). He has published extensively on research in this area, particularly in reference to preparing teachers in special education. He is an active lecturer with regard to the implications on causes and risk factors for abnormal behaviour concerns and treatments. Email: kamarulzaman@fppm.upsi.edu.my.

Pennee Kantavong is an Associate Professor in International and Development Education at the Faculty of Education, Khon Kaen University, Thailand. She has conducted research on inclusive education continuously. Her interest is in helping primary school teachers to develop skills for helping students with special needs in the inclusive classroom. Email: pennee@kku.ac.th.

Gwang-jo Kim is Director of UNESCO Office in Bangkok since 2009. He served as South Korea's Deputy-Minister of Education and Human Resources Development from 2005 to 2008. As educational and social policy advisor to former President Young Sam Kim (1995–1997), he played a key role in the planning of the nationwide education reform initiative "531 Education Reform", aimed at restructuring the entire Korean education system. Email: gj.kim@unesco.org.

Sin-yee Law is the Course Consultant of the Attachment Program for the in-service teacher education course for inclusion. She started promoting integrated education in Hong Kong in 1989 by teaching pertinent modules for initial teacher education courses. She is currently involved in a Macau policy research on inclusive education. Email: anghon@ied.edu.hk.

Johan Lindeberg joined UNESCO Bangkok as Associate Expert, and was later appointed as Programme Specialist during which he managed UNESCO's regional activities in inclusive education, human rights and multi-lingual education. He served as resource person in various regional conferences covering these areas and helped organize the international conference on "Language, Education and the Millennium Development Goals" in Bangkok in November 2010. He returned to Sweden in early 2011. Email: jlindeberg@hotmail.com.

Cathy Little is Lecturer of Special Education at the University of Sydney. She has extensive experience in working with students with an autism spectrum disorder and in the design and delivery of teacher education programs in the area of Special and Inclusive Education. Email: cathy.little@sydney.edu.au.

Pattie Yuk-yee Luk-Fong is Adjunct Associate Professor in the Department of Special Education and Counselling at the Hong Kong Institute of Education. She specializes and researches in areas such as school guidance, personal and social education, globalization and hybridities, gender identities and family changes. Email: yyluk@ied.edu.hk.

Olli-Pekka Malinen is a PhD candidate at the University of Eastern Finland. He is preparing his thesis in an international comparative research project on teachers' roles in inclusive education in China, Finland, South Africa, Slovenia, Lithuania and the United Kingdom. In the project he is mainly involved in research conducted in mainland China and Finland. Email: olli-pekka.malinen@uef.fi.

Lawrence Mundia teaches educational psychology in the Hassanal Bolkiah Institute of Education at the University of Brunei Darussalam. His main research interests are in psychological assessment, educational testing, special education, and school guidance and counselling. Recently, students with mental health problems have received more research consideration, attention and priority. Email: lawrence.mundia@ubd.edu.bn.

Renato Opertti is a Programme Specialist and coordinator of the Capacity-Building Programme at UNESCO IBE, Geneva. He holds a master's degree in educational research and sociology. He has coordinated several educational programmes in Uruguay at the ministerial level, and has worked as an international consultant for ECLA, UNESCO, UNICEF and the World Bank. He has published numerous studies on social policy, educational policies and curriculum issues. Email: r.opertti@unesco.org.

Humberto Rodríguez is a Director and Professor at Escuela Normal de Especialización in Monterrey, México, which trains Special Education Teachers, and leads a Master Degree Programme on Inclusive Education, under the auspices of the Department of Education. He has experience in teacher preparation programs, inclusive education and curricula design. Email: hrodriguezh@enehrl.edu.mx.

Karen B. Rogers is Professor of Gifted Studies, Curriculum and Instruction at the University of St Thomas, Minneapolis. She has published extensively on research with gifted learners, particularly in matching programs to the child's needs. She consults broadly with schools, parents and community groups on inclusion of gifted learners. Email: kbrogers@stthomas.edu.

Martyn Rouse is Professor Emeritus at the University of Aberdeen where previously he held the Chair in Social and Educational Inclusion and was the Director of the Inclusive Practice Project. He has extensive international research and has published widely on the impact of school reform legislation on the education of children with special needs. Email: m.rouse@abdn.ac.uk.

Hannu Savolainen is a Professor of Special Education at the University of Eastern Finland and is currently involved in a project researching and implementing inclusive education practices in Finland. He has recently published on teachers' perceptions on inclusive education and the social and academic outcomes of learning difficulties in late adolescence. Email: hannu.savolainen@uef.fi.

Kuen-fung Sin is the Director of the Centre for Special Needs and Studies in Inclusive Education at the Hong Kong Institute of Education. He coordinates a number of courses on inclusion. He has a wide range of consultancy on special needs and inclusion in Hong Kong, Macau and Mainland China. Email: kfsin@ ied.edu.hk.

Christine Skelton is Professor of Gender Equality in Education at the University of Birmingham, UK. She has published widely on male teachers and primary schooling. Christine has also researched into gender and under/achievement and contributed to the government publications on "Gender and Education – Mythbusters" and "Gender Issues in Schools". Email: c.skelton@bham.ac.uk.

Kathleen Tait is a registered psychologist and Associate Professor at the Hong Kong Baptist University. She has published widely in the areas of physical, developmental and intellectual disabilities. Dr. Tait actively researches and consults in: functional communication, applied behaviour analysis, functional life-skills, and inclusive teacher education in international settings. Email: ktait@ hkbu.edu.hk.

Wilma Vialle is Professor of Education, specializing in gifted education, at the University of Wollongong. She has published extensively on her research with gifted learners. She works closely with preservice and practicing teachers on inclusive practices that engage and extend gifted learners in the school system. Email: wvialle@uow.edu.au.

Amanda Watkins is Assistant Director of the European Agency for Development in Special Needs Education, responsible for project implementation. Holding a PhD and an MA in Education, and a BEd in Special Education, she has co-ordinated international projects on teacher education for inclusion, and mapping the implementation of policy for inclusive education. With UNESCO IITE, she recently completed a practice review on ICT in education for people with disabilities. Email: amanda@european-agency.org.

Jia-cheng Xu is Dean and Professor of Special Education at Beijing Union University. He is director of the Committee of Rehabilitation for People with Intellectual Disability as part of China's Association of Rehabilitation for People with Disabilities, and Vice Chairman of Chinese Association of Rehabilitation for People with Disabilities. Email: xujiacheng123@263.net.

Editorial board

All chapters in the text have been peer reviewed by two academics or practitioners in the field of teacher education for special and/or inclusive education. These reviewers formed the editorial board for this text.

Foreword

In December 2010 the *Global Round Table 'Teacher Education for Inclusive Education'* was hosted by the Hong Kong Institute of Education. Teacher educators, researchers and policy makers from across the world used the occasion to continue the debate about how teacher education might address some of the challenges in creating more equitable schooling systems. This book is the result of those conversations. As the chapters in the book suggest, the challenges are substantial. Across the world, national systems of education are struggling to meet the aspirations of the United Nations Education for All (EFA) agenda. EFA is an essential element in achieving the Millennium Development Goals, not only because education is seen as being crucial to human and social development, but also because more than 70 million children currently do not have access to education (UNESCO, 2011).

Many children are at risk of not attending school, or of receiving a sub-standard education. There are many reasons why children do not attend school, including high levels of mobility, conflict, child labour, poverty, gender and disability. In some parts of the world, schooling is not available because of a shortage of school places, a lack of quality teachers, or because schools are too far from where children live. Sometimes families choose not to send their children to school because of fears about safety and security, the poor quality of the schooling that is available, or because of the economic costs. Such costs include school fees, having to buy uniforms, books and materials, and so-called 'opportunity costs' that arise when young people are not economically active because they are in school. In some countries families are forced into a 'cost–benefit' analysis and they decide that the benefits of sending their children to school do not outweigh the costs. Clearly this raises questions about variability in the quality of provision, which is associated with the availability and quality of teachers. In turn, the quality of teachers is associated with their status and the ways in which they are prepared and supported.

Access to quality education is important because of the power of education to reduce poverty, to improve the lives of individuals and groups, and to transform societies. Developing 'schools for all' is crucial because schooling is linked to human, economic and social development goals. Education is not only a fundamental human right; it is the means through which other important human rights can be achieved. But at the same time, it is apparent that many school systems perpetuate existing inequalities and intergenerational underachievement. The reasons for this are complex, but it is often associated with deeply embedded attitudes to, and beliefs about, human differences. Failure to develop schools capable of educating all children not only leads to an educational underclass, but also a social and economic underclass which has serious consequences for society now and in the future. Dealing with exclusion, marginalisation and underachievement, whilst difficult, is not only the right thing to do, it makes sound economic and social sense. Therefore, the development of successful inclusive schools, 'schools for all' in which the learning and participation of all children is valued, is an essential task for all countries. It is hardly surprising, therefore, that tackling underachievement and increasing inclusion are part of a worldwide agenda.

In recent years the concept of educational inclusion has widened, moving beyond disability and special educational needs to incorporate broader issues of social inclusion. There is now greater awareness of the exclusionary pressures associated with migration, mobility, language, ethnicity and intergenerational poverty. The reciprocal links between poor health, poverty, disability, special needs and underachievement are now clearer, but these links manifest themselves differently in different places and at different times, for historical, cultural and policy reasons.

Barriers to learning and participation for some children arise from institutional structures, inflexible or irrelevant curricula, inappropriate systems of assessment and examination and negative attitudes, together with negative beliefs about some children's worth and ability to learn. Even in so-called 'well-schooled' countries, not all children are in school and even when they are, not all have positive experiences, nor do they have much to show for their time in school. Most school systems have children who are excluded, who do not participate in meaningful learning, or who underachieve, giving a new impetus to the call for more inclusive education and for improving the ways in which teachers are prepared to work with all children (Florian and Rouse, 2009).

Inclusion was the theme of the United Nations Educational, Scientific and Cultural Organization (UNESCO) 48th International Conference on Education (UNESCO-IBE, 2008). The recommendations of the conference stressed the importance of preparing and supporting teachers to work in inclusive ways, an objective that has been embraced by many governments as a strategy for improving access and equity. It would seem that there is widespread acknowledgement that teachers play a crucial role in providing high quality education, especially for children who experience difficulties in learning. Indeed, it is argued that the barriers to inclusive education are exacerbated by inadequate preparation of teachers, particularly in the area of 'special educational needs' and for working in inclusive schools (Forlin, 2001). But criticisms of the ways in which teachers are educated are not new. Preparing teachers for inclusive education has been a longstanding but elusive goal of teacher education, especially in countries where special education teachers are prepared separately in their initial training. In many countries, there is separate certification and accreditation for teachers preparing to work in special education; in other countries there is not the same requirement, in part because having a separate cadre of special teachers is seen as a barrier to inclusion because it absolves the rest of the education system from taking responsibility for all children's learning. Nevertheless, the absence of separate routes and certification does not mean that teachers trained to work in regular schools are well prepared to teach all the children who they will meet in their classrooms.

For many years there has been a debate about what all teachers need to know and should be able to do in response to children's difficulties in learning (Forlin, 2010; Rouse, 2008). Internationally, criticisms of ways in which teachers are prepared to work in inclusive schools have two distinct, but often overlapping, strands. First, there are those who claim that there is a specific body of knowledge and a set of skills for working with 'special' children and that initial training courses do not adequately cover these matters (Hodkinson, 2005) and beginning teachers do not have the necessary knowledge, skills and attitudes to carry out this work in inclusive schools (Forlin, 2001). The second argument (Slee, 2001) claims that because inclusion is not only about 'special' children, teacher education should focus on improving teaching and learning and should help young teachers to reduce the barriers to learning and participation. The argument here is that the elective modules on special education in initial teacher education courses that are taken by some students only reinforce the sense of separation that characterises special education and leads to the belief that such children are the responsibility only of those who have undertaken specialist courses.

Both these views are right to an extent, but they are also insufficient in helping to articulate what might be required to address the challenges of creating inclusive schools. A new way of thinking about the problem is required which does not deny human differences, but attempts to respond to difference within what is ordinarily available in schools rather than by marking some children as different (Florian, 2007). It is important to move beyond the debate about whether beginning teachers only need to know how to improve teaching and learning or whether they need more specialist knowledge about disability and children's learning needs. In the short time that student teachers are in initial training it is impossible to anticipate every type of difficulty they might meet in their professional lives. The task of initial teacher education is to prepare people to enter a profession, which accepts individual and collective responsibility for improving the learning and participation of *all* children. Therefore any debate about teachers' professional learning has to take a career-long perspective.

There have been some attempts to restructure the curriculum of initial teacher education so that issues of difference and diversity are infused throughout the programme, but very few institutions have radically reformed their programmes using the principles of universal design to ensure that inclusion is an essential element that is addressed throughout the programme with the intention of improving and extending what is generally available (Florian and Rouse, 2009). Similarly there is an urgent need to look at how teachers might be supported throughout their careers by providing opportunities for coherent professional development. Crucially, there is an urgent need to build an evidential base, not only to ensure developments in the field are incremental, but also to defend teacher education from the more extreme views of politicians and policy makers who want to undermine the long struggle to enhance the status of teachers and teaching. Too many reforms of teacher education have taken place with no research into their consequences. Without evidence that teacher education makes a difference to children's learning and participation, the whole enterprise is vulnerable to those who seek simple and inexpensive solutions to complex problems.

The chapters in this book present different ways of dealing with the challenges of preparing teachers to work in schools for all. The various contributions provide a range of insights into challenges that are faced and the diverse ways that different regions have addressed these. The organisers of the Round Table have brought together a wide variety of perspectives, and they are to be congratulated on including voices from countries and parts of the world that are underrepresented in the international literature on teacher education and inclusion. As the contributions to this book demonstrate, we have much to learn from each other.

Martyn Rouse
Professor Emeritus, University of Aberdeen, United Kingdom

References

Florian, L. (ed.) (2007) "Reimagining special education", *The SAGE Handbook of Special Education*, London: Sage.

Florian, L. and Rouse, M. (2009) "The inclusive practice project in Scotland: Teacher education for inclusive education", *Teaching and Teacher Education*, 25(4): 594–601.

Forlin, C. (2001) "Inclusion: Identifying potential stressors for regular class teachers", *Educational Research*, 43(3): 235–45.

Forlin, C. (ed.) (2010) *Teacher Education for Inclusion: Changing Paradigms and Innovative Approaches*, London: Routledge.

Hodkinson, A. J. (2005) "Conceptions and misconceptions of inclusive education: A critical examination of final year teacher trainees' knowledge and understanding of inclusion", *International Journal of Research in Education*, 73: 15–29.

Rouse, M. (2008) "Developing inclusive practice: A role for teacher education?", *Education in the North*, 16: 6–13.

Slee, R. (2001) "Inclusion in practice: Does practice make perfect?", *Educational Review*, 53(2): 113–23.

UNESCO, United Nations Educational, Scientific and Cultural Organization (2011) *Education for All: Global Monitoring Report*, Paris: UNESCO.

UNESCO-IBE, United Nations Educational, Scientific and Cultural Organization, International Bureau of Education (2008) *Conclusions and Recommendations of the 48th Session of the International Conference on Education (ED/BIE/CONFINTED 48/5)*, Geneva: UNESCO-IBE.

Preface

> If I am walking with two other men, each of them will serve as my teacher. I will pick out the good points of the one and imitate them and the bad points of the other and correct them in myself.
>
> (Confucius)

As educators, the best innovative ideas are often born from experience. Combining these with creative new approaches provides the best medium within which to cultivate the type of teacher education that will meet the needs of the next generation of teachers.

Teachers' work is based on a personally developed philosophy that is informed by their own background and schooling experiences, layered by tertiary level education, and refined by extensive practice. Teacher educators have no direct control over a teacher's prior experience, but they have considerable influence on the preparation they provide them to become effective inclusive practitioners.

Effective teacher educators are both reflective and future focused. Adopting the philosophical understandings from those of the past, the best practices from the present and by critically evaluating potential options for the future, a relevant teacher education program that will form the foundation of training for the next decade can be constructed.

This book shares insights into the multiplicity of current practices for teacher education by adopting a global perspective on the preparation of teachers for inclusion and focusing on future directions for improvement. The first section of the book considers how a range of different regions have responded to the changed training needs of teachers. The second section reviews the various practices that are being employed throughout a selection of regions to assist teachers to cope with the changed school landscape and increased diversity of the student population. The final section of the book provides some pertinent perspectives about the type of training that is perceived as essential for the future development of inclusive teachers. This book can be seen as a sequel to *Teacher Education for Inclusion: Changing Paradigms and Innovative Approaches* (Forlin, 2010), which focused on innovative programs being implemented in different institutions internationally and *Reform,*

Inclusion and Teacher Education: Towards a New Era of Special Education in the Asia-Pacific Region (Forlin and Lian, 2008) which was centered specifically around the changes within the Asia–Pacific region.

In the first chapter in each section I provide an overview of the topic to be discussed, drawing wherever possible from regions other than those explored in detail within individual chapters. These sectional introductory chapters provide the link for the remaining chapters in each section. They also aim to bring the book together to form a cohesive dialogue informed by current practices globally but focused on future directions for teacher education for inclusion.

Section I: Global perspectives on teacher education for inclusion

> One test of the correctness of educational procedure is the happiness of the child.
>
> (Maria Montessori)

The first section of the book reviews existing international practices for teacher education and the different approaches to be found between and even within jurisdictions. While the regions represented have initiated some form of teacher training for inclusion, the authors concede that this is insufficient to meet the demands to educate all teachers about the inclusive process. Each region similarly reports that negative attitudes of teachers still prevail and that in all instances more work is needed to improve the preparation of teachers for inclusion.

This section commences with a broad coverage of key issues associated with teacher education for inclusion. Chapter 1 explores the impact of inclusion on the training needs of teachers and identifies three major challenges faced internationally in relation to political agendas, maintaining equity, and the role of universities. Examples are drawn from an eclectic range of regions which portray the different directions taken and how the challenges of teacher education for inclusion have been met.

In Chapter 2 the current climate in Malaysia is reviewed by Haniz Ibrahim. Although inclusion has been promoted for the past 15 years in Malaysia, Ibrahim suggests that there are still many challenges with including all learners. A major issue is that of teacher attitudes. These are considered to be quite negative, with regular teachers who have not been trained for inclusion still expressing grave fears and anxiety and a strong reluctance to include learners with special needs.

The movement towards inclusion in Thailand has experienced similar difficulties. Pennee Kantavong explores the changing expectations for Thailand's schools and teachers in Chapter 3. Even though promoted by the Thai Government, inclusion is still not an accepted concept by many schools. In many ways Kantavong suggests that the slow inclusive movement is due not only to a lack of resources and negative attitudes, but also to a lack of suitably qualified teachers who can provide appropriate services and overcome what she considers outdated practices. Limited early identification or suitable intervention programs, inequitable access to education for different socioeconomic groups, and a lack of a common understanding of inclusion or strategic leadership in schools are all compounded by regular teachers' lack of appropriate knowledge and skills.

With similar challenges faced by China, Jia-cheng Xu explicates three developmental stages that teachers have progressed through as China embodies a model of "learning in regular class" to implement inclusion. In Chapter 4, Xu explains the initial voluntary or free phase of teacher education where no formal training requirements existed. This was followed by the conscious stage, whereby regular class teachers were provided with basic school-based training on inclusion. The final stage is what Xu describes as the "insert" stage when universities began offering specialized training. He acknowledges, though, that while this is meeting the training needs of some teachers, very few universities have adopted this approach and actual demands for training heavily outweigh the availability of courses.

Teacher education for inclusion in Israel, similar to Thailand, Malaysia and China, focuses on preparing teachers to work in a dual system of regular and special schools. The major difference is that in Israel inclusion has been practiced more extensively for nearly 20 years and that teacher education about inclusion is now mandated for all initial training courses. Gilada Avissar reviews the mosaic of models that have thus been developed to meet these mandated requirements and focuses on three approaches in detail in Chapter 5.

Akin to the earlier support of inclusion in Israel, the expansion of support for learners with special educational needs within a comprehensive educational system in Finland has undergone a major national level overhaul in the past five years. Olli-Pekka Malinen and Hannu Savolainen explore in Chapter 6 how as part of this educational reform teacher education for inclusion needs a greater emphasis on the education of regular teachers rather than the dominant reliance on special educators to meet the needs of learners with special educational needs.

Unlike other regions which have been practicing inclusion for several decades, Negara Brunei Darussalam aligns more with those which are gradually adopting more inclusive practices in recent years. Kathleen Tait and Lawrence Mundia utilize their personal experiences of teacher education in this region to review in Chapter 7 how teacher training programs have undergone several major recent reforms in Negara Brunei Darussalam and to identify the challenges that remain to ensure an equitable educational system for all learners.

Chapter 8 is the last in this section and Michael Gerber uses this to review teacher education in the USA which is where the first Public Law on the education of children with handicaps (sic) emerged. After nearly three decades of promoting and adopting integrated, or more recently, inclusive practices, he acknowledges that there is now a presence of comparable content across the States for teacher education for preparing teachers for inclusion. He also stresses, though, that there is still little empirical evidence and a dearth of research that links the content taught in preparation courses to the implementation of effective inclusive practice. Gerber discusses a number of influences on the preparation of teachers for inclusion in the

USA. He highlights the importance of teacher educators explicitly preparing both regular and special educators to employ cooperative learning strategies for evaluating their own practices to ensure meaningful inclusion.

Section 2: Diversity and its challenges

> The function of education is to teach one to think intensively and to think critically. Intelligence plus character – that is the goal of true education.
>
> (Martin Luther King, Jr.)

The second section of the book reviews teacher education from the perspective of preparing teachers to include learners who present with a range of learning needs. A broad approach is taken to review a sample of international practices that focus specifically on different aspects of diversity. Consideration is given to fostering both social and academic inclusion and to the role teacher educators must play in helping to prepare teachers to facilitate resilience for young people with disabilities.

As an introduction to this section in Chapter 9, a review is provided of what is guiding the change internationally towards inclusion and the development of competences and strategies required by teachers to support an inclusive approach. Three fundamental challenges are raised that are faced by schools that impact on a teacher's capacity to implement an inclusive pedagogy. The focus on how teachers can find time to support individual learners within the "crowded curriculum"; how to support learners who are marginalized due to cultural differences or socioeconomic status; and the development of positive attitudes towards inclusion. These are linked to the importance for regional approaches that can be contextualized for local training needs.

Learning to embrace diversity is explored in Chapter 10 by Gwang-jo Kim and Johan Lindeberg. Drawing from various programs and activities of UNESCO, they describe the importance of teacher education for inclusion and provide some suggestions as to how to achieve this. This chapter is underpinned by the right to education for all children as the foundation of an inclusive education system. Four dimensions of this right to education, namely, availability, accessibility, acceptability, and adaptability, are proposed, to ensure quality education for all learners.

In Chapter 11, Humberto Rodríguez identifies seven essential components that are necessary for effective teacher preparation for inclusion. While based on his extensive work in Mexico from which he includes practical examples for implementation, these are equally applicable to other areas as they encompass global perspectives of inclusion. By combining federally mandated teacher education curricula with a complimentary program developed to address local needs, Rodríguez articulates a universal approach to better prepare inclusive teachers.

Whilst the center of attention for inclusion is usually on learners with special educational needs related to an academic, physical, or social difficulty, in Chapter 12 Wilma Vialle and Karen Rogers raise the importance of also preparing teachers to cater for the needs of learners at the other end of the spectrum who have been identified as "gifted". They propose a strong argument for including "gifted-ness" in teacher preparation courses to ensure that teachers accept responsibility for educating gifted students. Acknowledging that preservice teachers tend to have more positive attitudes towards including gifted learners, they suggest that this does not necessarily predispose them to employ evidence-based strategies for supporting gifted students' development.

Further to the training of pedagogical skills for inclusive teachers, Ming-Tak Hue also suggests that teacher education must include three dimensions of preparation in school guidance and counseling. In Chapter 13 Hue discusses the importance of preparing teachers in developing inclusive counseling strategies; inclusive strategies for behaviour management; and in dealing with the impacts of the wider education system. Hue provides a range of practical strategies and stresses the importance of working collaboratively with professional organizations to ensure effective teacher preparation.

Preparing teachers to support gender equity is an issue raised by Becky Francis, Pattie Yuk-yee Luk-Fong and Christine Skelton in Chapter 14. Discussing gender discrepancy in the two contexts of the UK and Hong Kong, they unravel some of the myths surrounding the underachievement of boys. They propose that the com-plexities associated with avoiding projecting trends to stereotype particular students need to be carefully explored during teacher preparation courses to ensure that new graduates are able to deliver inclusive gender equitable practices for their students.

The importance of preparing teachers to facilitate the social inclusion of students as well as catering for their academic learning needs is explored by Cathy Little and David Evans in Chapter 15. Though conceding that many teacher preparation programs emphasize social constructivist pedagogy and schools are likewise domi-nated by the social constructivist model, they reaffirm that it is the responsibility of all teachers to create environments that are conducive to developing positive social interactions. They recommend that it is consequently the responsibility of teacher educators to ensure that teacher preparation courses provide the necessary skills to enable teachers to facilitate this.

In Chapter 16, Fuk-chuen Ho explores the importance of supplementing theo-retical and university-based training for teachers with practice and authentic oppor-tunities to implement newly acquired skills. By employing a collaborative model of professional learning Ho suggests that a field-based mode of training can strengthen theoretical learning input. The approach he articulates incorporates new knowl-edge into existing practice by developing a sense of community among teachers through collaboration, reflection, and open dialogue.

The final Chapter 17 in this section reviews the role of teachers in helping vul-nerable students within inclusive settings. Nur Aishah Hanun, Wayne Hammond and Kamarulzaman Kamaruddin focus on the importance of evaluating areas of concern for building resiliency in potentially disadvantaged youths. By employ-ing a resiliency framework to understand the key components that contribute to resiliency development in children, they propose that teachers can be guided to better prepare students to enable them to function in society. They suggest that understanding the resiliency processes is essential if teachers are to be able to effect inclusive practices for the most vulnerable children.

Section 3: Future directions: What is needed now?

> Education is a human right with immense power to transform. On its foundation rest the cornerstones of freedom, democracy and sustainable human development.
>
> (Kofi Annan)

The final section of the book aims to explore a way forward for advancing teacher education for inclusion, by reviewing some of the fundamental challenges faced by teacher educators and by providing examples of opportunities for change. Many of these chapters are informed by major national and international Conventions and policy about the rights of all learners to an inclusive educational experience.

Framed by an initial review of the current transformative role for teachers, Chapter 18 commences by identifying two conflicting spheres of influence related to equity and accountability that impact on preparing teachers for inclusion. An "*Inclusive Wheel*" model is proposed as a metaphor for the interactive nature of inclusion and the way to keep the teacher training agenda for inclusion moving forward.

The second chapter in this section reviews the impact of the 48th UNESCO International Conference on Education on informing future directions for teacher education for inclusion. In Chapter 19 Renato Opertti, Jayne Brady and Leana Duncombe explore issues surrounding the importance of equipping teachers with the appropriate competences and tools to teach all learners and the significant role teachers play in developing inclusive curricula. Education reform is considered as an important aspect of preparing teachers for inclusion and they propose that expectations and recommendations regarding the role of teachers must embody greater consideration of the principles of inclusive curricular reform.

Amanda Watkins and Verity Donnelly utilize Article 24 of the *United Nations Convention on the Rights of People with Disabilities* as a means of informing their discussion in Chapter 20. They review the key recommendations within this Convention for the need for the training of all teachers in inclusive practices and they raise some of the challenges posed across the different educational systems within Europe. A project on the development of a profile of inclusive teachers is enunciated, highlighting how they set out to address two questions related to what kind of teachers we need for an inclusive society in a twenty-first century school, and what are the essential teacher competences for inclusive education.

In response to the need for intensive upskilling of teachers about inclusive education Kuen-fung Sin and Sin-yee Law discuss in Chapter 21 a major training program that was initiated nationwide by an education system in order to provide relevant training for teachers. Recognizing that traditional models of teacher education have become outdated, they propose an Institute–School–Community partnership of teacher education for addressing current and future training needs.

The final Chapter 22 in the book provides a synthesis of the reflections of 86 teacher educators from a range of widely different regions about future directions for teacher education for inclusion. These teacher educators all participated in a *Global Round Table* held at the Hong Kong Institute of Education in December 2010, convened specifically to debate this critical issue. Commencing by recognizing the multiple interpretations and the difficult and complex issues associated with preparing teachers for inclusion, Lani Florian sets out to map a course for addressing some of the challenges and conflicting demands frequently cited as key difficulties for teacher educators. The final discussion is firmly embedded in the need for a much stronger research agenda upon which to formulate the future training needs of teachers.

Inclusive education has changed the professionalism of teaching in a fundamental and significant manner, which undeniably impacts on the role of teachers in unprecedented ways. This change simultaneously imposes a duty on teacher educators to ensure that the programs they offer are doing more than providing discipline knowledge; but that they are really meeting the needs of teachers faced with heterogeneous classes in a rapidly changing techno-social world.

When looking forward to the direction teacher education should take for the future, decisions require a close and detailed appraisal of practices both globally and locally, as any program for the future must use its current practices as a starting point for change. Clearly, approaches taken will vary enormously between regions based upon different cultures, social norms, societal expectations, financial status, leadership and governance, stability, sense of citizenship, commitment to reform, empathy, and a willingness to engage with an ideology of equity for all.

This book aims to assist individuals and education systems in their transformation of teacher education by providing the reader with a wide array of alternative approaches that may be considered for supporting the training of effective inclusive practitioners. Even though it is possible to read and to absorb a range of innovative ideas from these teacher educators, with respect to the final exploration for a decision about the way forward within your own region bear in mind what Julius Caesar said: "*Experience is the teacher of all things*".

Chris Forlin

References

Forlin, C. (ed.) (2010) *Teacher Education for Inclusion: Changing Paradigms and Innovative Approaches*, New York: Routledge.

Forlin, C. and Lian, J. (eds) (2008) *Reform, Inclusion and Teacher Education: Towards a New Era of Special Education in the Asia-Pacific Region*, New York: Routledge.

Part I

Global perspectives on teacher education for inclusion

Chapter 1

Responding to the need for inclusive teacher education
Rhetoric or reality?

Chris Forlin

Keywords: inclusion, rights, ethics, international, teacher, teacher educators, politics, curriculum, legislation

Chapter overview

The focus of this chapter will be on a broad coverage of the key issues associated with teacher education for inclusion. In particular, it will concentrate on the impact of inclusion on the role of teachers and the need for better teacher education to support them. There is considerable variation in international approaches to preparing teachers for becoming inclusive practitioners. Examples will be drawn from different regions to indicate how systems are responding to the urgent need for better training to address the increasingly diverse classrooms that teachers need to work in. It is acknowledged that teacher education for inclusion, though, has such enormous variation between and within countries, regions and states, that this can only be a relatively cursory summary of some of the issues which would seem to be global concerns at present.

Introduction

Teacher education for inclusion has become an important debate that has resulted in some positive outcomes by way of forwarding the agenda for deliberating on existing programs and planning changes that better meet the new training needs of teachers. Some systems are actively involved in re-evaluating existing training models by developing and trialing new approaches through greater collaboration between training institutions and schools (Florian and Rouse, 2011). Others have legislated at state level minimum requirements for initial teacher training, and training institutions are required to register to ensure they meet these requirements. In some systems, such as in the UK and US, post initial training is a requirement for newly qualified teachers to upscale during their first few years of teaching. Yet there are still numerous regions where teacher education has not yet changed to accommodate the need to work in progressively more diverse classrooms.

There are many factors that interact in the development of teacher education for preparing teachers to work in an inclusive school. In response to global pressures, regions are keen to be seen to be adopting international conventions that focus on equity and education for all students. Many new policies and legislation have, thus, appeared that replicate the terminology of these global directives and expect schools to become inclusive, and teachers to adopt inclusive pedagogies (Donnelly and Watkins, 2011). Nonetheless in numerous instances these are not reflected in the pragmatics of implementation. Under the guise of establishing an 'inclusive' educational system promoted by national edicts, local interpretation and implementation has in many instances been far from the original intention. Likewise, teacher education for inclusion in most regions has been tokenistic at best and non-existent at worst.

Generalist teachers are now required to be able to cater for the needs of the most diverse student populations both academically and socially. School populations world-wide include students with special educational needs such as a disability or learning difficulty but also have learners with an enormous range of other needs that can impact on their learning. These can include students from different social economic backgrounds, racial minorities, asylum seekers, refugees, and those who have mental health issues caused by internal or external influences, with many youngsters being completely disenfranchised with school. Alongside this enormous diversity of student needs, teachers are being held accountable for student outcomes in ways they have not been previously. There are many stakeholders who monitor the capacity of teachers to support all learners. Together with the emphasis on achievement which is frequently still measured by narrowly defined examination results, these all make teaching a very challenging and demanding job, and teacher preparation an extremely important role.

Three areas of key global importance in relation to teacher education will be discussed in greater detail. The first section will focus on inclusive education and include a review of the impact this has had on teachers and what we are preparing teachers for in the new millennium. The second section will consider the training needs of teachers, the challenges faced in providing authentic practice, and the role of teacher educators. The third section will conclude with a summary of three key challenges faced in teacher education for inclusion, namely, political implications; the competing forces of government v. private schooling; and the role of universities in preparing teachers for inclusion.

Inclusive education

Inclusion is seen by many as the most equitable and encompassing method for educating all children (Ainscow *et al.*, 2006). An international definition of inclusion that was provided as a Conference Resolution of the 'Return to Salamanca' conference (2009) stated that:

> We understand inclusive education to be a process where mainstream schools and early years settings are transformed so that all children/students are

supported to meet their academic and social potential and which involves removing barriers in environment, communication, curriculum, teaching, socialisation and assessment at all levels.

(Inclusion International, 2009)

Access to mainstream environments has improved for many children. Nevertheless insufficient training and a lack of resources to enable teachers to develop the appropriate mindset or attitude have been considered impediments to enabling full inclusion in many regions (Forlin, 2010; Watson, 2009). One of the biggest challenges for preparing teachers for inclusion is the enormous variation in the ways in which inclusion is defined. An earlier, widely acceptable designation was generally limited to the placement of children with disabilities into regular schools, either within the regular classroom or within a special resource class or center for part or all of the school day (Florian, 2009). In the past few years inclusion has gradually encompassed a much broader definition. It is commonly accepted internationally as meaning the placement of students with disabilities, learning difficulties, or other potentially marginalized groups into a regular school within the least restrictive environment so that no child is marginalized, alienated, shamed, embarrassed, rejected, or excluded. Inclusion should enable equitable participation in order for all students to achieve full potential in all aspects of education (Loreman, 2010). Inclusive education poses a duty upon schools to provide a curriculum that ensures all students are able to access an appropriate, relevant, and suitable education in order to reach their full potential. It further poses a duty on teacher training institutions to ensure that new teachers are effectively prepared to teach within inclusive classrooms.

Impact on teachers

In response to the earlier dual system of regular and special education, inclusive education is clearly a changed paradigm in the way that learners with special learning needs are educated. Evolving from a medical model of disability, there has been a distinct transition internationally towards a social model that encourages and supports the education of all learners regardless of need, within the same school and in the same classroom. Such a change in philosophy has resulted in new models of education that are more complex and often require difficult changes in the way schools function and in the expectations for teachers. In many instances teachers have reported a strong reluctance to support inclusion, and they are particularly concerned when the level of support needed for individual children increases (e.g. Woolfson and Brady, 2009). Preparing teachers for this new way of thinking and of practice has been addressed in many different ways globally, ranging from compulsory or elective preservice courses involving stand-alone or infused programs on inclusive education, to school-based or government-funded professional learning courses for inservice teachers (Florian, 2011; Forlin, 2010a).

The training needs of teachers

Even where major educational reforms are happening in schools to pursue more democratic and equitable education, there has been a rather slow and lagging parallel change in teacher education reform to support these new developments (Forlin, 2010a). Teacher education requires consideration at both pre- and inservice levels and good quality and appropriate training are imperative if inclusion is to be effective.

During initial training, preparation for inclusion is recognized as a critical factor in addressing attitudes and in promoting a greater commitment (Sharma *et al.*, 2008; Sze, 2009). Yet newly qualified teachers in many jurisdictions still rate their training as ineffective, for example, in Australia (House of Representatives Standing Committee on Education and Vocational Training, 2007) and suggest that they are unprepared for working in inclusive schools. Many training institutions are also considered to be out of touch with the reality of how new teachers need to be prepared (O'Keefe, 2009). Even where governments are spending considerable sums of money to upskill existing teachers in basic information about inclusive education, for example, in Hong Kong, in 2009 this still only met the training needs of less than 10 per cent of existing teachers (Sin *et al.*, 2010).

As a means of ensuring quality teacher education, some training institutions are being required to meet national expectations for course content and duration. The announcement of national professional standards for teachers in Australia, for example, has led to the development of arrangements for the accreditation nationwide of all initial teacher education programs. Every program will be assessed by expert trained panels against the same national standards (see www.aitsl.edu for further information).

Finding appropriate practicum placements

A further difficulty in many regions is the necessity to provide authentic quality practicum placements, so that teachers can acquire the competences needed to become inclusive practitioners through observation and participation in effective schools. For regions that are embracing inclusion for the first time, there is a lack of schools demonstrating inclusive methodologies where preservice teachers can be placed. In regions where inclusion is more firmly grounded, and where more inclusive mentoring models do exist, schools, however, may be reluctant to take on preservice teachers as they are frequently overwhelmed with other priorities. The difficulty in securing inclusive schools for placements is invariably further heightened by the number of universities and teacher training institutions competing for the few available school places.

The role of teacher educators

There is much debate about the competences required by teachers to become successful inclusive teachers (e.g. in Ireland (Watson, 2009)), yet there is a dearth of dialogue about the training of teacher educators so that they are able to provide this knowledge in an effectual and timely manner. To assume that teacher educators are able to provide relevant training by using innovative and applicable approaches, without themselves having received any such preparation, is rather unrealistic. Much greater emphasis must be placed on ensuring that those who are charged with the business of preparing teachers for inclusion are themselves appropriately trained to meet this demanding role.

Challenges faced in teacher education for inclusion

A political challenge

Teacher education is in many jurisdictions a key political issue that is being affected by the need to better prepare teachers, while at the same time working within limited budgets, fiscal constraints, and increased accountability. In response to international conventions, governments are required to give assurances that disability and diversity are being addressed, especially within an inclusive educational domain (Donnelly and Watkins, 2011).

The issue of equity has been the major force underlying the movement towards a more inclusive educational system. Through this approach, policy makers and governments have endeavoured to embrace a range of practices that will further inclusion. Definitions of equity, like those of inclusive education, vary broadly with there being a focus on identification and solution. There has been little research on the causes of inequities or on the potential effectiveness or otherwise of borrowed ideas for intervention from other jurisdictions (Reid, 2011). Government education policies focus on greater accountability, assessment, and improved outcomes.

I believe it is germane to reflect globally that while inclusive education has been led by international proactive rights groups and supported by parents, that implementation in almost all regions has been a political decision. Such decisions are increasingly made away from educators who have tended not to be consulted or involved in the development of inclusive policy. Further, education is progressively being led by economists and politicians who focus more on the fiscal implications and the political kudos that can be achieved by supporting current idealisms such as inclusion in education. Many would argue that commitments to equity are being undermined by the emphasis on the economic goals of education (Reid, 2011). Few decision makers have any educational background and, in addition, governments are increasingly turning to entrepreneurs to provide business style solutions for educational problems.

Inclusive education is a complex issue, especially as it has now broadened to reflect the right to include all learners with diverse needs to access education within their chosen school environment (Forlin, 2010). Policies for promoting inclusion are often difficult to enact and may be unrealistic in their expectations. According to Reid (2011, p. 4), who discusses the situation in Australia, "it is difficult to develop sophisticated policy approaches to address complex equity issues when education discourse is simplified". Reid calls for educators to become more active in public debates about the future for education. He posits that to sustain long-term change it requires policy processes that are:

- Based on a clear and articulated concept of equity.
- Thorough and systematic and recognize the complexities involved in achieving better educational outcomes for 'equity groups'.
- Founded on research and inquiry, and an appreciation of the different contexts in which educational practice operates.
- Trialed and evaluated before being spread widely.
- Wary about reinforcing the very inequities that they are designed to address.

(Reid, 2011, p. 4)

Thus, to ensure that education policy actually addresses the reality of inclusion and is not purely a rhetoric and that implementation ideas through school-based development are manageable and practicable, a more proactive and leadership role is needed by those who are involved daily in the execution of inclusion. The principal is a key player in supporting inclusion and enabling a positive outcome for all. Teachers and other staff are also critical to the successful implementation and sustainability of an inclusive approach. Of key importance, thus, teacher education courses must be more related to the practicality of implementation, rather than simply focusing on the theoretical underpinnings of the paradigm, or government policy that dictates the direction for change. Course content must also take greater account of the opinion of principals and teachers and the approaches that they have found useful and manageable in supporting inclusion within their local context.

Competing forces: An equity battle

Maintaining equity in education is fraught with many other new challenges. For example, an increasing trend throughout the world is the very noticeably strong movement in the past decade towards the establishment of international private, non-government schools and also local independent government schools which are considered to be stand-alone schools. While the international schools catered initially for expatriate children, many are now becoming sought-after options for indigenous students with local enrolments far exceeding international students (e.g. Hong Kong). Thus, they are directly competing for students, offering scholarships to the most able and enrolling those from the most affluent areas of society. This is setting up a hitherto limited schooling dichotomy, which now has the potential to expand exponentially and in doing so to counter all movements towards equity in education.

In particular, there has been an explosion of the number of these schools in regions such as Asia, especially China and Hong Kong, the Middle East including the United Arab Emirates, Qatar, Kuwait, and Thailand. This poses a number of challenges for educational systems where government schools are competing for students. Such issues include, but are not limited to, the following:

- Quality control of all aspects of schooling.
- Maintaining quality standards for teachers.
- Ensuring positive outcomes for all students.
- Monitoring curriculum.
- Replacing teachers who have moved to the private schooling system.
- Losing the best teachers.
- Positional advantages with better post school options and job access.
- Furthering equity and access for learners with diverse learning needs.

It is estimated that by 2020 the international school market will double. It is predicted that there will be approximately 11,000 international schools including up to five million students, and these schools will need to employ half a million teachers (Belardi, 2011). The bulk of the teachers for these international schools currently come from the US, UK, Canada, Australia, and New Zealand. As each of these jurisdictions is reportedly unable to fill all their current teaching positions, such a movement will only exacerbate the difficulty in employing suitable teachers.

The biggest concern in regard to the inclusion movement and the need to ensure equity of education for all learners, however, is the ability of international schools to be highly selective in offering places to students. Unlike government schools in regions where it is legislated that schools must accept all children who wish to enroll in them, such as in Australia, Canada, New Zealand, and the US, there is no such policy for international schools. Indeed, by definition in their prospectus they are highly exclusive, as the fees are generally prohibitive to many parents and places are only offered after intensive selection, almost always involving personal interviews.

As their specific role is to provide education which is grounded on achieving high examination results, and their existence is predicated on a financial model, there is no incentive for them to accommodate the needs of learners who require additional support that may be more costly, and who may lower the standards on examination results. Thus, teachers will not be encouraged to be inclusive and the focus of education will be on an elitist examination–oriented system. As demand for teachers qualified to teach content in narrow discipline areas will continue to be sought after, time spent on preparing teachers to focus on inclusive approaches may not be as well supported by employing authorities.

The role of universities

What then is the role of universities in preparing teachers for inclusive education and in catering for diversity, while supporting an equitable educational system for all? It is apparent that the underlying direction of universities has changed dramatically in the past few decades and even more so in the current millennium. Universities have moved from a moral role of discovery and dissemination of knowledge to contribute to the general good of society, to one that is being designed to exploit knowledge for its fiscal gains (Schwartz, 2011).

There is a unanimous call by governments everywhere for greater investments in education, not only to contribute to knowledge, but also to support economic progress. Selection of university course offerings are no longer based on what educators consider relevant, but are designed to meet job specifications being determined by multinational organizations. The number of courses offered has increased dramatically as universities grapple to gain the student edge by maintaining their enrolments in difficult financial times. Institutions are facing severe cutbacks in staffing, while concurrently being heavily pressured to produce outcomes by way of research publications and patents that are more likely to bring much-needed funds to help them cope with this changing dynamic. Many universities have established partnerships with retail groups and large corporate businesses, and accepted sponsorships to help them keep afloat.

Within this new movement for fund seeking and university entrepreneurship, one of the biggest challenges for teacher education is that this area is not seen as a particularly lucrative market. There are few large organizations that perceive that partnerships or sponsorship with teacher education sectors will bring them financial gain. Such perspectives highlight the undervaluing of teachers and the role they play in society. There are few countries where teachers are really valued as professionals and where their training and support is esteemed. One such country, for example, is Finland, where teachers are highly respected, teaching standards are high, and teaching is seen as a prestigious career (Burridge, 2010). Cultural issues would seem to clearly impact on this in a positive way. Unlike many other regions, Finland has low levels of immigration, so when students commence school the majority have Finnish as their native language. The many difficulties faced by learners from alternative cultures, ethnicity, and experiences have therefore been eliminated.

If teacher education is to be improved and if teachers are to be effectively prepared to teach in inclusive schools, then not only do universities have to accept greater responsibility for providing courses that meet their needs, but they also need to lead the debate by enacting more research into the outcomes for teachers engaged in inclusive schooling. Much of the evidence obtained to date regarding preservice teachers' preparedness and support for inclusive education is limited and has been anecdotal, gleaned from small samples in specific and fairly narrow contexts (Sze, 2009). Until decisions regarding course content for teacher education for inclusion are based on a stronger research foundation, it will be very difficult to justify ad hoc restructuring of courses, or to expect that these new versions will meet the needs of teachers. Courses need not only to provide appropriate content using innovative methodologies (Forlin, 2010a), they must also be based on extant research that justifies that they will lead to the desired outcome of teachers having appropriate knowledge, skills, and attitudes to become inclusive practitioners (Florian, 2011; Loreman, 2010).

Conclusion

Improving teacher education must surely lead to improved school effectiveness for all children. This will only occur, though, when there is a greater connectedness between the governments and policy makers, the training institutions, and the schools in which teachers work. Most regions have adopted a range of different training models to prepare teachers for inclusion. These are underpinned by international and/or local legislation and policy that is rights based, focusing on the need to cater for all children by providing equitable educational opportunities.

In increasing numbers, government systems are trying to have a greater input into course development for teacher training by determining the content through specifying key competences or skills that all teachers should acquire, and requiring program registration and accreditation. To improve teacher education requires consideration of how these key competences will subsequently be addressed by changes in the curriculum, pedagogy, and practical aspects of training courses for preparing teachers for inclusion.

It is clear that some form of national or state accountability and overall monitoring of the quality of courses is important; nonetheless, too much direction regarding the curriculum calls for caution. Too narrow a requirement can take away the strength that universities and teacher-training institutions have always had in being able to modify their courses to meet the different needs of their students. As they prepare teachers for inclusion, governments should also acknowledge the diversity in the training needs of different students and ensure that there is still sufficient flexibility in their policy and guidelines to allow teacher educators to make decisions based on their own local knowledge about how best to prepare teachers to work in their schools.

The educational arena has actively moved towards embracing an inclusive approach to educating all children. To ensure support by all stakeholders for inclusion, though, a public and community awareness program is also important and should be developed concomitantly with teacher training. People fear what they do not know, and this is often the case with inclusion. If support is to be gained from all stakeholders then they need to have an understanding about the proposed process and an opportunity to raise questions and to discuss expected outcomes. Further to this, an inclusive education system cannot be enacted successfully without a similar process to develop an inclusive society. Although education can take a leading role, it needs to be supported by the development of a more inclusive society if it is to be maintained and defensible in the long term. Given the high value placed on education for the future, the amount of money put into schooling at a global level, and the number of years dedicated to training teachers, it is crucial that we get teacher education right.

References

Ainscow, M., Booth, T. and Dyson, A. (2006) *Improving Schools, Developing Inclusion*, London: Routledge.

Belardi, L. (2011) "Going global", *Education Review*, June: 8–10.

Burridge, T. (2010) "Why do Finland's schools get the best results?" Online. Available at: http://news.bbc.co.uk/2/hi/programmes/world_news_america/8601207.stm (accessed on 7 April 2010).

Donnelly, V. and Watkins, A. (2011) "Teacher education for inclusion in Europe", *PROS-PECTS Quarterly Review of Comparative Education*, UNESCO IBE, 41(3): 341–53.

Florian, L. (2009) "Preparing teachers to work in 'schools for all'", *Teaching and Teacher Education*, 25(4): 533–34.

Florian, L. (2011) "Introduction – Mapping international developments in teacher education for inclusion", *PROSPECTS Quarterly Review of Comparative Education*, UNESCO IBE, 41(3): 319–21.

Florian, L. and Rouse, M. (2009) "The inclusive practice project in Scotland: Teacher education for inclusive education", *Teaching and Teacher Education*, 25: 594–601.

Forlin, C. (2010) "Teacher education reform for enhancing teachers' preparedness for inclusion", *International Journal of Inclusive Education*, 14(7): 649–54.

Forlin, C. (2010a) "Re-framing teacher education for inclusion", in C. Forlin (ed.), *Teacher Education for Inclusion: Changing Paradigms and Innovative Approaches*, London: Routledge, pp. 3–10.

House of Representatives Standing Committee on Education and Vocational Training (2007) *Top of the Class: Report on the Inquiry into Teacher Education*, Canberra: The Parliament of the Commonwealth of Australia.

Loreman, T. (2010) "Essential inclusive education-related outcomes for Alberta preservice teachers", *Alberta Journal of Educational Research*, 56(2): 124–42.

O'Keefe, D. O. (2009) "Learning at the chalkface", *Education Review*, (February) 10–11.

Reid, A. (2011) "What sort of equity?", *Professional Educator*, 10(4): 3–4.

Schwartz, S. (2011) "The quest to re-moralise the modern university", *Professional Educator*, 10(4): 27–8.

Sharma, U., Forlin, C. and Loreman, T. (2008) "Impact of training on pre-service teachers' attitudes and concerns about inclusive education and sentiments about persons with disabilities", *Disability and Society*, 23(7): 773–85.

Sin, K. F., Tsang, K. W., Poon, C. Y. and Lai, C. L. (2010) "Upskilling all mainstream teachers: What is viable?", in C. Forlin (ed.), *Teacher Education for Inclusion: Changing Paradigms and Innovative Approaches*, London: Routledge, pp. 236–45.

Sze, S. (2009) "A literature review: Pre-service teachers' attitudes toward students with disabilities", *Education*, 130(1): 53–6.

Watson, S. F. (2009) "Barriers to inclusive education in Ireland: The case for pupils with a diagnosis of intellectual and/or pervasive developmental disabilities", *British Journal of Learning Disabilities*, 37: 277–84.

Woolfson, L. M. and Brady, K. (2009) "An investigation of factors impacting on mainstream teachers' beliefs about teaching students with learning difficulties", *Educational Psychology*, 29(2): 221–38.

Chapter 2

Including children with disabilities in regular classes

Current climate and future direction in Malaysia

Haniz Ibrahim

Keywords: Malaysia and inclusive practice, integration, inclusion, functional integration, partial integration, vision, skills, incentives, resources, action plans, teaching skills, collaborative skills, regular teachers

Chapter overview

Malaysia is a signatory to the "*Salamanca Statement*" (UNESCO, 1994) and thus, is committed to include its children with disabilities into regular classrooms. For the last 15 years, efforts have been made by the Malaysian Ministry of Education (MMOE) to include children with disabilities in regular classes. According to the *Federated School's Inspectorate Report* (1998), including children with disabilities has yet to be widely practiced in Malaysia. Not much has changed since the report was published based on discussion with teachers, teaching these children. On average only two to three children with disabilities are being included per school. Thus, the main aim of this chapter is to explore the current status of inclusion in Malaysia, and to discuss possible future directions, focusing on teachers' training requirements.

Introduction

The United Nations Convention on the Rights of the Child (United Nations, 1989), *Education For All* (UNESCO, 1990), *Standard Rule on the Equalisation of Opportunities for Persons with Disabilities* (United Nations, 1993), and the *Salamanca Statement* (UNESCO, 1994) have directed national states to educate as far as possible (within the national education system) children with disabilities in regular classes. Where previously these disadvantaged children who experience difficulties were excluded from regular education, the recent past has seen a major effort to include them nationally in Malaysia. The notion that children with disabilities should be included, educationally, with children in the same classes has generated debates in Malaysia regarding the nature of inclusive practices and what changes to the national educational system are necessary to accommodate these children.

Malaysia's concept of inclusion

In Malaysia, the inclusion of children with disabilities (sensory impaired and intellectually challenged) has evolved from the practice of integration that aimed to move these children from segregated settings to regular classroom environments in order to increase their participation in the educational and social life within the context of the "whole school system" (Ainscow, 1997). The term "inclusion" was widely used in 1994 as the result of Malaysia subscribing to the *Salamanca Statement* (UNESCO, 1994). The 1997 *Education (Special Education) Regulations* states that inclusive education is a program for pupils with special needs who are able to attend normal classes together with normal pupils (MMOE, 1997).

Thus, inclusion in Malaysia is the process of placing children with disabilities who are under the responsibility of the Ministry of Education into regular classes to be educated alongside their peers of the same age group, with or without additional support, and within the present school system. This concept of inclusion might not be in line with the ideal concept of inclusion based on acceptance, belonging, and about providing school settings in which all children with disabilities can be valued equally and be provided with equal educational opportunities (Thomas, 1997), but in the Malaysian context (with its limitations and constraints) it is most suitable and practicable.

In terms of implementation, inclusion in Malaysia is more functional integration (Warnock, 1978) than total inclusion (acceptance of children with disabilities in regular classes without conditions). Two modus operandi are used to include children with disabilities in regular classes: (i) full inclusion, i.e. these children are being placed in all regular classes; and (ii) partial integration, i.e. these children are being placed in regular classes for certain subjects only (in Malaysia this form of integration is also considered as inclusion practice, officially referred to as partial inclusion).

Status of inclusion practice in Malaysia

The MMOE provides two types of special education for children with disabilities: (i) special schools, and (ii) integrated programs in regular schools (Special Education Division, 2008). The integrated program involves the establishment of special education classes in regular schools. Children in special education schools are segregated totally from regular learning. Special education schools sharing the same compound and physical facilities as regular schools do experience some form of social integration, but from the perspective of teaching and learning they are excluded entirely.

Inclusion for children with a disability in Malaysia is commonly practiced in regular schools with integrated programs. Children with hearing impairment who are following integrated programs in technical/vocational secondary schools are included for technical/vocational subjects and excluded for languages and religious subjects (Special Education Division, 2009). Only a limited number of children with hearing impairments (usually those with residual hearing) who are able to learn independently without the assistance of a sign language interpreter are included in regular classes. Generally, children with hearing impairments who do require sign language interpreters are excluded because this service is currently not available in schools in Malaysia.

The majority of children with visual impairments are normally fully included. They are excluded only for subjects that rely heavily on visual abilities. Intellectually, these children are able to cope with regular learning and their ability to follow verbal instruction makes their inclusion practicable. These children follow the national curriculum.

Children who are intellectually challenged are usually segregated from regular learning. Discussions with state education officers indicate a substantial number of these children are included in regular classes, but presently no data are available to substantiate this. The main reason cited for inclusion is to enable these children to sit public examinations. As for children with specific learning difficulties such as dyslexia, all are included in regular classes (Special Education Division, 2009).

A study undertaken by the Federal School Inspectorate (1998) to investigate the implementation of inclusion at the primary level of schooling reported on average only two to three children with disabilities were included per school. The criterion for inclusion was based on a school's authority's perception of the child's ability to cope either fully or partially with regular learning.

In 2005, the Special Education Division working with the National Autistic Society of Malaysia initiated the inclusion of children with autism from the society into the MMOE primary schools (Special Education Department, 2005). This project is still ongoing and currently six primary schools are involved.

It can be concluded that inclusion is being practiced in Malaysian primary and secondary schools, but there are still hiccups in its implementation.

Future direction and teachers' training

The inclusion of children with disabilities has been widely discussed in Malaysia since the Salamanca Declaration (UNESCO, 1994) and efforts have been made to implement it in Malaysian schools. Inclusion is being practiced in Malaysia, but has yet to be widely accepted by the school community.

Earlier studies (Haniz, 1998; National Audit Department, 1999) indicated that regular primary school teachers in Malaysia tend to resist the inclusion of special needs children. Recent studies by Manisah et al. (2006) show that, at least in theory, regular teachers are reasonably positive towards implementing inclusion. Efforts, therefore, have to be made to convince all teachers that children with special needs deserve the chance to participate in regular learning from the social–ethical, legal–legislative and psychological–educational perspectives.

Making inclusion work is not an easy task for Malaysia. Clough and Lindsay (1991) remind us (and it is true in the Malaysian context) that "change itself does not happen simply, immediately, and unilaterally, but is a much more awkward, less predictable, and often painful affair" (p. 5). The real world of regular education in Malaysia is complicated and there are limitations and constraints that cannot be ignored, especially teachers' acceptance of the inclusion concept, whether they are regular or special education teachers.

To achieve coherent implementation of inclusion in Malaysia, the Knoster model of managing complex change (LeRoy and Simpson, 1996) will be used as a guideline to forward suggestions for future action, especially for educators involved in teacher education. According to this model a combination of vision, skills, incentives, resources, and action plans are required for change to occur in a systematic and positive manner. If any of these five factors of change is missing, the restructuring process will lead to confusion, anxiety, resistance, and frustration. This could be demoralizing not only to teachers but also others involved in implementing inclusion.

Vision

The first requirement is vision. Part of this vision is to initiate inclusion in Malaysia (School Division, 1994). This vision is reinforced by the MMOE with the implementation of the *1996 Education Act* (MMOE, 1996) and *Education Regulation (Special Education) 1997* (MMOE, 1997). National policy to develop a 'caring' Malaysian society by the year 2020 (Wan Mohd Zaid, 1993) also triggered the MMOE to start implementing inclusion in 1994. The vision at the Special Education Division has resulted in the inclusion of children with hearing impairment in technical/vocational secondary schools, the inclusion of almost all children with visual impairments, and also the inclusion of children with specific learning difficulties such as dyslexia and children with autistic tendencies (Special Education Department, 2005). The MMOE does not mandate inclusion but is strongly encouraging all regular schools with special education classes to include children with disabilities. The Ministry's top-down vision of inclusion has yet to be properly embraced by those most involved in its implementation process, i.e. the schools' personnel. Discussion with regular teachers indicates that they still harbour negative perceptions of inclusion. This is not surprising since special education components are not compulsory for preservice regular teachers in Malaysia. Most teacher training institutions do not offer special education as part of the regular teacher's curriculum and this has resulted in these teachers lacking knowledge and awareness about inclusive education.

Most head teachers (the individual most responsible in the implementation of inclusion in regular schools) do not have any planning experience for inclusion either. The majority of these head teachers have minimal knowledge on special education and normally delegate the responsibilities of managing the school's special education class to the special education supervisor. Over the years, the Special Education Division has intensified its outreach program to explain to head teachers the Ministry's rationale, aims, and objectives of inclusion. A better understanding of inclusion, hopefully, will help develop head teachers' personal visions of inclusion. Schools have been allowed, thus far, to formulate their own vision of inclusion (within the broader vision of the MMOE), hence the present policy to strongly encourage the implementation of inclusion.

Teaching skills

The second requirement is to equip regular teachers with the relevant teaching skills through pre- or in-service training in special education. International studies (Burke and Sutherland, 2004; Janney et al., 1995; and Leyser et al., 1994) show that training in special education is significant in making teachers supportive of inclusion. Without training, regular teachers may experience fears and anxieties about inclusion.

Regular teachers in Malaysia usually insist that children with disabilities come to regular classes after mastering certain prerequisite skills (Haniz, 1998). If the criterion for inclusion is readiness, then there will probably be children with disabilities who will never be part of regular learning. It might, therefore, be necessary to place these children in regular classes, maybe for their secondary education (after being educated in a special education class or special education schools at the primary level), whether they are deemed to be ready or not. Regular secondary teachers will just have to work with these children in their classes. If this action is preferred, as advocated by Thomas and Webb (1997), regular teachers will need to be convinced that inclusion is all about good teaching and that they have the skills to teach any child with disabilities placed in their classes. Regular teachers have been asked to view inclusion as not being specialized teaching for children with disabilities (even though specialized skills in Braille for children with visual impairments and sign language for children with hearing impairments are necessary) but 'normal' teaching for regular children. Both can co-exist inside the classroom. It is therefore necessary for all teacher training institutions to reevaluate their teacher training curriculum and make special or inclusive education components compulsory for all would-be regular teachers.

Haniz's study (1998), using the three-component model of attitude, shows there is a positive relationship between these three components and inclusion. Thus, it may be necessary to reconsider the training of future regular teachers so as to inculcate them with the awareness and knowledge of special education and inclusion. Components of inclusion incorporated in the preservice teacher trainee's curriculum would increase their knowledge of inclusion, and would alter the cognitive element of their attitudes towards it. Trainees need to be given direct experiences of teaching children with disabilities in order to challenge the affective component of their attitudes. These in turn might influence favourably their conative component of attitudes, thus resulting in positive general attitudes to inclusion. In order to incorporate inclusion components in teacher trainee curricula, part of the present curricula will need to be removed. Since all elements of the present curricula are considered to be important, which elements should be removed? If removed, will this have a negative effect on subject matter?

Besides specific skills, as suggested by Fullan (1993), regular teachers should also be given inquiry and collaboration skills. Regular teachers encounter many problems when practicing inclusion. Effective inquiry skills, i.e. their ability to solve problems encountered and to experiment with different styles of teaching children with disabilities, are essential for the success of inclusion. Training in collaborative skills for regular teachers would enable them to work with, as well as learn from, other teachers about teaching children with disabilities. It would also enable them to work with special education teachers and other personnel in their everyday dealing with these children. The Special Education Division has organized many in-service training sessions for regular teachers in inclusion, but these are usually just one-shot workshops and offer disconnected training. It should be a continuous process.

Incentives

The third requirement is incentives. Incentives have been helpful in encouraging regular teachers to accept inclusion. Making it compulsory for regular teachers to implement inclusion will speed its implementation but this could have the repercussion of regular teachers being frustrated and/or angry. This could do more harm than good to the program.

Providing incentives in the form of personal gain (e.g. monetary rewards, scholarships, etc.) and reduction of workloads, as suggested by some teachers, are difficult to fulfill because of limited funding. Thus incentives offered should relate to regular teachers' professional status as teachers.

What has yet to emerge from the last 15 years of trying to implement inclusion is an ideal model within the Malaysian context. The MMOE have yet to provide guidelines on how inclusion should be implemented. Currently, schools are given the freedom on the best ways to implement inclusion. Thus, different schools have different ways of including children with disabilities. One of the most frequent requests made by regular teachers is an example on how inclusion should be done in Malaysia. Regular teachers currently have limited understanding on the practicality of having children with disabilities in their classes. They often complain that these children (especially those with behavioural problems) have disruptive influences. The Special Education Division needs to identify schools with good inclusion practices for others to emulate. The reduction of workload, support by head teachers and peers, being given material and human support, have thus far sweetened inclusion acceptance by regular teachers. An even bigger incentive would be a monetary reward. The most affordable financial incentives, however, that could be given to regular teachers within the Ministry's limitations is to make their participation in the inclusion program a substantial part of their yearly teaching appraisal.

Another issue that worries head teachers is the school's performance league tables based on a school's population and exam results. Head teachers are concerned that including children with disabilities (especially those who are intellectually challenged) would drag their school's performance down the tables, since these children would also be sitting these examinations. The MMOE have not taken inclusion practices as part of the evaluation criteria when evaluating a school's performance.

Resourcing

The fourth requirement is the availability of resources. Resource support is essential to avoid regular teachers being frustrated with implementing inclusion. Studies (Hilgendorff, 2007; Haniz, 1998; LeRoy and Simpson, 1996) show that teachers tend to exhibit positive attitudes to inclusion if they are given appropriate resource support. The two most common resource supports are: (i) learning materials and physical facilities, and (ii) human resources.

Regular teachers involved in inclusion (in schools with special education classes) are usually supported by special education teachers (to provide them with teaching and learning materials, especially for children with visual impairments, and to be a sign language interpreter for children with hearing impairments) and teacher assistants. Regular teachers involved in inclusion could easily seek advice from these special education teachers who are acting as resource teachers.

The post of teacher assistant (in Malaysia they are commonly known as student management assistants) was created by the MMOE in 2006. Currently, the MMOE allocates one teacher assistant for every 10 students with disabilities. The big issue is that many of these assistants have minimal experience and knowledge in dealing with children with disabilities. The majority of these assistants have only attended a one-week in-service exposure course in special education organized by the state education departments. Nevertheless, they are required to assist regular teachers involved with inclusion. Malaysia currently lags far behind other developed nations in the development of its teacher assistant resource services.

Action plan

The fifth requirement is an action plan. An action plan is necessary to support regular teachers in defining clear realizable objectives, targets, and producing the means of evaluating inclusion as well as assessing needs. The action plan should involve: (i) producing standard criteria for inclusion, and (ii) strategies to introduce inclusion or to reinforce current inclusion practices from the ministerial, state, district, and school levels. Implementation strategies, acquiring and distributing resources, training of regular teachers, and method of monitoring inclusion progress need to be planned carefully by the MMOE.

The Special Education Division encourages regular schools to develop their own inclusion modus operandi. Currently it would seem impractical to practice total inclusion, and to involve all regular schools in inclusion because this would cause massive administrative and financial problems. Efforts are, therefore, being undertaken by the relevant Malaysian educational authorities to strengthen the present practice of inclusion in regular schools. It is noted that regular teachers in schools that have tried inclusion are significantly more receptive towards its implementation than in schools that have not tried inclusion (Haniz, 1998). Regular teachers are usually given the necessary experiences in the education of children with disabilities before being asked to accept these children in their classes. Non-contact with children with disabilities at the professional level sustains ignorance of these children's educational needs, and this ignorance is damaging to inclusion innovation. Schools normally organize in-house training for regular teachers involved with inclusion.

The whole school approach (Ainscow, 1997) to inclusion needs to be given due consideration. Everyone associated with schools is encouraged to play their part. Teachers involved in inclusion need to be supported if they are going to be willing to accept children with disabilities in Malaysia.

At the stage of initiating or strengthening inclusion implementation, children with disabilities should be included in classes with regular teachers who are at least willing to try inclusion or are committed to make it work. Regular teachers involved in inclusion need to be persuaded and not directed by their head teachers to accept children with disabilities (Zalizan, 2000). Adopting this option has raised the issue of fairness among regular teachers. Is it fair not to involve regular teachers in inclusion just because they are disinterested or hostile towards it?

The gradualist approach has been utilized as the modus operandi in implementing inclusion in Malaysia. At the initial stage of implementation, inclusion has to be part-time and involve non-academic subjects only, so as not to exert undue pressure on children with disabilities, regular children and regular teachers. Including children with disabilities for academic subjects is done gradually to appease regular teachers' anxieties and to build up their confidence in their ability to teach academic subjects to these children.

Conclusion

In a society that is trying to create a caring outlook by the year 2020, the school system needs to look beyond a simple understanding of resources and incentives if it is to achieve this. Efforts have been made to reconstruct a vision of the schools' community on inclusion, and different approaches in presenting the school curriculum have been discussed at length in seminars and in intellectual discourse during the last 15 years of trying inclusion in Malaysia. Rethinking the process of educating children together in regular classes has also been widely debated. The process of bringing children with disabilities and regular children together within the existing regular school settings has still a long way to go before Malaysia can proudly proclaim to the world that it has successfully implemented the requirements prescribed in the Salamanca Declaration (UNESCO, 1994). Fundamental reviews of existing education systems, methods of resourcing, and processes of teaching have been made to encourage inclusion. For inclusion to be successful, positive attitudes amongst regular teachers towards its implementation is a must.

References

Ainscow, M. (1997) "Towards inclusive schooling", *British Journal of Special Education*, 24(1): 3–6.

Burke, K. and Sutherland, C. (2004) "Attitudes towards inclusion: Knowledge vs Experience", *Education. Chula Vista: Winter 2004*, 125(2): 163–73.

Clough, P. and Lindsay, G. (1991) *Integration and the Support Service: Changing Roles in Special Education*, Windsor: NFER-Nelson.

Federal School Inspectorate (1998) *Pelaksanaan Pendidikan Inklusif di Sekolah rendah* [Implementation of Inclusive Education in Primary Schools, Ministry of Education], Kuala Lumpur: Government Printers.

Fullan, M. (1993) *Change Forces: Probing the Depths of Education Reform*, London: Felmer Press.

Haniz Ibrahim (1998) *Inclusive Education in Malaysia: Teachers' Attitudes to Change*. Ph.D. Exeter University.

Hilgendorff, C. (2007) *General Education Teacher Readiness for Adapting and Modifying Curriculum for Special Learners in Their Classroom*, Ann Arbor, MI: Proquest Information and Learning Company.

Janney, R. F., Snell, M. E., Beers, M. K. and Raynes, M. (1995) "Integrating children with moderate and severe disabilities into general education classes", *Exceptional Children*, 61(5): 425–39.

LeRoy, B. and Simpson, C. (1996) "Improving students' outcomes through inclusive education", *British Journal of Learning Support*, 11(1): 32–6.

Leyser, Y., Kipperman, G. and Keller, R. (1994) "Teachers' attitudes towards mainstreaming: A cross-cultural study in six nations", *European Journal of Special Needs Education*, 9(1): 1–13.

Manisah, M. A., Ramlee, M. and Zalizan, M. J. (2006) "An empirical study on teachers' perceptions towards inclusive education in Malaysia", *International Journal of Special Education*, 21(3): 36–44.

MMOE, Malaysian Ministry of Education (1996) *Undang-undang Malaysia. Akta Pendidikan 1996 (Akta 550)* [Malaysian Laws. Education Act 1996 (ACT 550)], Kuala Lumpur: Government Printers.

MMOE, Malaysian Ministry of Education (1997) *Education Regulation (Special Education) 1997*, Kuala Lumpur: Government Printers.

National Audit Department (1999) *Laporan pelaksanaan Program Pendidikan Khas, Kementerian Pelajaran Malaysia* [Reports on the implementation of inclusive education program, Ministry of Education], Kuala Lumpur: Government Printers.

School Division (1994) *Inclusive Education. Plan bertindak* [Action plan: Ministry of Education, Malaysia], Kuala Lumpur: Government Printers.

Special Education Department (2005) *Kertas kerja pelaksanaan pendidikan Inklusif bagi kanak-kanak autistic* [Working papers to implement inclusive education for autistic children]. Working Paper. Unpublished paper submitted to Ministry of Education Malaysia.

Special Education Division (2008) *Data Pendidikan Khas* [Special education data: Ministry of Education, Malaysia], Kuala Lumpur: Government Printers.

Special Education Division (2009) *Maklumat Pendidikan Khas* [Special education information: Ministry of Education, Malaysia], Kuala Lumpur: Government Printers.

Thomas, G. (1997) "Inclusive schools for inclusive society", *British Journal of Special Education*, 24(3): 103–7.

Thomas, G. and Webb, J. (1997) *From Exclusion to Inclusion: Promoting Education for All*, Essex: Barnardos.

United Nations (1989) *The Convention on the Rights of the Child*. Online. Available at: http://www.unicef.org/crc/ (accessed 22 February 2012).

United Nations (1993) *Standard Rules on the Equalisation of Opportunities for Persons with Disabilities*. Online. Available at: http://www.un.org/esa/socdev/enable/dissre00.htm (accessed 22 February 2012).

UNESCO, United Nations Educational, Scientific and Cultural Organization (1990) *World Declaration on Education For All and Framework For Action to Meet Basic Learning Needs*, Thailand: Jomtien.

UNESCO, United Nations Educational, Scientific and Cultural Organization (1994) *The Salamanca Statement and Framework for Action on Special Needs Education. World Conference on Special Needs Education: Access and Quality*, UNESCO.

Wan Mohd Zaid Mohd Nordin (1993) *Penghisian wawasan Pendidikan* [Fulfilling the education vision, Main paper, National Education seminars, Ministry of Education Malaysia], Kuala Lumpur: Government Printers.

Warnock, H. M. (1978) *Special Educational Needs: Report of the Committee of Enquiry into the Education of Handicapped Children and Young People*, London: Her Majesty's Stationery Office.

Zalizan, M. J. (2000) "Perceptions of inclusive practices: The Malaysian perspective", *Educational Review*, 52(2): 187–95.

Chapter 3

A training model for enhancing the learning capacity of students with special needs in inclusive classrooms in Thailand

Pennee Kantavong

Keywords: training model, enhancing capacity, inclusive classroom, Thailand

Chapter overview

The *National Education Act* of Thailand focuses on educating all children together in inclusive classrooms. The movement toward inclusive classrooms also means that schools and teachers need to adjust their services to accommodate children with diverse learning needs. This chapter describes a training model for teachers who work in inclusive classrooms in Thailand and examines its result on teachers and their students. Problems encountered and suggestions for implementation of similar programs are also presented.

Overview

The status of special needs education in Thailand may not be much different from other countries in Asia. Thailand began with separate schools for each disability condition. For example, there are separate schools for the blind, the deaf, and for students with intellectual disabilities. These are not the only groups of children with special needs. There are other learners with special needs who find it difficult to succeed in regular schools. In recent years, there has been an increased awareness by the government that it has the responsibility to provide an education to all groups of children. The policy of the government moved to target education for all, including children with special needs, which ushered in a new phase in Thailand. Based on the philosophy of "education for all", the Thai government enacted a constitution establishing the right to education for all citizens of Thailand. Concurrently, the *National Education Act* (1999) was implemented, which aims to provide equal opportunities for every child. Together, both laws and Acts seek to eliminate all forms of disability discrimination (Office of the National Education Commission (ONEC), 2009).

Chapter 2 of the *1999 National Education Act* specifies the rights and duties in the education of Thai citizens and establishes that the education scheme must provide equal opportunities for every citizen to receive a basic education that is no fewer than 12 years. As for the underprivileged, and those with learning, emotional, and physical disabilities, the government is mandated to provide a special education to them. The second chapter also emphasizes that special education has to be provided in appropriate form according to individual needs as stated in Chapters 8–14, 22, 24, and 28–9 (ONEC, 1999).

Special needs education

The 1997 Constitution addresses the importance of education for all as the right to a basic education for every child. This right includes education for various groups of children, namely: gifted, intellectually limited, physically limited or impaired, and health impaired. The main concept is that instructional approaches for these groups of students are not the same as for ordinary students, i.e. teaching materials, teaching procedures, content, curriculum, and intervention techniques. The *National Education Act* specifies nine types of special needs which are as follows: "visually impaired, hearing impaired, intellectually limited, physically limited, learning disabled, speech impaired, behavioural or emotional disorders, autistic and multiple handicapped children" (Arayawinyoo, 1999, p. 5).

The *National Education Act* legislates the national system to become inclusive and that schools have to enroll all children into their classes without any discrimination. To prevent discrimination against students with special needs, this Act eliminates the use of entrance exams to determine eligibility for programs offering a basic education to Thai students. It is anticipated that schools will gradually offer inclusive education, which in turn will increase participation of school-age children. Schools, therefore, need to adjust greatly in order to accommodate children with diverse needs.

With the establishment of local Acts and policies, schools in the Asia–Pacific are acknowledging the need to move towards inclusive school communities and implement a more inclusive whole-school approach (Forlin, 2008). However, in Thailand, the inclusive school is still not an accepted concept as many teachers continue to emphasize academic achievement, and some schools still view students with special needs as a burden. Carter (2006) points out that the development of education services for students with disabilities in Thailand seems to be slow due to limited resources and attitudinal barriers. The attitude toward children with disabilities seems to have a mixed impact in the development of special education services. The educational policy in Thailand appears to have moved quickly to a more inclusive practice toward individuals with disabilities, but the difficulties seem to be associated with a lack of qualified educators who can provide appropriate services and overcome outdated practices.

In the same vein, Ainscow (2008) concludes in relation to successes of inclusive cultures in schools that: (1) there is likely to be a high level of staff collaboration and joint problem-solving and similar values and commitments may extend into the student body and parent body and other stakeholders in school, (2) respect for diversity by teachers may be understood as a form of participation by children within a school community, (3) the presence of leaders who are committed to inclusive values and a leadership style which encourages a range of individuals to participate in leadership functions is essential, and (4) the local and national policy environment can act to support or undermine the realization of schools' inclusive values. In order to enforce the law in Thailand, the ONEC (2003) also established a policy guide for implementation. The policy guidance set the target and implementation framework as follows:

1. The school age population, particularly the underprivileged, which includes the poor, the disadvantaged living in remote areas, at risk groups, the crippled and the disabled, will have access to a twelve-year basic education. Such education quality will be provided through diversified modalities and on a nationwide basis.
2. All groups of the disadvantaged will have access to and receive educational services and vocational training.
3. Autonomy in educational administration and management will be established so as to respond to the needs of learners and communities. The education provided will be of quality and meet the required standard.
4. Communities and community organizations will be strengthened and will be able to contribute to the collective conceptualization, decision making, monitoring, supervision, checking and provision of support for public activities affecting the communities and the local areas.

(ONEC, 2003, p. 20)

The ONEC also provides the following implementation framework:

1. Promotion and support for the underprivileged groups to have increased access to twelve-year basic education of quality.
2. Reform of the budget system for equality opportunity conducive to efficient provision of education which will be regarded as an investment in the solution of problems arising from poverty.
3. Reform of the administrative and management structure of education for diversification conducive to efficient provision of education.
4. Application of education measures as investments for strengthening the social foundations which lead to the happiness of the population.

(ONEC, 2003, pp. 6–10)

In Thailand, however, attitudes towards students with special needs continue to be a difficult issue to address. Thus inclusive classrooms are still considered an innovation in the country and in the early stages of development. The practice can be found mainly at the elementary level and there are various challenges that still discourage the move to inclusion. Since the government adopted "Education for All" as the target of educational policy in the country, inclusive education is the approach that has been adopted to increase the participation of students. The Ministry of Education has implemented the strategic plan since 2003. In compliance with the law, Kaennakam (2008) reviewed the state and problem of integrated education for special children in primary schools in the Khon Kaen province in Thailand. Kaennakam reported that most schools try to improve the learning environment to accommodate students with special needs. Most of the schools, though, had no resource room and no equipment to support students with special needs. Schools also promoted a positive attitude towards students with special needs among teachers and community, especially parents. Following a public relations exercise about inclusive education, the curriculum was adjusted to accommodate the different needs of students. However, there were not enough teachers to work in inclusive classrooms. Further, the teachers had no knowledge related to the implementation of curriculum for helping students with special needs and they had no background in using intervention techniques and in delivering teaching approaches to students in inclusive classrooms.

Inclusive education movement

Since the *Eighth National Social and Development Plan (1997–2001)* the concept of inclusive education in Thailand has been widely introduced in both Bangkok and in provincial schools. The approaches in providing inclusive education have been:

1. Full-time inclusive classrooms. This approach is operated under the conditions that students with special needs can manage learning materials, and have maturity levels closely to those of their peers and no disruptive behaviours.
2. Inclusive classroom settings with special education teachers providing guidelines for classroom management, e.g. suggestions for IEP development, classroom climate, classroom facilitation and evaluation.
3. Inclusive classroom settings with mobile special education teachers. These teachers move around from one school to the next.
4. Inclusive classroom settings with assistant teachers. These teachers help by teaching remedial topics for students with special needs.
5. Full-time and pull-in inclusive classrooms. This situation applies to students with similar impairments who mainly study in their own groups, but sometimes are educated in the classrooms with students without disabilities.

(Kaennakam, 2008, p. 9)

Ten years after the implementation of the education reform, work performance was evaluated and it was concluded that certain aspects of educational reform functioned at a satisfactory level, such as the education for students with special needs (ONEC, 2009). It was reported that in the year 2006, there were 3,075,341 underprivileged students attending schools. There was a one-time increase in the number of students when compared with attendance in the year 2004. There have been increasing numbers of students with disabilities attending school as well. In 2006, 223,211 students with a disability attended schools, a number considerably higher than in 2004 when there were 66,000 students (ONEC, 2009). This demonstrates that strategies for identifying students with special needs were enhanced and Thailand was moving towards the goal of education for all. Details related to the number of students with disabilities at different levels of education were as follows:

1. Twenty-three percent of 4–6-year-olds receive basic compulsory education.
2. Seventeen percent of 6–17-year-olds receive basic education. As for tertiary level, there were 998 students (880 bachelor degree, 16 master degree and 2 doctoral degree) (ONEC, 2009).

It was revealed, nonetheless, that there were still problems, especially with a lack of trained teachers in special education. The majority of teachers who work as special education teachers in inclusive classrooms are temporary staff. The schools which provide inclusive education also face various problems, namely a lack of trained teachers, inappropriate facilities, and inadequate funding. ONEC (2009) reported that teachers in schools with inclusive education classrooms do not have enough background knowledge. Most of these teachers have never been trained in special education. It was also pointed out that the policy for providing education for special needs groups is not clearly understood or adequately implemented.

ONEC further reported that even with a clear policy and activities for supporting special education, the country does not have a clear method of implementation to move the project forward. Although there are many organizations working on the projects such as NGO and the *Royal Patronage Charity Foundations*, they rarely communicate and collaborate with each other. At the same time, each organization that provides special education does not work systematically. Schools have problems in both budgeting for special education and having a full knowledge of the field. Most schools have no accurate database related to students with special needs. They have no screening test and lack knowledge about curriculum development for different student needs (ONEC, 2009).

Research reveals that inclusive education does not cover all disability groups and geographical regions. Kittiwathanakul (1998) reported that inclusive education in Thailand emphatically specifies that students with special needs have to be under the main curriculum with other students. Sometimes it is hard for students with special needs to cope with the regular curriculum, especially when teachers have no knowledge in organizing any interventions. Kasemsuk (2001) reported that teachers in inclusive classrooms want to receive ongoing training to work with students with special needs. He also found that teachers indicate that they prefer separate schools for students with special needs.

Thawiang (2006) found similar challenges to the implementation of inclusive education, reporting that schools are not ready to provide inclusive education for students with special needs. The problems include difficulty with curriculum adjustment, learning and teaching approaches, teachers' knowledge in special education, and lack of experienced personnel for supervising and monitoring the instruction.

In terms of public attitudes towards inclusive classrooms, parents of "normal" students in some schools in Thailand have expressed a strong opposition to integrating students with diverse needs in the same classrooms with their children because they are concerned that the academic achievement of their children would suffer. In addition, these parents are concerned that when teachers spend too much time with students with special needs, their children would receive less attention and less time for academic development. In the past, medical treatment was the preferred alternative for students with disabilities and/or learning difficulties.

When Forlin (2008) discussed the promotion of a whole-school approach to integration in Hong Kong, the schools involved were required to implement five strategies with school-based support. These strategies included: (a) early identification, (b) early intervention, (c) a whole-school approach, (d) home–school cooperation, and (e) cross-sector collaboration. Some schools are trying to implement a whole-school approach and the special education centers are supposed to provide the early intervention when these services are requested. As a result, home and school cooperation as well as early intervention are mostly provided only to upper- and middle-class families. To address this differential treatment of families by socioeconomic status, schools need to make sure that all families, including those from working-class backgrounds, understand the educational rights provided to them and their children. Cross-section collaboration is said to be one of the leading factors in the success of inclusive schools. Educators also need to adjust their services to make sure that the work schedules, time conflicts, transportation problems, and child care needs of families do not serve as barriers to the participation of families in the educational process.

An inservice training model for school teachers for helping students with special needs

An inservice training model was trialed for supporting learners with special educational needs in Thailand (see Kantavong and Sivabaedya, 2010 for a detailed review). Sample schools were selected based on screening assessments for students with special needs in LD, AD/HD and autism. The original model provided training for five days. Due to the teachers' overwhelming workload, the model was modified by adding the concept of collaborative work, which seemed to work better. A resource corner was also added to the new model since not every school could afford a separate resource room due to the cost and a lack of personnel to work in a separate resource room. When a separate room was available schools had to assign an existing teacher from their classes to teach students with special needs in the resource room.

The teachers, school directors, and parents were trained for three days during the month of January 2009. When working with students with special needs in inclusive classrooms, school administrators and parents are also key factors for the success of the program (Salend, 2011). In order to develop these tasks, school leaders and teachers need to have knowledge of and an understanding about special education. In the three-day training session 84 teachers, 8 school directors, and 85 parents were trained both in instructional techniques and in producing teaching materials for students with special needs in communication, social skills, language,

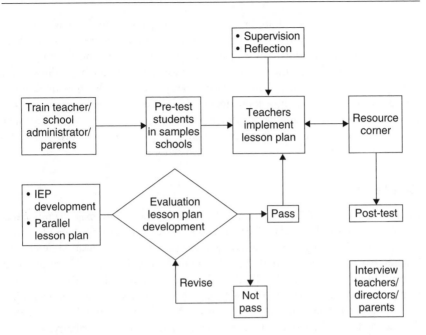

Figure 3.1 A training model

and mathematical skills. The group of parents was trained for one day. The training model is presented in Figure 3.1.

The concepts of the training procedures can be summarized as follows: teachers were divided into three groups based on their interests. The teachers had to analyze core curricula, learn about behavioural modifications, classroom management, intervention techniques, and parallel lesson plan development. The concept of a resource corner was also introduced. Videos were used for case study demonstration. The teachers were assigned to work in pairs or small groups to develop parallel lesson plans and subsequently present these to the whole group. Parents and administrators participated in the first day of the training session only. They did not need to participate in the workshop for instructional techniques.

After the training sessions teachers, parents, and administrators developed their own lesson plans and teaching materials based on the knowledge and techniques they learned from the training program. These lesson plans were then implemented in classrooms and data were collected by employing a classroom action research approach. During the period of working on their parallel lesson plan and teaching materials, teachers mailed or telephoned the researchers when they needed feedback and assistance.

The researchers also observed the teachers and their implementation of the prepared activities. These observations are reflected in the second and third cycles of the classroom action research approach. On the first round of visiting the classrooms, the teachers did not practice the quality parallel lesson plans they were trained to develop and implement, thus a re-training was conducted for them along with reflective observation. The teachers conducted a second and third round of their teaching, addressing the development of knowledge and understanding. From the reflective information and observation, it became evident that they understood the approaches for enhancing competency of students with autism, attention disorders, and learning disabilities. Unfortunately, as soon as they returned to their schools, the teachers encountered an overwhelming amount of work plus additional workload based on new policies in their schools.

Challenges

In order to develop inclusive education in a whole school, two major components are necessary. First, the head teachers or school directors and other stakeholders must support, cooperate, supervise, monitor, and evaluate inclusive education in schools. Second, development plans and activities should be established in school planning systems. In practice, though, in Thailand the academic standard agenda is the dominant policy in educational systems and every school will have to focus on increasing students' academic performance. This means that schools must provide teachers with the knowledge, skills, and time to help all students succeed in the mainstream.

In addition, communities generally aim to foster the high performance of their children, especially in secondary schools. When schools enroll all children with no academic test for entrance, teachers should have classroom management skills to organize instruction to meet the needs of all students. The standard agenda is quite demanding; from the National Quality Assurance Office, from the communities and from a competitive point of view among schools. The inclusive classroom is part of social justice as it is a scheme to help children who perform below average to achieve at much higher levels and to develop their social skills so that they can function as good citizens in society. As Ainscow *et al.* (2006) report, when schools are faced with the standard agenda on one hand and justice for the lower performers on the other, that "efforts to foster inclusive school development are more likely to be effective when they are part of a wider, systematic strategy" (p. 175).

Currently, various research agencies provide funding for educational scholars to work with schools for both knowledge related to special education development and to prepare teachers so that they can manage inclusive classrooms effectively. A compulsory course is also offered under the teacher–profession preservice degree program. As a result, public schools have grown more aware of children with special needs over the last five years in Thailand. For instance, people with high-functioning autism are now recognized as members of society, whereas before they were considered to be mentally limited or insane. Those with learning disabilities are also now well recognized by teachers and educators.

One important issue that needs to be addressed from the policy level is the values of the public and educators toward inclusive education. The majority of the general public still do not have a knowledge and understanding of inclusive education.

The public has been used to seeing students with special needs in separate institutions. Therefore, when they come across certain types of students with special needs in the mainstream, they do not understand or notice it. The policy level needs a lot of public relations work and public dissemination of information in communities and society as a whole.

One factor contributing to the movement of inclusive education in Thai schools is a strong policy from the Ministry of Education. It is evident that schools usually follow the policy of the Ministry. So when the Ministry views inclusive education as the major scheme to develop, school principals need to comply and make it easy for teachers to deal with inclusive classrooms. The teachers' training model as discussed in this chapter provides a channel to integrate into teachers' development plans to enable teachers to feel a greater confidence in working with all students. Inclusive education would then no longer be a new phase in education in Thailand.

Similarly, teacher educators should work continuously and develop a wider network based on their research strategies with schools and develop stronger relationships with local policy-makers. Through the educational process, if coupled with vigorous cooperation between stakeholders, educators, and academics, the awareness of the process and success of the program should inevitably be reached and obtained.

Acknowledgements

The author would like to extend her sincere gratitude to all 11 researchers, 84 school teachers, eight administrators and parents who made a great contribution to the testing of the training model and The Thailand National Research Council for funding support.

References

Ainscow, M. (2008) "Making sure that every child matters: Towards a methodology for enhancing equity within education systems", in C. Forlin (ed.), *Catering for Learners with Diverse Needs: An Asia-Pacific Focus*, Hong Kong: Hong Kong Institute of Education, pp. 11–28.

Ainscow, M., Booth, T. and Dyson, A. (2006) *Improving Schools, Developing Inclusion*, London: Routledge.

Arayawinyoo, P. (1999) *Learning Disabilities*, Bangkok: Wan Kaew.

Carter, S. L. (2006) "The development of special education services", *Thailand International Journal of Special Education*, 21(2): 32–6.

Forlin, C. (2008) *Catering for Learners with Diverse Needs: An Asia-Pacific Focus*, Hong Kong: Hong Kong Institute of Education.

Kaennakam, J. (2008) *A Study of the State and Problem of Integrated Education for Special Education in Primary Schools under Khon Kaen Provincial Primary Education Office*. MEd. Faculty of Education, Khon Kaen University.

Kantavong, P. and Sivabaedya, S. (2010) "A professional learning program for enhancing the competency of students with special needs", *International Journal of Whole Schooling*, 6(1): 57–67.

Kasemsuk, P. (2001) *A Comparison of Inclusive Schools' Management Problems between Special Education Centered Schools and Regular Primary Schools under Angthong Provincial Primary Education Office.* MEd. Faculty of Education. Thepsatreee Rajabhat University.

Kittiwathanakul, P. (1998) "The management of disabled students in regular school", *Journal of Education (Khon Kaen University)*, 12(1): 12–7.

Lim, L. and Quah, M. M. (2004) *Educating Learners with Diverse Abilities*, Singapore: McGrawhill.

ONEC, Office of the National Education Commission (1999) *The National Education Act,* Bangkok: Prig wan Communication.

ONEC, Office of the National Education Commission (2003) *Synopsis of the National Scheme of Education. B.E 2545–2559 (2002–2016),* Bangkok: Prig wan Communication.

ONEC, Office of the National Education Commission (2009) *Summary Report: 9 Years of Educational Reform (1999–2008)*, Bangkok: VTC Communication.

Salend, S. J. (2011) *Creating Inclusive Classrooms: Effective and Reflective Practices*, 7th edn, Columbus, OH: Merrill/Pearson Education.

Thawiang, D. (2006) *A Development of an Inclusive Learning Management: A Case Study of Nongkungpitayakom School under the Jurisdiction of Khon Kaen Educational Service area 5.* MEd. Loei Rajabhat University.

Chapter 4

Development of learning in regular class and measure of teacher education in China

Jia-cheng Xu

Keywords: Learning in regular class (LRC, 随班就读), teacher education in mainland China

Chapter overview[1]

The major form of inclusive education in China is "Learning in Regular Class (LRC, 随班就读)", that is children with disabilities learn in the mainstream school. The development of LRC in China began concurrently with the development of the modern school. It involved three developmental stages: spontaneity (自发期), experiment (实验期), and development (发展期) and has become the major form of inclusive education for children with disabilities in China today. Compared with the several developmental stages of LRC, teacher education in mainland China also underwent a number of changes: free stage (自在期), initial stage (萌发期), and "insert" stage ("镶嵌"期). Teacher education for inclusive education requires a new idea to promote the development of role specialization (角色分化) for teachers in inclusive education, professionalization (专业化), and team integration (团队合作).

Development of learning in regular class in mainland China

Inclusive education in mainland China is mainly called LRC, the development of which can be divided into the spontaneity, experiment, and development stages.

Spontaneity stage of learning in regular class

As recorded in 1835, Mr and Mrs Gurzlaff, a couple of preachers, set up a girls' school in Macau, where three blind girls studied by using protruding words to read（Braille, 点字盲文）(Guo, 2001). This was the earliest record of blind people studying in regular school and can be regarded as the beginning of LRC in China.

1 This chapter was originally written in Chinese.

Before 1987, the main form of special education in China was the special education school; however, a few children and teenagers with a disability learned in regular schools. Most of these children were physically disabled, and a few of them had a hearing disability, visual disability, intellectual disability, or other disabilities. There were no official enrollment verifications, education placement, education strategies, or remedial measures. Special education students were mainly scattered in regular elementary and high schools as individual cases, and a negligible number of them were able to enter colleges.

In June 2001, the author organized a seminar for the teacher training program for special education in Wushan County, Chongqing. One of the teachers, who came from a rural area, shared that in the 1970s, in a mixed class (i.e. where students of different academic levels study in the same class handled by only one teacher) at a school in the mountainous area of Wushan County, Chongqing, the teacher accepted a female student with a hearing disability. With the help of her younger brother, using an invented sign language, the student was able to complete six years of fundamental education. Similar cases existed in both rural and urban schools during the same period. Many people remember classmates who were handicapped in their elementary and high schools.

> In the 1970s, when our country was still closing her doors against the world, a significant trend appeared in deaf teaching circles, advocating the transfer of deaf students with certain hearing ability to regular schools based on their grades, so that they could practice speaking the language used in regular schools, and rapidly improve their speaking abilities and overcome deaf-mutism. At the same time, in this way, both deaf and healthy children could play and study together, which is beneficial for the integrated development and future of deaf children.
>
> (Zhang, 1990, pp. 44–5)

The above-mentioned cases make two important points. First, in a vast rural area children with a disability enroll in regular schools in their neighborhood. Second, deaf children learning in special education schools also attempt to leave their isolated environment and enroll in regular schools. These two basic reasons for promoting LRC in China will be discussed further.

Experiment stage of LRC

The initiation and experiment stage of LRC in China took place between 1987–1994. Since 1987, the Xu Bailun Visual Disability Education and Research Center has been promoting the "Golden Key Blind Children Education Plan" (金钥匙盲童教育计划), which is being implemented with the support of administrative departments for education in Beijing, Shanxi, Jiangsu, Hebei, Heilongjiang, and other provinces in China.

The core of the plan is to enable blind children to attend classes together with regular students once they have completed fundamental learning, which is in accordance with the requirement of entering the school in the neighborhood. In addition, other than teacher training, there are special requirements for school campuses and facilities.

(Su, 2010, p. 7)

This educational experiment has achieved desirable effects in all experimental areas. In 1990, it was named LRC. After the State Education Commission in China it was accredited by the Disabled Persons' Federation in order to promote it nationwide.

Special education for children with intellectual disabilities was started in the 1980s in China. It used to be referred to as a special education school, and is now known as Peizhi School. In 1988, the former State Education Commission conducted experiments in five provinces and cities: Beijing, Shandong, Liaoning, Jiangsu, and Zhejiang. In April 1992, the State Education Commission held the "Onsite Seminar on Mentally Retarded Children Learning in Regular Class" (弱智儿童随班就读现场研讨会) in Changle, Weifang, and Shandong, to enlarge and promote experiments with children with intellectual disabilities learning in regular class.

In 1994, the state education commission held the "Conference on Handicapped Children Learning in Regular Class in China" (全国残疾儿童随班班就读工作会议) in Yancheng, Jiangsu, to arrange LRC. The Yancheng Conference focuses on Chinese children who are blind, deaf, or have an intellectual disability learning in the regular class. LRC has gradually developed into a main form of special education in China.

Development stage of LRC

After the Yancheng Conference, LRC in China started to be implemented officially from being a pilot program. LRC entered its development stage, with the following manifestations.

Development of targets of LRC

At the end of the 1980s to the beginning of the 1990s, students learning in regular class were mainly three types of children with disabilities: those with hearing disabilities, those with visual impairment, and those with intellectual disabilities. Education targets have been gradually extended to children with cerebral palsy, infantile autism spectrum disorders, learning disability, and behaviour and emotional disorders.

Development of the number of children learning in regular class

Since 1994, LRC has been constantly promoted, with the number of students gradually increasing. According to the latest data, children learning in regular class account for more than 60 per cent of children receiving special education (Ministry of Education of the People's Republic of China, 2010).

Extension of length of service

Length of service of LRC develops from fundamental education toward both ends, with the front end extending to inclusive education in kindergarten, and with the back end extending to secondary education and higher vocational education. In 2003, three institutions, including the Ministry of Education, revised relevant regulations on enrollment in colleges and reduced the restrictions on physical qualifications of students participating in college entrance examination, so that more students with a disability could receive higher education in colleges, most of whom have physical disabilities, whereas a few have a hearing disability or a visual impairment. In 2011, the number of college students learning in regular class has surpassed the number of students learning in special education schools. According to 《中国残疾人事业发展统计公报》 (China Disabled Persons' Federation, 2011), "7,674 people were accepted by regular colleges, 1,057 people entered the special schools for learning" (Section 2, Education of people with disability, para. 3); the former is more than seven times greater than the latter.

Development of teaching model

Four types of pedagogical models have been developed to support children with special educational needs:

 i. Hierarchical teaching: using the experience gained from the initial stage of LRC to divide students learning in regular class and ordinary students into several hierarchies according to abilities, thereby enabling teachers to provide proper and appropriate guidance to students of different hierarchies.
 ii. Individualized teaching: compiling individualized education programs for students learning in regular class, adopting ability level grouping by merging the individualized teaching plan with the regular teaching program ("群点"教学) in ordinary classes based on individualized education programs, and providing individualized remedial instruction to the students.
iii. Cooperative learning: cooperative LRC is reflected as group cooperative learning and competition between different groups in order to enable some students in a group to assist those learning in regular class in their study; a partnership system is sometimes adopted, whereby outstanding students interact with those learning in regular class, providing necessary support.
 iv. Difference in teaching: 15 different systematic teaching and learning strategies based on personality characteristics and significant individual differences between cognitive levels are utilized to improve the students' learning effectiveness (Hua, 2009).

Development of the support system

When LRC started its implementation, a relevant support system was proposed, and the model of resource classroom or counseling classroom began to be built. After 2000, by implementing the national educational program, the Elementary Education Department of the Ministry of Education proposed the establishment of the "Support and Guarantee System of LRC" (随班就读支持保障体系). In Beijing, Shanghai, Zhejiang, Sichuan, and other cities and provinces, the basis of LRC, resource classrooms, and support systems were initiated. This provided students learning in regular class with social, professional, and natural support strategies suitable for their individual expectations, promoting their independence, learning effectiveness, social participation, and sense of happiness, as well as improving both the teaching and learning quality of LRC.

Development of LRC and response to teacher education

Corresponding to the development state of LRC, teachers transitioned from the free stage to the conscious stage, and faced the challenges of professional demands.

Voluntary stage (自在阶段)

Before 1986, LRC was still in the free stage, wherein there was no special education in the teacher education system in China. At that time, teacher education was called normal education and was composed of higher normal education (including two levels: undergraduate and graduate education), secondary normal education, pre-school teacher education, and other levels. In higher normal schools, teachers for secondary school and above are trained; secondary education is responsible for training primary school teachers; and pre-school teacher education aims to train kindergarten teachers. At this stage, there was no special normal education; therefore, teachers in special education schools were trained using two methods: teaching succession and school-based training based on receiving ordinary normal education. Since 1949, special education schools in China have mainly been providing primary education for students with a disability; therefore, teachers in special education schools are mainly graduates from secondary normal universities who have received theoretical and skill training in special education from special education schools.

In the spontaneity stage, understanding of special education of teachers in regular schools was voluntary (自在阶段). The way they treated children with a disability was due to their compassion and sense of justice. Special school teachers, however, had not received any professional training in special education.

Initial stage (蒙发时期)

From the beginning of the pilot project of LRC, teachers needed to enter the conscious stage, with most of them having their education ideas altered. A few teachers tried to reject the new system, reasoning that children with a disability should be educated in special education schools, and that LRC means separating the children with a disability from classes in regular school and giving them different requirements.

The global perspective and philosophy towards special education and putting this in practice have become the basic forms of teacher education of LRC.

China's reform and open policy provides an opportunity for teachers to understand international development trends and the spirit of special education. In order to change the teachers' educational orientation, improve the quality of LRC, and enhance teaching effectiveness, teachers involved in LRC are provided with opportunities of short-term training and project research. Short-term training is mainly an international operation project, whereas national and regular training involve continuous education.

Project research is closely related to school-based research and training. The exploration of special education in some regions, including the "Golden Key Blind Children Education Plan", pilots projects of LRC in five provinces and cities. These have promoted the growth and quality of teachers, as well as the first batch of learners in regular class, by completing certain projects, research, and school-based training.

Insert stage (镶嵌时期)

In recent decades, the curriculum and instruction on LRC have gradually developed into a domestic normal education system, and an inserting structure has been formed.

LRC, during its initial period, was mainly carried out in primary schools with teachers who were mostly from secondary teacher schools. In addition, with the financial support of the United Nations Children's Fund, the China Research Institute of Education Science has set up general courses for special education in secondary teacher schools.

When special education was offered as a major in higher normal education in China in 1986, the special education teacher training in China entered the stage of formal education (Chen, 2004). At the same time, with the financial support of the normal education development project through a loan from the World Bank, Chongqing Normal University has established both its special education course in higher education teacher training and public course in special education, with a major in regular normal education (Chen, 2004). With primary school teacher education being offered in undergraduate courses, Quanzhou Normal University has set up a course on special education in their major primary education (Zeng and Ye, 2004). The College of Special Education of Beijing Union University (2007) has established the optional courses of LRC and resource classroom, with a major in special education. As a result, the graduates are able to work in special education after completing their fundamental and pre-school education, understanding learning in regular kindergarten and resource classrooms.

In the modern Chinese teacher education system, teacher education related to LRC is still restricted to a few normal universities' cases in a huge system, which is far less than the actual demands of training teachers for LRC.

Expectation for teachers with the new trend and development

New background

Under the *United Nations Convention on the Rights of Persons with Disabilities* (2006), the right of children with a disability to receive education is stressed, and is used as a basis for including children with a disability in the regular education system. As an active proponent of and the first country to sign the convention, China is faced with the problem of realizing education for children with a disability and ensuring their right to receive education.

In *National Medium- and Long-Term Education Reform and Development Planning 2010–2020*, the strategic targets of education development in China for the future are proposed (The Central People's Government of the People's Republic of China, 2010). Equal access to education and education quality has become the main concern of development in the next century. LRC, as the main special education model in China, is faced with the problem of finding ways to enlarge the service objects of special education and improve education quality.

Challenges faced

With the latest development trend, LRC is faced with the following challenges:

Challenge 1: Taking all necessary measures to ensure the rights of children with a disability to receive education has public support. Many people take the problem of children with a disability receiving education, not as an inherent right, but as a benefit.

Challenge 2: Many people hold that children with a disability should study in special education schools, instead of learning in regular classes in regular schools.

Challenge 3: Courses in regular schools are mainly discipline-based courses and cannot meet the demands of students with disabilities learning in regular class.

Challenge 4: Teachers in regular schools are usually short of effective teaching strategies and methods aimed at children with special needs and lack support of professional rehabilitation talents.

Challenge 5: Poor teaching quality and effect of LRC.

New countermeasures of teacher education

The following updates are expected to be realized for teacher education design:

(a) In terms of education design: conversion from a discipline-based teacher role recognition to holistic humanity-oriented education.

(b) In terms of course concept: conversion from discipline-based curricular concept to multi-curricular concept.
(c) In terms of teaching: conversion from single teaching strategy to integrative strategies of teaching, rehabilitation, and support.
(d) In terms of teaching evaluation: conversion from teaching quality evaluation to education achievement evaluation.

Teacher role recognition and role specialization

(a) All the regular teachers need to recognize themselves as teachers involved in LRC.
(b) A new teacher type – resource teacher – needs to grow from the current regular teachers.
(c) A new group of teachers need to be trained in special education schools and undertake the responsibility of inspecting and guiding both resource classrooms and LRC in regular schools. Teachers of this type usually need to possess certain skills in special education, certain understanding of regular education, and at the same time, abundant teaching experience.

Teacher specialization development

Teachers of various types involved in LRC not only need to have their own specialization development strategies, but also need to form a professional team based on mutual respect and cooperation. These involve both specialty differentiation and team integration.

Specialty differentiation is mainly reflected in two types: resource teachers and inspecting and guiding teachers. Resource teachers trained to work in regular schools should develop their professional skills for teaching children with disabilities including those with learning disorders, language disorders, as well as behaviour and emotional disorders, and be trained in social work.

Specialty differentiation of resource teachers oriented for resource centers is mainly developing in the direction of rehabilitation majors, such as physiotherapy, occupational therapy, hearing evaluation, language therapy, and psychotherapy (including musical therapy, play therapy, and the like), as well as in the direction of professional services for children with multiple severe disorders. With specialty differentiation of teachers, special attention needs to be observed in forming teams, especially by the team leader. Someone with a certain level of authority, coordination ability between different majors, and promotion ability should be cultivated into the core of team construction to enable team integration.

Institutionalization of teacher education

The previous analysis shows that teacher education in China is facing great challenges in the new developmental trend of inclusive education. To cope with these challenges, the design and construction of teacher education institutionalization for LRC should be implemented. Institutionalization construction includes the following.

Special major education in pre-vocational education (education with record of formal schooling) for teachers

This should include an inclusive education course and resource teacher orientation for special education major. Special education courses should be created for all students of normal education, so that concept courses and teaching of special education could be included in the public course system of education. Medical schools, psychology, sociology, and other relevant majors should aim to cultivate professionals in rehabilitation and social work.

School-based research and continuing education implementing special education in vocational continuing education (in-service education)

Front-line teachers should be encouraged to conduct research about LRC. Systematic training on LRC should be implemented to meet the objectives of continuing education.

Conclusion

Analyzing the corresponding relationship between the developmental stages of LRC and the development of teacher education in China, this relationship reveals the interaction between the practice of LRC and professionalization of teacher education. Therefore, by promoting the professionalization of teacher education, it should be possible to effectively improve the quality of LRC in order to meet the increasing demand of LRC in China.

References

Chen, Y. Y. (2004) 中国特殊教育学基础 [*Introduction of Special Education in China*], 北京 : 教育科学出版社.

China Disabled Persons' Federation (2011) "2010 年中国残疾人事业发展统计公报 [Statistical Communique on Development of the Work for Persons with Disabilities in 2010]". Online. Available at: http://www.cdpf.org.cn/sytj/content/2011–03/24/content_30316232.htm (accessed 19 August 2011).

Guo, W. (2001) "基督新教与中国近代的特殊教育 [Protestantism and Chinese modern special education]", *Social Science Research*, 4, pp. 123–8.

Hua, G. (2009) 差异教学策略 [Different Teaching Strategies]. Beijing Normal University Publishing Group.

Ministry of Education of the People's Republic of China (2010) "2009 年全国教育事业发展统计公报 [2009 National Educational Development Statistics Bulletin]". Online.

Available at: http://www.moe.gov.cn/publicfiles/business/htmlfiles/moe/moe_633/201008/93763.html (accessed 19 August 2011).

Special Education College of Beijing Union University (2007) 特殊教育专业2007版人才培养计划 [*The 2007 Professional Training Program for Special Education*]. Internal Document.

Su, T. (2010, October 14) "徐白仑：白黑人生的多彩印迹 [Xu Bailun: The colorful traces of a life with white and black", *China Education Daily*, p. 1.

The Central People's Government of the People's Republic of China (2010, July 29) 国家中长期教育改革和发展规划纲要2010–2020年 [*National Medium- and Long-Term Education Reform and Development Planning (2010–2020)*], China: The Central People's Government of the People's Republic of China.

United Nations (2006) *Convention on the Rights of Persons with Disabilities*.

Zeng, Y. R. and Ye, Z. B. (2004) "Exploring on elementary teacher education for integrated classes", *Teacher Education Research*, 16(6): 45–9.

Zhang, N. (1990) "试论聋童一体化教育安置的心理条件 [A preliminary discussion on psychological conditions of integration education placement of deaf children]", 辽宁师范大学学报, 1: 44–5.

Chapter 5

A mosaic of models

Teacher education for inclusion in Israel

Gilada Avissar

Keywords: teacher education, teacher education in Israel, inclusion in Israel, infusion model, unification model, a unified practicum

Chapter overview

A study of the implementation of teacher education requirements in Israel shows a varied picture. While adhering to the official requirements, the different colleges have developed a mosaic of Initial Teacher Training (ITT) models. Three of these models will be presented in detail in this chapter: (1) the development and implementation of a mandatory course during ITT on the topic of 'Diversity in Education'; (2) the initiation of a mandatory ITT unit that includes introductory courses covering several areas of special educational needs (SEN); and (3) the creation of a unified ITT practicum which brings together students in the special education and elementary school education training programs.

Introduction

Education in Israel is provided in a dual system of 'regular' and special education. This division can be seen both in a parallel system of schools, as well as in teacher education programs. The inclusion of students with SEN in regular schools has been practiced on a voluntary basis since the mid-fifties and became mandatory in the early 1990s. Consequently, as of the mid-nineties, teacher training institutions began to respond and adapt their programs accordingly.

Most of the teacher education in Israel takes place in teacher training colleges that grant Bachelor of Education (BEd) and Master in Education (MEd) degrees. These colleges prepare kindergarten, elementary and middle-school teachers. High-school teachers are trained in the universities, after obtaining a Bachelor of Arts (BA) degree. A characteristic of the Israeli education system is that it is highly centralized, although it allows for some local and institutional autonomy. This autonomy has enabled the teacher education institutions to develop somewhat different approaches.

Two major factors influence teacher training for inclusion: (a) the mandate that every student teacher must take at least one course that pertains to the education of children with SEN and (b) the new *Guidelines for Teacher Training* (Council for Higher Education, 2008) that aim to diversify the training programs while cutting down the overall number of credit hours required. The new guidelines make special education courses accessible to all those who are interested and certification has been broadened to include a category for 'inclusive educators'.

Teacher education for inclusion

Teacher education worldwide today faces a complex reality and of late has been the target of steady scrutiny and criticism (see, for example: Forlin, 2010; Mevorach and Ezer, 2010; and the new AERA research volume edited by Ball and Tyson, 2011, which focuses on diversity in teacher education). In many countries central authorities such as ministries of education or local education authorities are initiating and leading reforms in teacher education in response to the ongoing reforms in education at large. As inclusion is understood to be "one of the more complex changes on the current education scene" (Fullan and Steigelbauer, 1991, p. 41), it is no surprise that over the last decade many have contributed to the discussion about training teachers to function effectively in inclusive educational environments (see, for example: Jordan *et al.*, 2009). Efforts have been made to ensure that regular education teachers are adequately prepared for inclusive teaching and learning environments. Stayton and McCollun (2002) provide an overview of research in this area. They have identified three models: (a) an infusion model where one or two special education courses are infused into the training program for regular education coupled with exposure to SEN during the practicum; (b) a collaborative training model where staff from both training programs (special education and regular education) collaborate in teaching the pedagogic course and in mentoring the practicum; and (c) a unified model where the training programs have been unified into one. The latter model seems to be based on the near consensus that "there is no compelling reason for general and special education to remain separate, at least in the initial level of teacher education" (York and Reynolds, 1996, p. 829).

Teacher education for inclusion in Israel: Historical and legal context

Israel is home to two nations, Jewish and Arab and to a growing number of immigrant Jews from all over the world. It was established as an independent democracy in 1948 and soon after, the founding fathers, responding to existing societal and political forces, created a general education system which is divided into four tracks: (1) state; (2) state-religious (Jewish); (3) independent; and (4) Arab. The language of instruction in the Arab schools is Arabic and the curriculum emphasizes Arab history, religion and culture. State-religious schools offer intensive Jewish studies programs and emphasize tradition and observance. There are also private independent schools (e.g. Democratic Schools, The American School or church sponsored schools). The majority of children attend state schools. Provision for students with

SEN is in a parallel system that is organized into the same tracks. The dual system of 'regular' and 'special' education can be found both in the parallel system of schools, as well as in teacher education programs.

Provision of education in Israel is governed by three major laws: *The Compulsory Education Law* (1949); *The State Education Law* (1953) and *The Special Education Law* (1988). The latter has been recently amended (2003) to emphasize the mandate to include children with SEN in general education settings. Higher education in Israel is governed by the Council for Higher Education Law of 1958. Teacher training colleges, the first of which were established as teacher seminars in 1914, were transformed into academic institutions of higher education beginning at the end of the 1970s.

Special education legislation in Israel supported ongoing practices and reflected commitments and concerns of legislators and educators worldwide (Al-Yagon and Margalit, 2001). By the 1998–99 school year all schools in Israel were expected to begin to enroll pupils with special needs. At this point, special education services are provided either in non-inclusive (segregated) settings that are detached from the mainstream of education (i.e. special kindergarten and special schools) or in self-contained special classes within mainstream schools. In addition, a growing number of children are included in mainstream education where they receive individual assistance in the classroom or in a 'pull-out' program in accordance with their Individual Educational Plan. The education ministry in Israel has not proposed closing its special schools, although it has increasingly pursued a policy of mainstreaming many students who would previously have been placed in special educational settings.

The policy for educating students with SEN was shaped during the 1990s. First, a task force was appointed by the Minister of Education and the Minister of Science in December 1996 to examine the issue of pupils with learning disabilities and to suggest ways and means to empower these youngsters so that they would be able to fulfill their potential. Second, in February 2000, the Minister of Education appointed a committee whose aim was to examine the implementation of the *Special Education Law*. Both committees recommended re-examining and amending teacher training programs so that every teacher, whether being trained to work in special education settings or in mainstream schools, would be trained to teach students with SEN, in particular students with learning disabilities. In accordance with these recommendations, the head of the department of teacher training within the Ministry of Education, addressing the heads of teacher training colleges, issued in March 1992 a policy statement which ended with a mandate to incorporate into their curricula at least one course on SEN. I suggest that this mandate had a major influence on teacher training for inclusion.

Another source of influence is the new *Guidelines for Teacher Training* (Council for Higher Education, 2008) that aims to diversify the training programs, strengthen the disciplinary studies component and emphasize the practicum while reducing the overall number of credit hours required (Council for Higher Education, 2008). These guidelines establish the structure for programs of teacher training in every academic framework recognized by the Council for Higher Education and every institution has to conform to them. One of the leading principles is having core topics common to the different training programs. One such topic is "teaching and learning for students with diverse needs and from different social and cultural backgrounds". Another principle mandated a baseline comprised of thirty credit hours that include courses in education, pedagogy and research literacy as well as a practicum, in either a traditional model or the Professional Development School (PDS) model. A third principle calls for facilitating different combinations of the course of study. Thus, the teaching certificate could either be granted in two disciplinary areas such as mathematics and science for elementary education or in a single discipline supplemented by two smaller units from other disciplines, for example, mathematics for elementary education along with smaller units in special education and in science. I therefore suggest that these guidelines make special education courses accessible to all who are interested. In addition, certification has been broadened to include a new category – 'inclusive educator' for pre-school and elementary school levels.

Although the Israeli education system is highly centralized, it allows for some local and institutional autonomy. This autonomy has enabled teacher education colleges to develop somewhat different approaches. A study of the implementation of these requirements shows a varied picture (Ben-Peretz, 2001; Avissar and Almog, 2003). While adhering to the official requirements, the teacher training colleges developed a mosaic of training models. Three of these models are now presented.

Following an infusion model

"This course was not only interesting but also an 'eye-opener'".

(Feedback from a student)
A mandatory course – 'Diversity in Education'

One of the challenges facing teacher education for inclusion is how to foster positive attitudes toward the accommodation of students with SEN in general education classes. A simple and most direct step is to add a course to the training program for general education as in an infusion model (Stayton and McCollun, 2002). There is a growing body of research pertaining to attitudinal changes of student teachers with regard to disability per se and with regard to inclusion (see, for example: Golder et al., 2005; Jung, 2007; Forlin et al., 2009). The courses described usually lasted for one semester and the participants were mainly general education student teachers. Some of these courses included a certain degree of direct contact with people with disabilities through site observations or individual tutoring. The overall aims of these courses were to influence attitudes positively and to improve the abilities, confidence level and a sense of self-efficacy of the participants. In general, these studies point out that such courses contribute to positive changes in preservice teachers' attitudes and that guided field experience plays an important part in the change process.

Partly in response to the mandate to incorporate a special education course in training programs for general education and partly as a consequence of local initiatives, courses pertaining to children with learning disabilities or SEN in general were introduced into teacher training curricula. In one of the colleges this development became part of an overall change in the structure of the curriculum. It was decided that along with the traditional introductory courses in education, a course pertaining to diversity in education should be offered to all preservice teachers. An interdisciplinary team of six lecturers that included two special educators, two sociologists and two anthropologists began planning the course in 2004. The planning process involved sharing of disciplinary knowledge and debating the possible objectives of the course, the target population and even its title. The decision was that the course would be entitled 'Diversity in education' and it would be mandatory for all except for special education student teachers. The objectives are:

1. To evoke awareness to diversity as a normal and normative social phenomena.
2. To become acquainted with aspects of diversity and modes of researching diversity and their relevancy to education.
3. To acknowledge the basic dilemmas of diversity.
4. To learn about the characteristics and the needs of learners with disabilities who are included in regular education classrooms.
5. To develop a sense of self-efficacy with regard to dealing with diversity in the classroom.

Obligatory content units include dilemmas of diversity, attitudes toward disabilities, the idea and the movement toward inclusion, inclusionary measures in the classroom and legal mandates with regard to diversity and disabilities. Depending on the disciplinary background of each lecturer, units on learning disabilities, gifted students, students with autism, social processes, heterogeneity in teaching and learning were developed and shared by means of continued meetings among the faculty and guest lectures in the respective classes. The group was led by a special educator but it was agreed that the context of this course is beyond that of students with SEN.

By the third year, the faculty of the department of early childhood education had developed their own course on special needs in early childhood. In addition, based on students' feedback, the pedagogic instructors as well as the lecturers of this course realized that a knowledge-based course was not enough. Also, the student teachers requested to acquire more skills needed in the classroom. After much debate it was decided to add a course titled 'Instructional strategies in the heterogeneous class' aimed at the practical aspects related to diversity in education and in the classroom.

At present, these are required courses for student teachers in the elementary-school and middle-school programs. The group of lecturers continues to confer, study and revise the course. Last year the course title was changed (again) and it is now called: 'Diversity as an educational challenge'.

Following a unification model

> "My colleagues and I have always fantasized that every student teacher will take courses in special education".
>
> (Head of the Special Education Department)
> A mandatory unit that includes introductory courses
> covering several areas of SEN

The need to implement the new *Guidelines for Teacher Training* resulted in structural as well as content changes in teacher training programs. The immediate need was to respond to the reduction in credit hours. In some cases this was an opportunity to re-think the vision and the mission of the programs.

One teacher training college underwent a prolonged process of redefining its vision and mission. One of the principal ideas was that the course of training for general education, pre-school, elementary and middle school should include a unit on SEN.

Personal communication with the respective heads of the programs revealed that this was both a vision shared by the staff of the special education department and the head of the school of education. The rationale was that mainstream education is currently the reality in schools all over Israel and educating mainstream students is by and large the responsibility of the mainstream teacher. The staff of the college felt obligated to take this into consideration when adapting existing training programs to the new guidelines.

Beginning in the 2008–2009 school year, student teachers from programs other than special education were required to take a unit of six to ten credit hours as part of their education course credits. This unit includes courses such as: Inclusion – theory and practice; learning disabilities; remedial teaching in reading; remedial teaching in math; classroom management; challenges in language acquisition; learners at risk; multi-lingual learners in early childhood classes and in elementary education; developing social skills; and others. In addition, the educational philosophy that recognizes diversity and inclusion and promotes it is evident from the revised structure of the practicum. In the first year of study the focus is on child development and it is accompanied by working with an individual child. During the second year the practicum focuses on working with a group of children and developing awareness of multi-culturalism and inclusion, and during the third year the focus is on classroom management emphasizing leadership qualities and management of diversity.

This model is still developing. No data has been collected yet as to the efficacy of this model but an evaluative follow-up study is planned for next year. Internationally, there are a number of reports on unified programs as summarized by Stayton and McCollun (2002) and a similar approach is described by Ford *et al.* (2001) with regard to the restructured teacher education program at the University of Wisconsin–Milwaukee.

The Israeli version of a unified model aims at strengthening the commitment of future teachers of all age levels to teaching a wide range of children and to having a better understanding of diversity and disability.

A unified practicum

> "I find it very difficult . . . it is a big class and the students are 'regular' and special-ed. put together".
>
> (A student teacher)

Practicums in PDS settings are common in Israel. Several training institutions use this framework to conduct a unified practicum where student teachers from the special education department collaborate with their counterparts from the elementary education department as do their respective pedagogic instructors.

The scarcity of reports on PDS and inclusive schools is well reflected in the March 2007 special issue of *The Journal of Educational Research* which describes seven examples of efforts to reform K-16 teaching and learning through PDS partnerships. Only one presents an overview including the *No Child Left Behind* legislation (Trachtman, 2007).

One of the teacher training colleges in Israel has conducted a unified practicum that utilizes the infrastructure of PDS since 1996. It exemplifies the characteristics of an academia–school partnership such as joint planning, feedback and evaluation, assignment of two student teachers to each class and a requirement to devote two days per week to the field placement (as opposed to the general requirement of a single day per week). The pedagogic curricula of the two training programs are integrated, as are the feedback sessions with the student teachers. The latter are attended by both pedagogical instructors and the classroom mentoring teacher.

This partnership began when the school principal approached the college looking for "somebody who will understand my needs and offer appropriate assistance". The college saw this partnership as an opportunity to realize its commitment to community involvement and to support educational progress of under-achievers and students with SEN. Thirty per cent of senior student teachers in each training program were selected taking into account their academic standing and their pedagogic performance. The idea was to assign outstanding students to this program and a group dynamic method was used to pair them. The mainstream home-room teacher acted as mentor for both and additional supervision was carried out by pedagogical instructors from both departments.

This model reflects collaboration, co-teaching and modeling (a detailed description can be found in Bashan and Holsblat, in press). Collaborative teaching is one of the more important factors of successful inclusive education and is considered a basic skill in teaching that is most appropriate for mainstream and inclusive classes. Modeling is highly important in teacher training as it links theory to the reality of the classroom (Lunenberg and Korthagen, 2003).

This collaborative model developed gradually. It involved the training of mentoring teachers as their role included working with two students who taught collaboratively as well as cooperating with two pedagogical instructors. It created several challenges: an average-size school can accommodate only a certain number of student teachers which means that the pedagogical instructors need to find appropriate practicum placement for the rest of the student teachers. The necessity for documentation and reflecting on the collaborative process put an extra workload on the pedagogical instructors. Finally, and most importantly, this model was rather expensive for the college as two staff members were employed whereas previously a group of this size would have had a single instructor. As of 2010, twelve years after the inception of this collaborative program, it was "put out to pasture" as a result of budget cuts.

Conclusion

A diverse range of models aiming to prepare teachers for inclusive education have been adopted in Israel. All the models described in this article pertain to ITT. These approaches might be relevant and of interest to colleagues in other regions to adapt, implement and investigate. A mosaic is defined in the Merrian-Webster dictionary (www.merrian-webster.com) as: "A picture or design made up of different pieces, fitted together by design to form a unified composition". Can teacher education for inclusion in Israel be considered a mosaic? Is this variety of models being implemented an indication of a diversified approach to teacher education for inclusion? What seems to be missing is a unifying conceptualization of what is needed to prepare teachers to implement inclusion. What is called for is research that will emphasize the local context and validate the steps taken by the various teacher training institutions.

References

Al-Yagon, M. and Margalit, M. (2001) "Special and inclusive education in Israel", *Mediterranean Journal of Educational Studies*, 6(2): 93–112.

Avissar, G. and Almog, O. (2003) "Hakhsharat morim be'metzioot shel shiluv: Me'ayin banu ve'le'an anu holkhim [Teacher training in an inclusive era: Where we came from and where are we heading?]", *Issues in Special Education and Rehabilitation*, 18(2): 5–18.

Ball, A. F. and Tyson, C. A. (2011) *Studying Diversity in Teacher Education*, Washington, D.C.: Rowman and Littlefield Publishers in partnership with AERA.

Bashan, B. and Holsblat, R. (in press) "Co-teaching through modeling processes: Professional development of students and instructors in a teacher training program", *Mentoring and Tutoring Journal*.

Ben-Peretz, M. (2001) *Hakhsharat hamorim be'Israel be'temurot hazman: Doch hava'ada kebedikat hakhsharat hamorim be'Israel* [Teacher education in Israel in changing times: Report of

The Commission for Examining Teacher Education in Israel], Jerusalem: Ministry of Education.

Council for Higher Education (2008) *Guidelines for Teacher Training*. Online. Available at: http://www.che.org.il/template/default_e.aspx?PageId=309 (accessed 19 August 2011).

Ford, A., Pugach, M. C. and Otis-Wilborn, A. (2001) "Preparing general educators to work well with students who have disabilities: What's reasonable at the preservice level?", *Learning Disability Quarterly*, 24(4): 275–85.

Forlin, C. (2010) "Reframing teacher education for inclusion", in C. Forlin (ed.) *Teacher Education for Inclusion: Changing Paradigms and Innovative Approaches*, London: Routledge, pp. 3–22.

Forlin, C., Loreman, T., Sharma, U. and Earle, C. (2009) "Demographic differences in changing pre-service teachers' attitudes, sentiments and concerns about inclusive education", *International Journal of Inclusive Education*, 13(2): 159–209.

Fullan, M. and Steigelbauer, S. (1991) *The New Meaning of Educational Change*, 2nd edn, New York: Teachers College Press.

Golder, G., Norwich, B. and Bayliss, P. (2005) "Preparing teachers to teach pupils with special educational needs in more inclusive schools: Evaluating a PGCE development", *British Journal of Special Education*, 32(2): 92–9.

Jordan, A., Schwartz, E. and McGhie-Richmond, D. (2009) "Preparing teachers for inclusive classrooms", *Teaching and Teacher Education*, 25: 535–42.

Jung, W. S. (2007) "Pre-service teacher training for successful inclusion", *Education*, 128(1): 106–11.

Lunenberg, M. and Korthagen, F. A. J. (2003) "Teacher educators and students – directed learning", *Teaching and Teacher Education*, 19(1): 29–45.

Mevorach, M. and Ezer, H. (2010) "Riding on a speeding train? How teacher educators perceive teacher education", *Teacher Development*, 14(4): 427–45.

Stayton, V. D. and McCollun, J. (2002) "Unifying general and special education: What does the research tell us?", *Teacher Education and Special Education*, 25(3): 211–18.

Trachtman, R. (2007) "Inquiry and accountability in professional development schools", *The Journal of Educational Research*, 100(4): 197–203.

York, J. L. and Reynolds, M. C. (1996) "Special education and inclusion", in J. Sikula, T. J. Buttery and E. Guyton (eds), *Handbook of Research on Teacher Education*, New York: Macmillan, pp. 820–36.

Chapter 6

The directions of Finnish teacher education in the era of the revised Act on Basic Education

Olli-Pekka Malinen and Hannu Savolainen

Keywords: Finland, special education, reform, Response to Intervention (RTI), collaboration

Chapter overview

Since the 1990s, special education has continued its expansion in Finland and it is evident that it has been used as a tool to respond to the increased diversity of learning needs in compulsory education classrooms. During the last few years, however, there has been a systematic attempt to change both the rhetoric and services of additional learning support towards a more inclusive direction through a new special education strategy based on the revised *Basic Education Act* and updated *National Curriculum Guidelines*. The reform implies many new requirements for all teachers. We give background to the current situation by referring to our recent research findings from a large-scale study (N = approximately 800) on teachers' perceptions of inclusive education and self-efficacy for inclusive practices. We analyze the reform by referring to discussion on Response to Intervention (RTI) models and the findings of meta-studies on effective teaching methods. Finally, we suggest what the key determinants for success may be in this reform and conclude with the discussion of future directions for Finnish teacher education.

Expansion of special education in Finland

The expansion of special education in Finland has been too large to be explained merely by factors related to students. There appear to be two major factors contributing to the expansion: the comprehensive school reform in the 1970s, and the regulation that linked the amount of government subsidy for the municipalities with the number of students defined as having special educational needs.

The Finnish school system was reformed in the early 1970s from the old twin track system into one comprehensive school for all. A new form of special education, part-time special education, became much more common after the reform (Kivirauma *et al.*, 2006). The idea of this model of learning support was to respond to the increased diversity of learning needs in comprehensive school classrooms.

Simultaneously with the growth of part-time special education the more traditional type of special education, which involves the identification of students as having special educational needs and an administrative decision for support, has also continued to expand. In 2009, 22.8 per cent of students in Finnish comprehensive schools received part-time special education and another 8.5 per cent had been transferred to special education (Statistics Finland, 2010).

During the 15-year period from 1995 to 2009 the number of students transferred to special education almost tripled. At least part of this growth was due to the regulations effective since 1998 that guaranteed a 50 per cent increase of government subsidy per student that was identified as having special educational needs. Therefore, this very rapid increase is not only an indication of the growing needs of students but also a sign of municipalities' policy to obtain more resources by means of administrative special education transfer decisions.

The comprehensive school reform acted as the background for reorganizing Finnish teacher education. In 1974 the training of class teachers, who have the main responsibility for teaching students from first to sixth grade, was transferred into universities. Before that, class teachers had been trained in teacher seminars or colleges. The university-based class teacher training started as a three-year program. In 1979, the training of class teachers as well as special education teachers was converted into a Master-level program that took approximately five years to complete.

The purpose of reforming Finnish teacher education in mid- and late 1970s was to give teacher education a more solid theoretical base. The aim was that every teacher would become an academic expert who could independently acquire new knowledge and apply it in his/her daily work. The Finnish teacher education reform from practice-oriented preparation to the more theoretical and science-based training provided by the universities was quite strongly criticized in the 1980s and 1990s. In the early 1990s it was even suggested that the training of classroom teachers should be transferred into universities of applied science. Nevertheless, in the last decade the criticism against academic teacher training has been much weaker. One important reason is the good rankings Finland has gained in the OECD-coordinated Programme for International Student Assessment (PISA). The PISA results seem to indicate that university-based teacher education has had a positive impact on Finnish comprehensive school students' learning outcomes (Scheinin, 2010).

National special education strategy, revised *Basic Education Act* and National Core Curriculum as tools to slow down the expansion of special education

As the increase in special education seemed almost uncontrollable, it is understandable that the national education authorities wanted to enhance the planning and organization of special education in Finland. As a result of this objective, a nation-

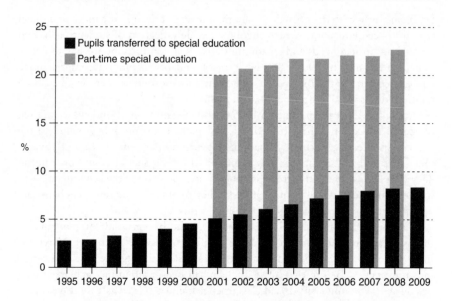

Figure 6.1 Shares of pupils transferred to special education and receiving part-time special education among all comprehensive school pupils 1995–2009

Source: Statistics Finland, 2010

Note: Comparable data on part-time special education are available for the period 2001–2008. The number of pupils transferred to special education and number of recipients of part-time special education cannot be added together because some of the pupils transferred to special education also receive special teaching part-time.

wide strategy for special education was developed (MOE, Ministry of Education of Finland, 2007). It may be surprising that this strategy was the first of its kind in a country that has probably one of the most widespread systems of special education in the world. The strategy was followed by changes made in the law that concerns special education and national curriculum guidelines that put into action the decrees stated in the renewed law. The Finnish Ministry of Education has supported the process by allocating about 45 million euros between 2008–2011 for municipalities to be used in development projects preparing for the changes required by the new law. The National Board of Education has also funded regional research and development projects that are carried out by groups of municipalities together with universities. The objective of these network projects is to identify and develop good inclusive and special educational practices and collect evidence from their outcomes. The purpose of the networking is to disseminate good practices nationally and offer teachers opportunities to share their experiences with other teachers in the region. For example, in Eastern Finland the regional network project has visited all of the approximately 50 participating schools and organized several one-day or half-day inservice training sessions in different municipalities. The program for these sessions has been designed by the university staff based on the feedback received from the schools. As part of the project, teachers also visit other schools in the region in order to benchmark and learn from their good inclusive practices. Furthermore, in the Eastern Finland region the project has actively recruited teachers to begin their own research and there are already a few teachers who have begun their PhD studies.

Changes and challenges of the special education reform

The developments in the last five years can be described as an attempt to make a total nationwide overhaul of special education services in Finland. We interpret this as a systematic attempt to change and turn both the rhetoric and services of additional learning support towards a more inclusive direction. The most important changes this process brings are as follows:

1. The spirit of the reform is that all students should go to and receive any additional services they need in their neighbourhood schools.
2. Special education support decisions are temporary and must be reviewed at least at the end of second and sixth grade.
3. The intensity of support given to students varies (general, intensified or special support) and does not necessarily go hand in hand with the placement of a student.
4. Support can be intensified only after the school shows evidence that despite good teaching arrangements and general support, the student does not reach the set objectives. This implies adoption of a Finnish version of an RTI model.

RTI model with Finnish characteristics

The reform implies many new requirements for all teachers. Perhaps the biggest change is that schools are now required to show evidence that they have taken measures to change the mainstream class environment so that all students can learn before any decisions for intensified support can be taken. This so-called general or universal support can be provided by teachers' differentiation of teaching, adding teacher's assistant resources in the classroom, or even by inviting special education teachers to support teachers' work in the classroom. If then, despite these efforts, a child does not seem to reach objectives set for his or her education, intensified support can be offered.

Intensified support can take many forms, but typically it would involve either support teaching outside school hours or a part-time special education teacher giving individual or small-group tutoring for the child in question either in class or outside of class for one to two hours a week, for example. Intensified support would then last for some time (none of the national level guidelines actually mention how long this kind of support should last) and the child may then return to normal teaching. If, regardless of intensified support, problems persist, the child may be moved to the next level, which is called special support. Identifying a child as needing special support involves making an administrative decision about the special need. In addition, a more detailed pedagogical review of the child's learning and the support given thus far have to be made.

When considering the need for special support, the child's situation is discussed in their school's multi-professional student welfare group and their parents must also be consulted. Finally, if a decision for special support is made, it must determine what type of support the child is entitled to and in what kind of learning environment the support will be provided. The pedagogical details of the support are written in an individual education plan that is made together with the special support decision.

It is interesting that the Finnish reform clearly adopted an RTI approach to special education without making any reference to the US discussions and critique of RTI approaches. This literature shows that not only are there different approaches to RTI (Fuchs et al., 2010) but also that RTI may well be criticized from an equity and inclusive education perspective (Artiles and Kozleski, 2010). It remains to be seen what approach to RTI will become the mainstream approach in Finland. What is clear now is that national guidelines will not determine this, but the responsibility to develop the approach remains with the institutions that provide education services and educate future teachers. We do not know yet what approach to RTI will become popular, but one of the key factors that will determine the inclusivity of the model lies in the interpretation of what constitutes universal support. Perhaps the most common procedure will be identifying students who have difficulties (e.g. through classroom-level screening) and then giving them additional support in class. This approach mainly targets individuals for support, although it is thought to be universal. The other alternative could be a more broad identification of key factors of barriers to learning in the school or the classroom and then launching a school-wide learning support program. This approach would target all students; an example could be a school-wide positive behaviour support program.

Challenges of the special education reform

The major new aspects in the process of reforming Finnish special education services are: (1) schools are now required more directly than before to show evidence of good and adequate teaching and learning support before any child can be given more intensive learning support; and (2) the decision about a child's need for special support (third level) is principally based on a pedagogical review of a teacher, whereas in the past such statements were routinely requested either from a psychologist or a medical doctor. These two changes imply new duties for both mainstream and special education teachers. However, thus far the national guidelines lack detail, particularly in two aspects. First, they do not describe how children's learning and the support provided to them should be monitored, and second, after what period of time a decision on intensifying support should be made.

The revised *Basic Education Act* has raised criticism among the Trade Union of Education in Finland (TUEF), which represents over 95 per cent of Finnish teachers. The Union has voiced fear that under the system, teachers may turn into "paper pushers" (Laaksola, 2011). The argument was that the new requirement for documentation of teaching and learning either reduces time spent with children or increases teachers' workloads remarkably. Also, while the new law clearly shifts most of the power in special education decisions from psycho-medical experts to teachers, thus promoting the role of pedagogical professionals in schools, the TUEF also interpreted this as a risk of increased work demands. Some stakeholders who commented on the draft law text also voiced concerns about whether teachers have enough professional skills to understand the pedagogical demands related to different disabilities.

When the restructuring of the Finnish special education system was planned and the revisions of the *Basic Education Act* were drafted, some interest groups saw it as too radical. The classroom teachers' association even stated that the special education reform would threaten to destroy the Finnish school system. When the final version of the Act and the revised National Core Curriculum were settled, another kind of criticism was voiced by advocates of inclusive education. Some claimed that the real change the new *Basic Education Act* brought was small or even minimal. One reason for such criticism may be the vagueness of the Act as well as the National Core Curriculum with regard to the principle of inclusion. These documents do not take a clear stance on, for example, the view that teaching in the mainstream class of the neighborhood school should be the primary place for any child to learn. This kind of statement was actually included in the first draft of the law but it was removed after the first round of comments cited above. Perhaps a more radical change was actually brought by the *2009 Act on the Financing of Education*. This Act repealed the former regulation that guaranteed municipalities 50 per cent higher government subsidy for each student identified as having special educational needs. While it is clear that the aforementioned former regulation resulted in a dramatic increase in the numbers of students identified as having SEN, it may be that in the future, municipalities are less eager to make the administrative decisions of identifying students with special needs, when there are no financial incentives for such policy.

Teacher education in the era of Finnish special education reform

In recent years, the context of inclusive education in Finland seems to be evolving significantly. What is needed from teachers in this new environment, where students with special educational needs are expected to receive most of their support in mainstream settings, and where classroom and subject teachers have more responsibility for evaluating their students' needs and providing support for all students in their class? What are the core skills and competencies that future preservice and inservice teacher training should address? Potential answers to these questions can be found by referring to the results of our ongoing research project funded by the National Board of Education.

Collaboration skills – Key to successful inclusion?

As part of our project we have collected a questionnaire data set of over 800 Finnish teachers from schools run by large, middle-sized as well as small municipalities. Among other things the questionnaire included the Teacher Self-Efficacy for Inclusive Practices (TEIP) scale (Forlin *et al.*, 2010) and the Sentiments, Attitudes and Concerns about Inclusive Education (SACIE) scale (Loreman *et al.*, 2007). The TEIP scale is designed for measuring teachers' self-efficacy related to inclusive education, and the SACIE for assessing attitudes toward inclusion. Our research investigated whether teachers' self-efficacy for inclusive practices (i.e. how good the teachers themselves think they are in teaching in inclusive classrooms with diverse learners) correlated with attitudes towards inclusive education and which type of self-efficacy for inclusive practices would be the best predictor of attitudes.

Our analyses revealed that there was indeed a positive relationship (correlation = 0.42, $p < 0.001$) between teachers' self-efficacy and their attitude toward inclusive education (Savolainen *et al.*, 2010). This indicates that teachers with a stronger sense of self-efficacy appear to hold more positive attitudes toward inclusion. In further analysis the teacher self-efficacy for inclusive practices was divided into three sub-dimensions: *efficacy to use inclusive instructions, efficacy in collaboration*, and *efficacy in managing behaviour*. From these sub-dimensions teachers' *self-efficacy in collaboration* (with colleagues, parents, etc.) had the strongest positive relationship (correlation = 0.46, $p < 0.001$) with attitudes toward inclusion. This finding illustrates that inclusive education is something that a teacher cannot manage alone. Those who see themselves as capable of cooperating with parents, colleagues and other professionals appear to hold less negative perceptions and vice versa.

Promoting cooperation in preservice teacher training

Our research results suggest that the future teacher training for inclusive schools in Finland should have a special emphasis on developing collaboration skills. In inclusive schools, teachers' ability to cooperate with parents, colleagues and other professionals may be even more crucial than other core competencies such as instructional skills, effective classroom management and subject knowledge. Effective collaboration is not just a set of certain tricks that can be easily learned and then quickly put into practice. In order to prepare teachers for inclusive schools, the Finnish teacher education system must also become more inclusive. The future curricula of Finnish teacher education institutions should, therefore, have courses that concentrate on learning the principles of fruitful cooperation. Furthermore, it is imperative that preservice teachers have more opportunities to try collaboration in safe settings where they are supported by their university teachers and clinical teachers of their teaching practice.

Collaboration should be embedded in all aspects of preparing future teachers for inclusive education. In practice, this means more training modules that are mutual to all future teachers. Cooperation and cross-fertilization between student teachers with different majors ought to be a penetrating theme of these shared modules. Currently, in many Finnish universities there are too many courses held separately for future class teachers, special education teachers and subject teachers without any reason other than tradition for such an arrangement. Kozleski and Waitoller (2010) point out that these types of separate preparation programs will easily lead to ill-developed collaborative and co-teaching skills as well as poor understanding of the skills and capabilities special and general educators bring to the design and implementation of learning. It is not surprising, therefore, that combining different types of teacher candidates for common courses has been used as a tool for promoting inclusive schools (Florian *et al.*, 2010).

An additional factor prohibiting the natural occurrence of cooperation is the system where the teaching practice of most regular education preservice teachers takes place in teacher training schools attached to universities, whereas the majority of special education majors' teaching practice is organized in other schools. In order to promote cooperation, for example, the preservice teachers should be sent to the schools in small groups with both general and special education majors. In these heterogeneous groups the teacher trainees would then be able to practice team planning of teaching, co-teaching, consultation with colleagues, and other inclusive practices.

Conclusions

Key to successful inclusive education in future Finnish schools is that universal support, i.e. support to all students in a school, works well. The understanding of universal support requires some work and testing of new models. It remains to be seen how long the reform and the change from the current situation will take. Many things have to change if we are to go from the situation where every third student is receiving individually oriented special education into a situation where all teachers understand their responsibility for providing universal support as a way for developing better inclusive practices. Having said this, we are still of the opinion that, in future Finnish schools, there is a need for teachers who have a strong background in special education. Our view derives from the fact that, even if all students would study in inclusive settings, it is unrealistic to expect all their special educational needs to disappear. Finnish special education teachers possess invaluable expertise on designing and implementing effective interventions that support students' learning and growth. The challenge is how to better utilize this expertise in ways that also help general education teachers to better accommodate their students' needs. Once again, this is a challenge where collaboration plays a key role.

References

Artiles, A. and Kozleski, E. (2010) "What counts as response and intervention in RTI? A sociocultural analysis", *Psicothema*, 22(4): 949–54.

Florian, L., Young, K. and Rouse, M. (2010) "Preparing teachers for inclusive and diverse educational environments: Studying curricular reform in an initial teacher education course", *International Journal of Inclusive Education*, 14(7): 709–22.

Forlin, C., Cedillo, I., Romero-Contreras, S., Fletcher, T. and Hernández, H. (2010) "Inclusion in Mexico: Ensuring supportive attitudes by newly graduated teachers", *International Journal of Inclusive Education*, 14(7): 723–39.

Fuchs, D., Fuchs, L. and Stecker, P. (2010) "The 'blurring' of special education in a new continuum of general education placements and services", *Exceptional Children*, 76(3): 301–23.

Kivirauma, J., Klemelä, K. and Rinne, R. (2006) "Segregation, integration, inclusion – The ideology and reality in Finland", *European Journal of Special Needs Education*, 21(2): 117–33.

Kozleski, E. B. and Waitoller, F. R. (2010) "Teacher learning for inclusive education: Understanding teaching as a cultural and political practice", *International Journal of Inclusive Education*, 14(7): 655–66.

Laaksola, H. (2011) "Opettajista ei saa tehdä paperinpyörittäjiä [Teachers must not turn into paper pushers]", *Opettaja – lehti [Opettaja – magazine]*, 106(1–2): 5.

Loreman, T., Earle, C., Sharma, U. and Forlin, C. (2007) "The development of an instrument for measuring pre-service teachers' sentiments, attitudes, and concerns about inclusive education", *International Journal of Special Education*, 22(1): 150–9.

MOE, Ministry of Education of Finland (2007) *Special education strategy*, Issue No. 47, Finland: Ministry of Education.

Savolainen, H., Engelbrecht, P., Nel, M. and Malinen, O.-P. (2010) "Understanding teachers' attitudes and self-efficacy in inclusive education: Implications for pre-service and in-service teacher education", documents presented at the 2nd East Asian International Conference of Teacher Education Research, The Hong Kong Institute of Education, December.

Scheinin (2010) "Opettajankoulutuksen haasteista [On the challenges of teacher education]", in A. Kallioniemi, A. Toom, M. Ubani and H. Linnansaari (eds), *Akateeminen luokanopettajakoulutus: 30 vuotta teoriaa, käytäntöä ja maistereita [Academic Class Teacher Education: 30 Years of Theory, Practice and MEds]*, Jyväskylä: Suomen kasvatustieteellinen seura, pp. 9–11.

Statistics Finland (2010) *Official Statistics of Finland: Special Education*. Online. Available at: http://www.tilastokeskus.fi/til/erop/index_en.html (accessed 19 August 2011).

Chapter 7

Preparing teachers to meet the challenges of inclusive education in Negara Brunei Darussalam[1]

Kathleen Tait and Lawrence Mundia

Keywords: Negara Brunei Darussalam, remote community, preliminary inclusive, educational initiatives, limited resources, Islamic faith

Chapter overview

In recent years the Ministry of Education (MoE), along with other interested parties, has taken various steps to develop a system that is more receptive to the educational needs of all students. As with any education system, change comes slowly when it requires a reform to previous systemic principles, standards, and practices. Consequently, Brunei is only beginning to pave the road to inclusive education. This chapter highlights the special education policies which are embedded within the framework of the inclusive education system, and documents the provision and delivery of special education programs and services to students with SEN in Brunei. It also provides a summary of the developments in special education teacher training since the inception of the *MoE Special Education Policy Guidelines* of 1997, and makes an attempt to point the way forward in the growth of inclusive education in this country.

Introduction

Negara Brunei Darussalam (Brunei) is a Malay Islamic monarchy state located in the northern part of the ecologically rich island of Borneo in Southeast Asia. Official government statistics from sources within this country are extremely difficult to obtain. However, according to the latest *Brunei Darussalam Country Report* (2011), Brunei has a population of about 401,890, comprising 66.7 per cent Malays, 11.1 per cent Chinese and 22.2 per cent from other races. While Islam is the official religion and is practiced by 67 per cent of the country, Buddhism, Christianity and other religions (including indigenous beliefs) are also practiced there.

---

1 Original title: Pandangan Mengenai Pendidikan Guru Untuk Pendidikan Inklusif Di Negara Brunei Darussalam.

Although Brunei has a long history of having students with diverse backgrounds in government schools, many students with special education needs (SEN) do not succeed at school, as the education system there is strongly oriented towards academic performance (Wong, 2005). Indeed, not long ago in this country it was not an uncommon practice for students with SEN to be kept at home due to their disabilities. In addition, it had been the practice of staff to turn children with disabilities away from Bruneian public schools due to the lack of special education resources to support such children's learning. This situation is further compounded by the scarcity of trained teachers in the field of special education in Brunei.

The impact of religious education on education provision in an Islamic state

There are three main tertiary institutions in Brunei which offer courses in teacher training. The Sultan Bolkiah Institute of Education (SHBIE), situated within the University of Brunei Darussalam (UBD), is the sole general education teacher education institute in Brunei. However, the University Islam Sultan Sharif Ali offers courses in Islamic religion studies and the Seri Begawan Religious Teachers University College trains the members of this traditional Muslim community who wish to become Imams (religious teachers and leaders) of the Islamic faith. There are several primary and secondary schools in Brunei which are run by Imams. These centres of learning are known as Madrasahs. The medium of instruction is Arabic. There are two types of Madrasah program on offer in Brunei. Children may either attend a Madrasah on a full-time basis, where the emphasis is on Islamic Studies and Arabic; or there are part-time (2:00pm–5:00pm) programs for children who wish to attend regular education or private schools in the morning.

Consequently, while all Bruneian children are eligible to attend a general education (or regular) school program from the age of six, it should be noted that in Brunei regular school classes taught in Malay and which offer an academic program are only run from 7:30am to 12:30pm each day. At 12:30pm, regardless of their religious faith, all children return home for lunch where they may remain for the rest of the day. General education teachers remain on campus, preparing lessons, and attending staff meetings, etc. However, in addition to a lunch break, Muslim children who attend regular schools in the morning are required to wash and change from their regular school uniforms into a pure white uniform. This outfit is known as a Jelabah, for boys; or a Hijab, which refers to the scarves and covering up of the body except for the face and hands, for girls.

This is the required preparation for an afternoon of religious instruction in the teachings of the Qur'an. Madrasahs are completely separate institutions of learning to the general education schools run by the MoE in Brunei. It is unknown how many children with SEN receive religious instruction in Madrasahs in Brunei. In general, children with intellectual impairments are not considered to be able to perform the necessary religious obligations of the Islamic faith. Nonetheless, Bruneian children with SEN are exposed to religious education to the maximum extent possible. Some parents engage Imams privately to teach the readings of the Qur'an to their children with SEN in their homes.

Overview of the general education system in Brunei Darussalam

Brunei has both government and private institutions of general education learning. According to the MoE (Special Education Unit, 2002) implementation of the national education system prioritizes the use of the Malay language as the official national language and the use of English and Arabic as the other mediums of instruction. In 2004, the Bruneian government adopted a 7–3–2–2 structure of education for its formal school system. This pattern represents seven years of primary education (including one pre-school year), three years of lower secondary, two years of upper secondary or GCE 'O' Level, and two years of GCE 'A' Level/ matriculation or pre-university (Bradshaw and Mundia, 2006).

Inclusive education: An educational agenda in Brunei Darussalam

Inclusive education has become a significant educational agenda in Brunei over the past decade or so. The roots of this development can be traced to a confluence of national and global trends in the education of children with SEN. For example, Brunei was one of the signatory countries at the *United Nations Convention on the Rights of the Child* in 1989 (United Nations, 1989). On the global stage, Brunei was one of 150 countries that attended the UNESCO's World Conference of Education for All, held in Jomtien, Thailand in 1990 (MoE, 1992).

What is happening on the local front?

A little under two decades ago the MoE introduced special education in regular (mainstream) schools as an initiative to arrest the failure of large numbers of students by providing needed assistance to help Bruneian children and youth with SEN cope better in the school system (Csapo and Omar, 1996). Recommendations of this initiative, encased in the *Special Education Proposal* (Special Education Unit, 1994), were adopted by the MoE in 1994, which marked a turning point in the development of special education towards a focus on inclusive education. Bolstered by worldwide trends towards inclusion and faced with the special needs of students within the regular school system, inclusive education was fostered further by the mounting of the First Special Education International Conference held in 1996. The following year the country passed and adopted a *National Education Policy* (MoE, 1997) which required that all children (including children with SEN) be provided with 12 years of basic education. This policy is Brunei's equivalent of an education for all (EFA) statement. This policy is not enforced.

The provision of education for students with mild learning difficulties in Brunei

While the country has an inclusive education policy, regular, religious, and special schools, several different government departments are responsible for the management and running of these various centres of learning. For example, while regular schools are registered by the MoE, the special schools and centres are registered either by the Ministry of Culture, Youth and Sports (MoCYS) or the Ministry of Health (MoH). This makes the integration of service provision very difficult. In keeping with the limited number of official government records kept on disability, the number of students integrated into regular schools is not known. Similarly, the exact number of children registered in special schools and centres is not known either. However, individual special education centres keep their own statistics. The *Brunei Darussalam Country Report* (2005) estimated the figure to be around 1,947. There are no official statistics on out-of-school children with disabilities.

The provision of education for students with high support needs in Brunei

For the moment, there is no tertiary training course on offer at either the undergraduate or postgraduate level for teachers to learn how to educate children with high support needs (HSN) in Brunei. In stark contrast to the country's economic wealth, Brunei is very much a developing country in relation to its capacity to cater for children with HSN such as autistic spectrum disorders (ASD) (Tait and Mundia, in press). Children with a medical record indicating a moderate to severe disability may be referred to the Special Education Unit, MoE, by parents, special education teachers, classroom teachers, and head teachers for further assessment. There are no government education services available to school-aged children with HSN in the country. However, there is one non-government organization (NGO) known as the SMARTER agency which offers part-time day services to children with ASD aged between 4–12 years.

Reform of the school curriculum to cater for students with HSN

The importance for schoolteachers in Brunei to have the relevant skills for intervening with students with high support needs was the subject of the 'Curriculum Guide for Students with High Support Needs' conference organized by the Special Education Unit in the MoE in September 2007. In conjunction with the Curriculum Development Department they produced a curriculum guide for students with HSN (Special Education Unit, 2008). The guide, which is in the form of intervention lesson plans, focuses on the following topics: communication; gross and fine motor skills; social skills; self-care; health and safety; Islamic religious education; self-direction; functional academics; leisure skills; work skills; information communication technology (ICT) skills; assessment; and individualized education plans (IEP). The guide had every potential to be a very good resource for Bruneian schoolteachers. However, to date, students with HSN remain in special centres which are run by NGOs.

Educational reform of teacher education programs in Brunei

Several key educational reform agendas for school curricula and curricula for Bruneian teacher education from the mid-1990s onwards helped advance the development of teacher education programs to enable the preparation and training of teachers for inclusive education. First of all, the University of Brunei Darussalam (UBD) undertook a total curriculum reform in the mid-1990s. At that time, all preservice teachers enrolled in the primary teacher education program at the Sultan Hassanal Bolkiah Institute of Education (SHBIE) were required to take a core course in inclusive education. This restructuring of educational programs allowed for a greater alignment with the preparation of teachers for inclusive education at the preservice, inservice, and postgraduate levels (Bradshaw and Mundia, 2006).

Further, in the mid-1990s the MoE introduced a number of major curriculum reforms at the school level in the areas of bilingual policy education, information technology, and curriculum revisions for various school subjects. These initiatives not only predisposed schools to expect and experience change, but also encouraged them to be open to and initiate change. Such initiatives would later serve to generate interest and support for developing a new core of personnel known as Learning Assistance Teachers (LATs) to assist regular teachers to work with children with SEN.

At the inservice level, SHBIE, in collaboration with the Special Education Unit at the MoE, jointly mounted the Certificate in Special Education in January 1995. The LAT's central role was to administer screening tests to identify students with SEN, develop individualized educational plans (IEPs), and collaborate with regular teachers in helping them design IEPs for students. The implementation of special education in regular schools is based on the Learning Assistance Model and LATs comprise the backbone of special education support within the regular education system. The first cohort of LATs completed their Certificate in Special Education in May 1996. The learning assistance program was implemented in a number of regular schools in June 1996. From August 1999, further higher educational opportunities existed at SHBIE for LATs who wanted to upgrade their qualifications by enrolling in the Bachelor of Education (Special Education) and the Master in Education (Special Education). Between 1995 and 2003, a total of 211 LATs had obtained certification and were allocated to 97 primary government schools.

The most recent change to Bruneian teacher education for inclusive education is that since 2007, all teacher education courses on offer at SHBIE are only offered at the postgraduate level. According to the policy of the MoE all postgraduate teachers at the university have to take courses in inclusive education. As a result, the

UBD (via SHBIE) currently offers a Master in Education (MEd, special education) program, a Master in Teaching (MTeach) program, and a Master in Counseling (MCouns) program.

Support offered via the Learning Assistance Program (LAP)

By the end of 2002, a total of 1,303 students with IEPs were receiving assistance via the LAP (Special Education Unit, 2002). Currently, the primary LAP provides assistance to approximately 3,000 lower and upper primary students (Mundia, 2009). The majority of students who receive learning assistance have mild learning difficulties in the basic skill areas of reading, writing, and mathematics. The bulk of these students are in lower primary classes, as the LAP focuses on early intervention. To support these students, LATs share and demonstrate appropriate remedial teaching strategies, as well as team teaching with regular classroom teachers. Unfortunately, students from the upper primary who need assistance are often not in a LAP in large primary schools. This is due to the large number of lower primary students with special needs in Brunei. Consequently, the LAT is less likely to be found helping out with the special educational needs of upper primary school students. There is even less evidence of LATs working in Bruneian secondary schools (Mundia, 2009).

Special Education Needs Assistant (SENA)

Early in 2009, the term LAT was changed to Special Education Needs Assistant (SENA) teacher. In addition, only teachers holding a certificate, diploma, or degree in education and who had taken inservice courses in special and inclusive education at the Sultan Hassanal Bolkiah Institute of Education (SHBIE), University of Brunei Darussalam (UBD), were recruited by the MoE as SENAs. Further, SENAs needed to have 3–5 years of teaching experience at primary or secondary school level. SENAs work only in government schools (i.e. not in international or private schools). In 2010 there were 116 SENAs (21 males and 95 females) working in 95 primary schools (24 primary schools had no SENAs). In the same year (2010) there were 26 SENAs of both genders working in 52 secondary schools (10 secondary schools had no SENAs). Unfortunately, the SENA training program was discontinued towards the end of 2009 when SHBIE at UBD was upgraded to a graduate faculty under the ongoing Brunei teacher education reforms.

Support for students with special needs in secondary schools in Brunei

The training of school counselors in Brunei is just as important as the training of teachers in special needs skills because at the secondary school level classes in most Bruneian schools are streamlined by ability. While there are core courses in guidance and counseling that trainee teachers are required to take, as yet there are no degree programs on offer in secondary school counseling at SHBIE. Despite this difference, some regular trainee teachers are appointed as school counselors after completing their university studies. This imbalance in the two skill areas needs to be addressed to enable school counselors (without a certificate or diploma in counseling) to function more effectively.

The teacher education programs in Brunei need to be adjusted to provide more counseling skills to novice secondary teachers. In addition, an inservice degree program in counseling needs to be mounted for those serving teachers who are interested in becoming secondary school counselors. The newly introduced MCouns program in SHBIE might serve in that respect. One noticeable concern is that the amount of collaboration between the Special Education Unit and the Division of Counseling and Career Guidance (both units in MoE) is not known. Consequently, there is no information on or about consultations between regular secondary education teachers, special education teachers, and school counselors.

Bruneian teachers' attitudes to inclusive education

Historically, studies have repeatedly found that many regular Bruneian school-teachers are opposed to having students with SEN in their classrooms (Csapro and Khalid, 1996). One possible reason for this resistance seems to be due to their lack of appropriate skills to properly help students with SEN. Among the students who are included, regular teachers prefer those students who have mild learning disorders and least prefer those with intellectual and behaviour management disorders (Bradshaw and Mundia, 2006). In addition, Bruneian teachers often think that the placement of children with SEN in regular classrooms might negatively influence their teaching effectiveness (Csapo et al., 2001; Namit, 2006). Therefore, advocates of inclusive education in Brunei may need to do a lot of advocacy work to press for the success of inclusive education in this country.

Other barriers to inclusive practice in Bruneian mainstream classrooms

In addition to negative teacher attitude, there are three other major barriers to including students with SEN in Bruneian classrooms. First of all, the current high teacher–student ratios in Brunei, which range from 1:30 to 1:40, should be reduced to between 1:20 to 1:30 so that teachers in inclusive classrooms may give reasonable individual attention to learners with SEN. Studies on the Bruneian education system have consistently shown that paying individual attention to students in large classes is very difficult (Baetens-Beardsmore, 1998; Haji Mohammad, 2006).

Second, a manageable number of children with SEN (e.g. two or three) should be included in each class to enable the teacher to give each child maximum individual attention. Inclusive education advocates will need to advise Bruneian teachers and school administrators on matters regarding making reasonable placements on an individual basis, to facilitate diagnostic teaching and effective learning.

Third, teachers, non-disabled students, parents of non-disabled students, and the Bruneian society in general should not only work to develop positive attitudes towards students with SEN, but they also need to have positive expectations of them. Inclusive education teachers will need to mount more sensitization/awareness campaigns in this country to reduce the current perfectionist attitudes and unrealistic expectations within the academically oriented, national assessment-driven curriculum in evidence among the above stakeholders.

Conclusion

With a rich oil-based economy and one of the highest capita GNP in the region, Brunei is fast developing economically and socially towards the levels of Singapore, Hong Kong, Taiwan, and South Korea (Brunei Darussalam Country Report, 2011). The main agent of change is of course education. The success of inclusive education practice in any country depends heavily on the attitudes of the teachers within regular schools towards students with special needs. Positive perceptions and feelings on the part of the teachers tend to encourage successful inclusive practice.

The establishment of the LAP to train LATs, and the development of the three-pronged strategy at SHBIE for preservice and inservice teachers to develop knowledge and skills about special needs have provided significant opportunities for Bruneian teachers to increase and upgrade their competencies for inclusive education. In practice, the Special Education Unit and the Division of Counseling and Career Guidance in the MoE are expected to work in liaison, but the degree to which this is happening is unknown. Similarly LATs and regular class teachers in the secondary education system are supposed to be working in close cooperation, but again the extent to which they do this is not clear.

While there is no doubt that inclusive education has become a major feature of current curriculum reform in Brunei, the current concern is how to improve equity in participation and access to quality inclusive education programs in the regular classrooms in Brunei. This can be established if educational institutions like SHBIE collaborate to establish a cohort of classroom teachers who are trained in inclusive education pedagogy in order to offer positive inclusive educational outcomes in Bruneian schools.

Teacher education programs in Brunei are in a position to ensure that preservice teachers acquire the knowledge, attitudes, and skills required to succeed in educating students with disabilities. As schools across Brunei move toward more inclusive models of education, both preservice and inservice teachers must be prepared to meet this challenge through a sound knowledge base and the development of appropriate attitudes and skills. Teacher educators must search for new avenues to pursue this goal and establish a field of study or a practical situation which meets the needs of the regular classroom teacher.

Mere identification of a child's special learning needs is not enough. This is where more effort and resources needs to be directed in this country. These constraints might become significant barriers to the provision of realistic, beneficial, and meaningful inclusive education in schools if not addressed. However, it must always be remembered that barriers are often temporal and that with determination, effort, resources, and time, their effects may be reduced and eventually eliminated. Further comprehensive research into inclusive education in Brunei is recommended to better understand the problem and its likely solutions.

Acknowledgements

The authors wish to extend warm thanks to Dr. Faridah Serajul Haq for translating the title of this chapter into Malay and for her advice on matters of the Islamic faith.

References

Baetens-Beardsmore, H. (1998) *Report to the Brunei Darussalam Ministry of Education on Second Language Learning*, Bandar Seri Begawan: Ministry of Education.

Bradshaw, L. and Mundia, L. (2006) "Attitudes to and concerns about inclusive education: Bruneian inservice and preservice teachers", *International Journal of Special Education*, 21(1): 35–41.

Brunei Darussalam Country Report (2005) *Case Study and Manual on Guidelines for Action to Include Children and Youth with Disabilities in School Systems and the EFA Monitoring Process*. Online. Available at: www.unescobkk.org (accessed 19 August 2011).

Brunei Darussalam Country Report (2011) *The World Fact Book*. Online. Available at: http://www.imf.org/external/pubs/ft/scr/2011/cr11140.pdf (accessed 1 September, 2011).

Csapo, M. and Omar bin Haji Khalid (1996) "Development of special education in Brunei Darussalam: The case of a developed/developing country", *International Journal of Special Education*, 11(3): 108–14.

Csapo, M., Mak, L., Zainab, Dk and Burns, R. (2001) "An evaluation of the effects of early intervention on the academic achievements of primary class 2 pupils in Brunei government schools", *International Journal of Special Education*, 16(1): 42–53.

Haji Mohammad, J. (2006) *A Survey of the Attitudes of Primary School Teachers towards the Implementation of Remedial Education Programs for Low Achievers in the Tutong District*. Unpublished thesis, University of Brunei Darussalam.

MoE, Ministry of Education (1992) *Education in Brunei Darusslam*, Bandar Seri Begawan: Special Education Unit.

MoE, Ministry of Education (1997) *Special Education Policy Guidelines*, Bandar Seri Begawan: Special Education Unit.

Mundia, L. (2009) "Implementation of inclusive education in Brunei Darussalam: Review of possible implications for school counselors", *Electronic Journal for Inclusive Education*, 2(4). Online. Available at: http://www.cehs.wright.edu/~prenick/Spring_Summer09_Edition/htm/mundia.htm (accessed 19 August 2011).

Namit, N. (2006) *The Needs of Remedial Reading Programs for Children with Reading Difficulties in Primary Schools*. MEd. SHBIE: University of Brunei Darussalam.

Special Education Unit (1994) *Proposal for Identifying and Meeting the Special Educational Needs of Students in Brunei Darussalam*, Bandar Seri Begawan: Ministry of Education.

Special Education Unit (2002) *Annual Report*, Bandar Seri Begawan: Ministry of Education.

Special Education Unit (2008) *Annual Report*, Bandar Seri Begawan: Ministry of Education.

Tait, K. and Mundia, L. (in press) "The impact on families of children with autism in Brunei Darussalam", *International Journal of Special Education*.

United Nations (1989) *Convention on the Rights of the Child*, New York: UN.

Wong, J. (2005) "Special education in Brunei Darussalam", *Brunei Darussalam Journal of Special Education*, 2: 1–15.

Chapter 8

Emerging issues in teacher education for inclusion in the United States

Michael M. Gerber

Keywords: special education policy, United States

Chapter overview

Despite thousands of published articles, chapters, and books purporting to provide authoritative guidance to teachers in how to be inclusive in their practices, and despite the now common presence of comparable content in teacher preparation programs, there remains little real empirical evidence that shows how or under what circumstances or at what scales these practices are "effective" or, indeed, in what sense they may be construed to be "effective". Part of the reason for the dearth of assuring research (e.g. see Simpson, 2004) over the past decade may be that "inclusion" (or "inclusive education") really refers to whole environments and is not merely the sum of specific practices taught to teachers in their professional preparation.

Indeed, it is difficult to assess emerging issues in teacher education for inclusive education in the United States without contextualizing what is taught to future and current teachers by the actual conditions of public schools and the constraints these conditions impose. Although it is almost universally true that American teacher education institutions give some attention to "best practices" for inclusive education, the distance between these "best" practices and the reality of everyday teaching is still significantly great to warrant concern (Cole *et al.*, 2004; Jackson *et al.*, 2009). Moreover, the observable divide between "best" and "actual" practices – I am tempted to write "idealized" instead of "best" – can no longer be dismissed as a result only of inadequate professional preparation. To be sure, there is little evidence that general education teachers, or special education teachers, for that matter, receive sufficient training in a number of critical teaching skills, e.g. systematic instruction, behaviour management, and design and evaluation of instruction. The skills needed to establish and maintain meaningful and productive inclusion of students with disabilities may represent a wholly different kind of expertise than has been presumed. Nevertheless, in the early twenty-first century, when national education policies form a major structural component of national economic imperatives, it ought to be recognized that inclusive education is a product of the rather complicated context in which teaching occurs in public schools as much as, or more so, than of the knowledge and enumerated skills that newly certified teachers possess (Gerber, 2002; Zigmond, 2007).

The policy context in the US

The modern era of special education in the US began with new legislation in 1975, the *All Handicapped Children Education Act* (now called the *Individuals with Disabilities Education Act*, or IDEA), and all aspects of its practices continue to be strongly influenced by public policy. Approximately, 9.2 per cent of all children aged 6–21, i.e. over six million, receive special education in the United States (Office of Special Education and Rehabilitative Services, 2010), managed by over 470,000 special education teachers (US Bureau of Labor Statistics, 2010). Of school age students in special education, at least 48 per cent are classified as having a learning disability. Students with learning disabilities generally receive most, if not all, of their education in general education classrooms and their special education programs (i.e. IEPs) are referenced to the same learning goals in the general curriculum that are set for their non-disabled peers. Despite the fact that students with learning disabilities are the single largest group of students who are included in general education, federal support for personnel preparation (i.e. about $90 million) tends to be aimed at programs that prepare teachers to teach students with moderate to severe disabilities, groups that collectively constitute only about 10 per cent of all students receiving special education.

What makes special education policy in the US unusual is that it has been justified by civil appeals, rather than education, rights. That is, there are no education provisions in the US Constitution. Formally speaking, the federal government has no specific role regarding education which is the responsibility of state government and locally elected boards of education. Therefore, IDEA mandates various practices related to identification, referral, assessment, and education programs and services following from primary consideration for equitable access to publicly supported education. It is fair to say that these various practices are informed by professional educators' opinions and views, but the statute was not established with much debate about the quality of education that might be achieved. Rather, the federal courts which oversee implementation of IDEA are primarily concerned with the achievement of standards that safeguard equality of educational opportunity. Special education policy does not guarantee the best possible education, but only an educational opportunity reasonably calculated to afford progress that is "satisfactory" (*Hendrick Hudson District Board of Education v. Rowley*, 1982). It is left to the professional educators who implement special education in each school to determine the quality of education that students with disabilities actually receive.

Two significant shifts occurred in public special education policy since 1975: reauthorization of the original legislation as IDEA in 1990 and reauthorization of important general education legislation (i.e. the *Elementary and Secondary Education Act*, or ESEA, originally intended to address the needs of children from impoverished homes) as the *No Child Left Behind Education Act of 2001*, or NCLB). Although maintaining the legal requirement that students with disabilities must be educated in the "least restrictive environment" possible, IDEA incorporated subtle, but important, presumption that schools should prefer to educate students with disabilities in general education settings. This policy shift inaugurated what has become known as the inclusion "movement".

The passage of NCLB aimed primarily to make schools accountable for federal money that was intended to close the achievement "gap" between (particularly) economically disadvantaged students and typical, middle-class students. ESEA, which was first implemented a decade before IDEA, also was grounded in legal concepts of equality of opportunity more than quality of education. Aside from targeting children from low-income families (to "compensate" for their presumed lack of family-provided preparation for school achievement), ESEA also represented a distinctively different theory and strategy for federal involvement in local public education. In simplest terms, ESEA allocated additional resources to schools which then implemented programs for a qualifying class of students (i.e. those at risk for underachievement due to poverty). IDEA, on the other hand, allocated additional resources to provide specialized education programs tailored for individually qualifying students (i.e. those with certified disabilities).

This distinction created two major streams of federal money, each with elaborate criteria for implementation and accountability. School personnel were strongly pressed to comply with these separate, but often overlapping, mandates finding it often difficult to maintain attention of quality of education over requirement to comply with rules and regulations. NCLB began a significant shift towards placing one unified framework around all federal education policy and began the politically volatile process of reconciling differences that historically had developed, both intentionally and unintentionally, between ESEA and IDEA. In early 2011, the American Congress is looking towards a new round of reauthorizations of both laws with an eye towards further harmonizing their frameworks for federal assistance to states and local schools.

Influences on the preparation of teachers for inclusive education

Both of the major federal policies described exert powerful influences on how American states and territories manage their schools, including how teachers are trained and licensed, and under what conditions with what requirements are they employed by local schools. For example, in the 1990s, when IDEA urged for dramatically greater effort to integrate students with disabilities, teaching practice in the schools began to shift noticeably. General educators were frequently expected to accommodate students with disabilities in their classrooms, sometimes merely managing their physical presence, but sometimes managing their instructional program to some degree as well. Special educators, likewise, were expected to support such inclusion. These changes in expectations produced significant changes in school environments, procedures, employment patterns, and the observable practices within classrooms and schools.

Professional teacher education programs similarly changed to align with these new expectations, providing more opportunity for general education teachers to learn about students with disabilities and how they might be involved in general classroom activities, and more emphasis in the professional preparation of special education teachers on strategies and methods for supporting inclusion, both for students with disabilities and classroom teachers, as opposed to providing direct instructional services. Thus, special education teachers were taught "strategies" and methods to facilitate "cooperation" and "partnership" and "co-teaching" with their general education colleagues, to manage IEPs when students with disabilities were distributed among many classrooms rather than concentrated in a single, special education classroom, and to mediate relationships between school authorities, families, and teaching colleagues.

To a large extent, the content of these modified professional education programs was grounded more in emerging practical experiences of "best practices" by teachers, schools, and teacher educators than on empirical evidence. Indeed, the research literature is still astoundingly impoverished when it comes to scientifically valid evidence in support of practices that are regularly taught to pre-professionals under the rubric of "inclusion".

This was the circumstance roughly in 2001 when NCLB became the dominant national education policy in the US. The structure and specific provisions of NCLB are complicated and largely beyond the scope of this chapter. Its major impact on local public education, though, was to assert the narrowing of achievement "gaps" between several sub-populations of students who were or might be substantially disadvantaged compared to white, middle-class students, e.g. students from economically disadvantaged homes, students who were learning English as a second language, students who because of gender might be susceptible to less equal opportunity to achieve, and students who had disabilities. The chief mandate of NCLB was for schools in all jurisdictions to focus their efforts on reaching similar and measureable (i.e. tested) learning outcomes for all such disadvantaged students. Moreover, graduated and potentially serious penalties were to be imposed on schools and districts that failed to make timely progress towards ultimate equalization of achievement among these groups.

By including students with disabilities as a targeted group, NCLB took a major step towards "including" IDEA within a larger framework for federal involvement in public education. Simply stated, whoever received federal assistance, states, districts, and local schools, needed to be accountable by demonstrating by objective measures substantial improvement in desirable educational outcomes (e.g. in the language arts, mathematics, and science). Thus, two major changes have occurred in how individual classroom teachers must try to manage inclusion. First, inclusion is now understood to mean substantive inclusion not only in learning activities but also learning outcomes. Second, teachers are to focus concretely on all students deemed to be "at risk" because of their relatively lower achievement test scores, regardless of the perceived cause for their lack of achievement.

Needless to say, within the constraints imposed by their specific working conditions, available resources, administrative and other support and, of course, their professional preparation and opportunities for further development, teachers find these expectations extremely challenging. With regard to inclusion of special education students, keeping in mind that this now means inclusion in academic lessons (perhaps modified to accommodate specific limitations), as well as formal assessments of academic progress – the burden teachers may experience may be particularly difficult. For parents of students with moderate to severe disabilities (e.g. ASD), emergence of such stringent academic standards may be viewed as threatening to the quality of the social inclusion in classrooms, e.g. proximity to normally achieving peers, access to good learning and behaviour models, and potential for friendship development. For parents of students with more mild to moderate disabilities (e.g. dyslexia), this changed emphasis on high levels of testable achievement may be perceived as increasing both psychological and social stress on their children because of the higher expected pace, rate, and level of achievement. Moreover, in the time of economic recession, reasonable expectations for supplemental resources to meet these higher goals seem indefinitely undermined, leaving fewer teachers to accomplish more across a broader range of student differences with far smaller budgets to support their efforts.

Increasing dependency on paraprofessionals

Interest in inclusion of students with disabilities in general education classrooms may have had some unintended consequences. Without increase in the number of special education teachers employed, distribution of students among many classrooms to promote inclusion also means that special education resources, particularly those embodied in special education teachers, must be similarly distributed across locations and time during the workweek. Because the special education teacher does not control time or group size for instructional purposes, inclusion demands a set of skills that are markedly different from those employed when these teachers delivered instruction directly. To a greater extent special education teachers must negotiate the nature of individualized program and program delivery with general education colleagues. It is these colleagues who manage both the students and their instruction for most or all of the school day.

Two developments over the past 20 years have worked in tandem with the preference to have students with disabilities included in general classrooms. First, physical inclusion has come to mean *academic* inclusion as well, i.e. in general curriculum, achievement goals, and high stakes assessments. The mandated "individualized" planning for students with disabilities is constrained somewhat by expectation that learning objectives and activities will be framed within the context of the standard, general curriculum. With an emerging emphasis on systems of universal progress monitoring and triggers for supplementing or intensifying core instruction, a certain ambiguity is developing around if and when referral for special education is indicated. This broadening of the meaning of "individualization" marks a significant departure from the specialized or personalized curricula that once characterized special education and indicates a new allocation strategy, one that diverts attention as well as resources away from classical special education towards what will arguably be greater organizational efficiency for schools.

Second, the distribution of students across classrooms is accommodated to some degree by the exchange of time from paraprofessionals (instructional assistants) for that of credentialed teachers. Schools in the US have dramatically increased the numbers of paraprofessionals who work especially with students who have moderate to severe disabilities. For example, there were 373,466 full-time special education instructional assistants in 2007, a ten-fold increase over the previous decade (National Center for Education Statistics, 2009).

However, redefining of "individualization" in terms of general curriculum standards, as well as the growing dependency on paraprofessionals to "manage" inclusion, have not occurred without potentially significant costs. Typical "inclusion" in the US today may provide less learning than advocates might hope and less social normalization than they believe they should achieve. The idea that included students could have both greater (higher level) learning and (normalizing) socialization in public schools given their current capacity is, generally speaking, not true. The idea that schools would "learn" to provide effective special education in general education settings is not borne out by the facts, and these have substantial implications for preparing teachers not only to support but also to manage *full* inclusion (i.e. substantive learning as well as socialization) most effectively.

For example, "exposure" to the "normal" curriculum guarantees little substantive learning opportunity by itself. Teachers, and in most cases this means general classroom teachers, must learn to tailor lessons grounded in general curriculum not only to provide opportunity for social participation but also so that a justifiable amount of substantive learning will occur. Moreover, increased time in "normal" environments has meant more time with less skilled paraprofessionals and less direct instructional attention by the more skilled credentialed teachers in the environment. Instead, teachers often must manage instructional opportunity indirectly through their management of paraprofessionals who have the most time and proximity to these students.

These are skills not generally taught in professional preparation programs. Moreover, these requisite skills involve more than managing paraprofessionals, they also imply an ongoing and highly individualized training program tailored both to the learning needs of the paraprofessional as well as those of students with disabilities. Classroom teachers are reluctant and often not well prepared to take on this role, while special education teachers are deeply challenged not only by the increased number of settings in which students are included but also the significant variations in classroom climates as well as among the paraprofessionals themselves.

Paraprofessionals are meant to facilitate effective inclusion in a number of ways. For example, they are intended to be contingent on classroom opportunities, provide direct instruction in academics, manage (teach) student behaviours, assist with personal care, facilitate social interactions between peers, collect student data, and generally supply highly individualized emotional, physical, and motivational "support" for students. Unfortunately, there is mounting empirical evidence that what they actually do is maintain "on-task" behaviour, monitor and correct some errors (while rarely teaching new skills), stop disruptive (but rarely systematically train adaptive) behaviours, maintain an unnecessary and unproductive proximity (hovering) to students that actually prevents many learning and socialization opportunities. Moreover, they rarely exchange information with general education teachers while being rarely supervised by special education teachers. Finally, they tend to receive little or no systematic professional development from school authorities while being among the lowest paid staff in the school.

Although the circumstances described above might be used to argue for initiatives to increase the professionalization (and salaries) of paraprofessionals, schools are hard-pressed to fund their central functions, and any substantial increase in the professional skills (and attendant costs) for paraprofessionals would negate the economic advantage that their employment initially provided.

Looked at differently, these problems imply a major reorientation of professional education of teachers for inclusion. The problems described above might be addressed, at least in part, by refocusing to this to enable teachers to become more skillful managers of instructional *environments*, both within and across classrooms, and in ways that explicitly include systematic progress monitoring and multiple tiers of supplementary instructional intervention (e.g. "response to instruction", or RTI), systematic supervision of skill acquisition and application by paraprofessionals (Giangreco *et al.*, 2010), and a return to an emphasis on having special education teachers act as highly skilled resources to, not co-teachers with, general education staff (Zigmond, 2007).

Systemic reorientation of professional preparation for inclusion

How will a reoriented professional preparation look? Such training will be predicated on an understanding that instructional environments in modern schools that are committed to inclusion must view teaching as a finely crafted *group* enterprise (Zigmond, 2007) and no longer the classical one-teacher-per-class model that arose in the Industrial Age. The original imperative to identify and respond to *individual* differences has yielded to a persistent effort to reorient public education itself. This latter effort is aimed more narrowly at *general* low achievement and poor, but non-specific, developmental outcomes across a broad range of individual differences. Meanwhile, the rapid growth in neuroscience and behavioural genetics promises a continuous wave of new knowledge that current preparation programs are ill-prepared to digest. These developments also imply the need for training teachers in a far more intensive kind of self-management of one's own professional development. Against all of these systemic demands, it is unclear now how special education ultimately will emerge, or how it can continue to act as the formal framework for setting aside resources and specialized instruction to support individualized programs. Meaningful inclusion involves an environment characterized by complex professional transactions, one which demands more expertise than can reasonably be expected of any single teacher at current levels of training.

What seems clear is that an increasing emphasis on accountability for student learning outcomes in the US likely will force adoption of new technologies, intelligent computer applications, but also in the sense of more research-based instructional repertoires and management tools that will permit more intensified instruction. That is, given relatively fixed, or even diminishing, resources, teachers will have to find or develop new efficiencies in managing diversity in school environments. Teacher education for inclusion, therefore, will have to adopt strong emphasis on meeting accountability demands through more rapid adoption of new technologies.

Greater focus on curriculum standards, high-stakes assessments of students' achievement, and value-added models of teacher evaluation also will impose itself on all teacher preparation. A consensus is forming to embrace national curriculum standards in practice, if not in name. Computer administered tests aligned to these standards that are vertically scaled across age and grade will increase testing efficiency, but also elevate the general curriculum as the basis for special education design. As Zigmond (2007) pointed out, special education teachers are not and should not be subject-matter experts. That is expertise that general education teachers should be expected to possess. But "successful" inclusion in this atmosphere will require significant pedagogical expertise related to individual differences, expertise that general classroom teachers cannot be expected to possess in equal measure. Moreover, the alignment and scaling of testing also will create the necessary conditions for value-added strategies for teacher evaluation. Neither general nor special education teachers possesss all of the requisite knowledge and skill to promote meaningful learning by all students, and both will be evaluated and compensated based on empirically measured outcomes for these students. Therefore, programs seeking to prepare teachers for inclusive education in the US and elsewhere will need to evolve models of training that explicitly address mutual support and contribution from both professionals.

With increased and articulated measurement schemes both for professionals as well as students, it is clear that teacher training programs themselves will be subject to new accountability to produce teachers with appropriate and demonstrable skills at managing meaningful inclusion. Moreover, given increasing attention to evaluating teachers based on student outcomes, teachers cannot afford to passively await generic top-down professional development opportunities. Rather, training programs should explicitly prepare special and general education teachers to employ cooperative evaluation strategies, like "lesson study" (Lewis et al., 2006), as a basis for ongoing review and assessment of their perspectives and skills for implementing inclusive education.

References

Cole, C. M., Waldron, N. and Majd, M. (2004) "Academic progress of students across inclusive and traditional settings", *Mental Retardation: A Journal of Practices, Policy and Perspectives*, 42: 136–44.

Gerber, M. M. (2002) "Reforming special education: Beyond inclusion", in J. Soler, J. Wearmouth and G. Reid (eds), *Contexualizing Difficulties in Literacy Development: Exploring Policy, Culture, Ethnicity, and Ethics*, New York: Routledge Falmer, pp. 303–20.

Giangreco, M. F., Suter, J. C. and Doyle, M. B. (2010) "Paraprofessionals in inclusive schools: A review of recent research", *Journal of Educational and Psychological Consultation*, 20(1): 41–57.

Hendrick Hudson District Board of Education v. Rowley (1982) 458 US 176.

Jackson, L. B., Ryndak, D. L. and Wehmeyer, M. L. (2009) "The dynamic relationship between context, curriculum, and student learning: A case for inclusive education as a research-based practice", *Research and Practice for Persons with Severe Disabilities (RPSD)*, 33–4, 175–95.

Lewis, C., Perry, R., and Murata, A. (2006). "How should research contribute to instructional improvement? The case of lesson study", *Educational Researcher*, 35(3), 3–14.

National Center for Education Statistics (2009). *Schools and Staffing Survey*, Washington, DC: National Center for Education Statistics.

Office of Special Education and Rehabilitative Services, Office of Special Education Programs (2010). *29th Annual Report to Congress on the Implementation of the Individuals with Disabilities Education Act, 2007*, Washington, DC: US Department of Education.

Simpson, R. L. (2004) "Inclusion of students with behavior disorders in general education settings: Research and measurement issues", *Behavioral Disorders. Special Issue: Elucidating Precision and Rigor in EBD Research*, 30(1): 19–31.

US Bureau of Labor Statistics (2010) *Occupational Outlook Handbook 2010–11*, Washington, DC: US Bureau of Labor Statistics.

Zigmond, N. (2007) "Delivering special education is a two-person job: A call for unconventional thinking", in J. B. Crockett, M. M. Gerber and T. J. Landru (eds), *Achieving the Radical Reform of Special Education. Essays in Honor of James M. Kauffman*, New York: Taylor and Francis Group, LLC, pp. 115–38.

Part II

Diversity and its challenges

Chapter 9

Diversity and its challenges for teachers

Chris Forlin

Keywords: diversity, inclusion, equity, legislation, school, teacher education, Article 24, key competences

Chapter overview

This chapter will initially provide a review of what is guiding or leading the change towards inclusion and how this is progressing from an international perspective. Preparing teachers for diversity is considered by discussing competences and strategies needed to support an inclusive approach. Finally, some key challenges are presented that are faced by schools and impact on teachers' capacity to implement an inclusive pedagogy.

Introduction

In many jurisdictions there are standards or policies that are established to ensure that teachers cater for the needs of all learners. For example, in Australia the *Disability Standards of Education* (2005) states that classroom teachers are expected to make reasonable adjustments when including students with disabilities. Likewise, the expectation of the *No Child Left Behind Act* (2001) undeniably has had a high impact on the role of schools in the US (Harvey *et al.*, 2010). Similar expectations are embedded within the UK *Code of Practice* (Department for Education, 2001) and in many other regional policies and regulations. Alongside a standards-based reform in many regions such as these, inclusion has challenged educators to achieve high standards for all students, including those with disabilities and other special learning needs (Voltz and Collins, 2010).

Leading the change

One of the most powerful conventions to be enacted in recent years regarding equity and equality for people with disabilities has been the *Convention on the Rights of Persons with Disabilities* (Office of the United Nations High Commissioner for Human Rights [OHCHR], 2006). Under the Convention there are eight guiding principles for expounding the rights of persons with disabilities and for establishing an implementation framework to facilitate these rights to be endorsed through the development of suitable policy and local legislation; of which some are predominantly pertinent in the field of education. Though this Convention focuses only on the rights of people with disabilities, this has clearly impacted on the inclusive movement which adopts a broader understanding of ensuring equity by providing support for all learners who may be excluded from access. Inclusive principles include full and effective participation; respect for difference and acceptance of persons with diverse needs; and equality of opportunity and access.

Within the Convention, Article 24 focuses on education. This has become the international foundation for improving the inclusion of children and youths with disabilities in regular schools as it expressly calls for an inclusive education system at all levels that provides equal access to primary and secondary education, vocational training, adult education, and lifelong learning. In order to accomplish this, it states that systems must employ appropriate materials, support, and inclusive techniques, as deemed necessary.

In Section 4 of Article 24 of the Convention it unequivocally states that, "State Parties shall take appropriate measures to employ teachers, including teachers with disabilities, who are qualified in sign language and/or Braille and to train professionals and staff who work at all levels of education" (OHCHR, p.15). Yet this is confounded by the bigger issue of achieving the proposed universal primary education by 2015, whereby an additional 1.9 million teachers are needed in order to do this. For example, this would mean an estimate of a further 2.1 million teachers needed in East Asia and the Pacific alone (United Nations Educational, Scientific and Cultural Organization [UNESCO], 2010, p.116). It seems extremely unlikely that this will be attained as a global achievement, particularly if consideration is given not only to the rate of newly graduating teachers but also the number of existing teachers who are expected to retire or leave the profession in the next few years.

How are we doing?

The Education For All (EFA) Global Monitoring Report *Reaching the Marginalized* (UNESCO, 2010) suggests that while at a global level great strides have been made towards the EFA and Millennium Development Goals adopted in Dakar 2000, there is still a long way to go in combating global inequality. While on a positive note it would appear that out of school numbers have fallen quite dramatically, declining by 33 million for primary school-aged children since the 2000 agreement, there are still at least 72 million children who cannot access education; millions of young people continue to leave school without appropriate skills to enable them to access the workforce; and one in six adults are illiterate.

There is still considerable concern that minority students are overrepresented in special education provision. This is not necessarily associated with the identification of students with specific disability types, though, as in many regions such as the

UK, students are assessed on their individual rather than categorical needs. Some minority groups – students from low socio-economic areas, those from different ethnic groups, living in poverty, and males, as well as those with disabilities – tend to be more frequently identified as having special educational needs.

Who are the learners?

It is difficult to obtain data that quantifies the number of learners of school age that are potentially marginalized and who may require additional support to receive an equitable education. Many vulnerable groups continue to be identified including those with disabilities, racial minorities, asylum seekers, refugees, disaffected youths, those in poverty, from developing countries, or in war-torn regions, among many others. Undoubtedly, the type of learners requiring additional support will vary enormously between jurisdictions, with some areas having larger cohorts of learners with regionally unique needs (e.g. refugees or displaced persons).

In regard to the number of people with disabilities, the *First World Report on Disability* (World Health Organization, 2011) suggests that more than a billion people in the world experience disability. It indicates that disability prevalence is high and growing and it estimates a population worldwide of 15 per cent. The range of disability is very diverse but it provides widespread barriers to people in accessing education, and it disproportionally affects vulnerable populations such as those from poorer areas, women, and older people.

Preparing teachers for diverse classrooms

Teacher education continues to be a critical aspect for improving both access to and the quality of education for young learners. As highlighted in the first *Global Monitoring Report on Disability*:

> Teachers are the single most important education resource in any country. From early childhood through primary and secondary school, the presence of a qualified, well-motivated teacher is vital for effective learning . . . In many countries, shortages of trained teachers remain a major barrier to achieving the Education for All goals, especially among marginalized groups.
>
> (UNESCO, 2010, p. 114)

Yet there has been much debate and little consensus over what should constitute the content of initial teacher preparation courses for preparing inclusive teachers (e.g. Harvey *et al.*, 2010; Pearce and Forlin, 2005). Consequently, in an attempt to ensure that all teachers are better prepared for inclusion, many regions are now focusing on developing their own key competences for teachers at national levels, with some aiming to use these as a means of assessing teachers' preparedness for teaching.

Initial teacher education

Initial training and ongoing professional learning for teachers and other paraprofessionals involved in schooling is critical in order to produce quality teachers who need not only have the knowledge and skills but also appropriate inclusive dispositions that are positive and welcoming (Sharma *et al.*, 2008). A review of the literature on inclusion identifies many competences teachers need to facilitate successful inclusion (Pearce and Forlin, 2005). These include knowledge of disability and legislation, strategies, interpersonal communication skills, curriculum development and differentiation among others. It has been found, though, that simply increasing knowledge about legislation and policy related to inclusion, and improving levels of confidence in becoming inclusive teachers, does not likewise address teachers' concerns (Forlin and Chambers, 2011).

It is generally accepted that from a broad view teachers need knowledge, skills, and appropriate attitudes for becoming inclusive practitioners (Berry, 2011). Rouse (2008) proposes that this relates to the head, hand, and heart. Some of this knowledge and skills can be provided during preservice training. Others are best provided at the 'chalkface' during inservice training where socio-cultural characteristics, ethnic differences, and localized needs can be best considered. The skills of school principals and special education administrators also need to be developed if they are to provide appropriate leadership for teachers to work in inclusive and culturally diverse settings (Voltz and Collins, 2010).

Alongside preparing teachers for diverse classrooms, there are many other areas that need to be addressed within teacher preparation courses. Although new expectations for content are continuously being added, nothing seems to become redundant or deleted, so the list is constantly increasing. It is clear that teachers have to be prepared in pedagogy, psychology, and discipline content. In addition, though, they need to be able to understand and implement a range of other areas. These include but are not limited to the use of interactive learning, new technologies, collaborative teaching, diagnostic assessments, a learning outcomes-focused approach, response to intervention, referrals, multidisciplinary teaming, school-based curriculum development and assessments, social skills training, differentiating curricular, universal design, etc. The challenge for teacher educators is to determine how many of these to include in their courses, and how they will assess the effectiveness of these in facilitating the development of inclusive teacher practitioners.

Regardless of the content or model of teacher training, the effectiveness of existing teacher preparation for inclusion has been found lacking in many regions (for example, in the US: Grskovic and Trzcinka, 2011; Asia-Pacific region: Forlin, 2008; India: Hodkinson and Devarakonda, 2009). In Macedonia, teachers perceive themselves as inadequately prepared as they suggest that the competences they require are not systematically developed (Spasovski, 2010). The findings and recommendations of a recent exploratory national study in the US concluded that in addition to focusing on knowledge, skills, and attitudes to more effectively prepare teachers for inclusion, teacher-educators should establish integrated programs that involve special and discipline faculty working collaboratively to develop a shared vision of philosophy and practice (Harvey *et al.*, 2010).

Professional learning in schools

By listening to the voices of experienced inclusive teachers more appropriate support can be provided to new teachers once they join a school. The provision of information about school and district policies and procedures are essential for obtaining local practice knowledge in order to comply with government requirements (Berry, 2011). To provide more of the skills believed to be crucial for effective inclusion, Berry further suggests that schools should establish communities of practice which can offer support within the narrow local context of individual schools. Further, because of this support being localized and school-specific this may be of greater use than generic information obtained during preservice preparation.

In order to facilitate effective education teachers are required to identify appropriate outcomes for all children, which can then guide the differentiation or modification of the curriculum to enable every child to achieve these. This relies heavily on the ability of the teacher to undertake these modifications by knowing what is needed and how to achieve this. Effective inclusive teachers have been found to employ a range of good pedagogies to include all children in active learning. These include among others, clearly communicating expectations that engage all students in learning, setting high expectations for all students, establishing routines that free up time for small group and individual instruction, and spending time working with learners who are struggling (Jordan *et al.*, 2010).

Use of paraprofessionals

The additional pressure of teaching in inclusive classrooms where student diversity requires more detailed planning and differentiation on the part of teachers has led to an increased demand for greater classroom support. There remains, nevertheless, an inconsistency with regards to the development of what is perceived as an essential role. Where available, such support has relied, internationally in many instances, on the employment of qualified special education teachers or, more frequently, unqualified teaching assistants (TA) whose role has been to support a particular child.

As inclusion has expanded there has been a concurrent and significant increase in the designation of additional adults into supportive roles in classrooms (Rose and Forlin, 2010). In a lot of schools the earlier roles of administrative support and individual guidance have been changed to reflect a more pedagogical and instructional approach. Despite this, in many situations it is the untrained adults who are given the most challenging students to help; either with or without guidance from the teacher. According to the *Lamb Inquiry* in England:

The research refers to underpinning differences between teachers and TAs in subject knowledge and pedagogical knowledge; and in approaches to explaining to and questioning pupils. In addition the core understanding of how children learn, why they don't learn and what to do about it, which is at the heart of teacher training, is largely missing in the preparation that TAs receive.

(Lamb, 2009, Section 2.34)

Best practice strategies

When determining the best possible intervention and support for learners with special educational needs, this cannot be resolved in advance during initial teacher training as:

Decisions need to be made in the context and setting of a child's school by persons who are knowledgeable about children, resources, and issues of how to analyze the amount of effort and intensity required to accelerate the child's academic performance or sustain appropriate behaviour.

(Barnett et al., 2004, p. 77)

Teacher education, therefore, needs to provide teachers with a range of possible strategies that could be adopted, while ensuring that teachers realize that final decisions must be based more on a response to intervention approach, rather than by simply applying a predetermined set of interventions. The development of school-based strategies and curriculum-based measurements that respond to local need can much more readily accommodate the minority groups of students who require additional learning support.

A variety of teaching modes are being promulgated as best practices for supporting all learners within an inclusive classroom. Such approaches frequently include the use of team teaching or co-teaching as an inclusive strategy. In Turkey, for example, a pilot project to investigate the use of co-teaching in a mainstream system was found to be useful. Although the Turkish trial was only preliminary and limited, it was clear that to be effective, training in inclusive education and cooperation skills and time to plan collaboratively are essential elements for co-teaching to work (Gurger and Uzuner, 2011). Another frequently used instructional model is that of differentiated instruction. Adopting both of these strategies, though, requires effective leadership by principals who are able to lead while also empowering teachers to embrace these new ideas (Harpell and Andrews, 2010).

Meeting the challenges

Even when teachers are well prepared for becoming inclusive practitioners they are still faced with many challenges that can inhibit them. In Australia, for example, primary principals suggest that inadequate funding and resourcing is making the delivery of relevant inclusive education to the most disadvantaged students significantly challenging (Reid *et al.*, 2011). Further, issues such as a crowded curriculum, increased cultural differences and ethnically disadvantaged youths, and negative attitudes and beliefs can all be particularly challenging for teachers. While demanding, these do not deter good teachers from aiming to become inclusive practitioners.

The crowded curriculum

Endeavouring to provide flexibility in a curriculum for learners with special educational needs has been compounded in many regions by what is referred to as a 'crowded curriculum'. Societal demands on educational authorities has resulted in schools being required to include much more non-traditional content so that teachers have found they do not have the time to dedicate to extensive individual planning. There seems to be an expectation that it is the role of education, which for many students is the only stable environment in their lives, to fill in for the ails of society. To counter societal problems, schools are thus frequently being asked to include topics that should be, but are not, being dealt with by families and the community. Curricula about community awareness issues such as drug education, obesity, racism, suicide prevention, mental health, and homophobia, among others, are increasingly being added to a school's program. In some areas local problems are being brought into schools so that teachers are being required to address environmental issues such as surviving bush fires, floods, tsunamis, coping with post-traumatic stress, or recognizing and avoiding terrorist threats. This has resulted in little time left for the basics of education and even less time for supporting learners with special needs. In many regions there is a push for greater parental involvement in schooling. Perhaps the time has come for better parent education so that these issues can be addressed within the community, rather than added onto the already overloaded and crowded regular curriculum.

Including culturally and ethnically disadvantaged students

Catering for learners who are marginalized due to cultural differences or low socio-economic status is progressively a challenge for many educational systems worldwide. To overcome these challenges, schools have to consider innovative ideas and to look to their communities for support. In many areas in Australia, for example, where there are large indigenous populations, students have been frequently marginalized when it comes to completing high school and they are severely underrepresented in further education.

An idea to link universities with schools to help support indigenous students to complete high school and go on to further study has seen the development of a pioneering program in Australia called the 'Australian Indigenous Mentoring Experience' (AIME). Beginning with one university in 2005 and 25 university students acting as mentees for aboriginal high school students, this has now been adopted by 10 Eastern state universities. In 2011 it is matching 1,250 indigenous high school students with the same number of university mentees (O'Keeffe, 2011). This program has already reported huge increases in the number of students completing junior and senior secondary schooling (see www.aimementoring.com). Such a partnership between schools, that have traditionally found it extremely difficult to provide a learning environment that ensures indigenous students can be included and achieve comparable outcomes with their peers; and university students who are able to provide individual ongoing one-on-one support, has supported an inclusive approach.

Teacher acceptance, beliefs, and attitudes

Employing teachers who have the necessary skills and attitudes towards inclusion is, nonetheless, not easy, particularly in countries where they have had no prior opportunities to experience inclusive education. While teachers generally appear to be accepting of inclusion as an equitable educational philosophy, the lack of support to effectively adopt an inclusive pedagogy has continually been raised. For example, throughout the Asia-Pacific region teachers accept the ideology but disagree in practice, citing many concerns about it being unworkable for regular teachers to cater for students with disabilities and other special learning needs in their classes (Forlin, 2008). Likewise, in countries of the South which are just starting to employ an inclusive approach, such as Botswana, findings of a recent study indicate that many teachers feel unprepared and are fearful about inclusion and that they compensate for this by displaying frustration, anger, and negative attitudes (Chhabra et al., 2010). Even in developed countries such as England, recent governments have queried the policy of inclusion and have begun to offer a range of alternative options as the best practice approach.

Conclusion

Schools and classrooms are considerably more diverse than they have ever been. The role of teachers has expanded to include not only catering for increased student diversity, but also to embrace additional work that is outside their traditional direct teaching duties. Teachers have to liaise with a large range of stakeholders both within and outside schools. They need to provide individual planning for many students, prepare students for national benchmarking assessments, and become involved in extracurricular activities. They have to work collaboratively with parents, producing student portfolios to demonstrate each child's learning, and support any feedback with evidence. Above all of these they are held accountable for each child's achievement and progress. How effectively can they really manage this?

Many governments and researchers who have attempted to determine the effectiveness of teachers as inclusive practitioners usually focus on a narrow field of inquiry. In order to do this effectually requires evaluation of multiple dimensions of practices, witnessed within classrooms (Jordan et al., 2010). Jordan et al. (2010) report that epistemological understandings brought to the classroom by teachers may have significant implications for how teachers develop their inclusive skills and practices.

Recently there has been what Reid (2011) calls an 'equity revival'. This is likely to impact further on the diversity of school populations and the role that teachers must inevitably play in supporting this. If teachers are bringing with them beliefs and attitudes that are formed during initial teacher preparation as found by Jordan *et al.* (2010), and if schools continue to place extraneous demands on teachers to perform a range of non-teaching duties, it is unclear as to how teachers will cope with all of these challenges.

To ensure that teachers are able to enact inclusive pedagogies in increasingly diverse and demanding schools, they must be given the correct preparation during their training, ongoing support and professional learning once they have graduated, and time to collaborate and learn from other teachers how best to implement this knowledge and skill. Each region should develop their own set of competences that ensure that all teachers are being trained in appropriate skills to meet the needs of local learners. Effective ongoing professional learning must also be provided for all teachers to keep them abreast of best practices, policy, and ideas for enabling inclusion. With effective preparation and ongoing professional learning support teachers will more likely endeavor to become effective inclusive practitioners.

References

Barnett, D. W., Dally III, E. J., Jones, K. M. and Lentz, Jr, F. E. (2004) "Response to intervention: Empirically based special service decisions from single-case designs of increasing and decreasing intensity", *The Journal of Special Education*, 38(2): 66–79.

Berry, R. A. W. (2011) "Voices of experience: General education teachers on teaching students with disabilities", *International Journal of Inclusive Education*, 15(6): 627–48.

Chhabra, S., Srivastava, R. and Srivastava, I. (2010) "Inclusive education in Botswana: The perceptions of school teachers", *Journal of Disability Policy Studies*, 20(4): 219–28.

Department for Education and Skills (2001) *Special Education Needs: Code of Practice.* Online. Available at: https://www.education.gov.uk/publications/eOrderingDownload/0581-2001-SEN-CodeofPractice.pdf (accessed 20 February 2012).

Forlin, C. (2008) "Education reform for inclusion in Asia: What about teacher education?" in C. Forlin and M.-G. J. Lian (eds), *Reform, Inclusion, and Teacher Education: Towards a New Era of Special Education in the Asia-Pacific Region*, London: Routledge, pp. 61–73.

Forlin, C. and Chambers, D. (2011) "Teacher preparation for inclusive education: Increasing knowledge but raising concerns", *Asia-Pacific Journal of Teacher Education*, 39(1): 17–32.

Grskovic, J. A. and Trzcinka, S. M. (2011) "Essential standards for preparing secondary content teachers to effectively teach students with mild disabilities in included settings", *American Secondary Education*, 39(2): 94–108.

Gurger, H. and Uzuner, Y. (2011) "Examining the implementation of two co-teaching models: Team teaching and station teaching", *International Journal of Inclusive Education*, 15(6): 589–610.

Harpell, J. V. and Andrews, J. J. W. (2010) "Administrative leadership in the age of inclusion: Promoting best practices and teacher empowerment", *The Journal of Educational Thought*, 44(2): 189–210.

Harvey, M. W., Yssel, N., Bauserman, A. D. and Merbler, J. B. (2010) "Preservice teachers' preparation for inclusion", *Remedial and Special Education*, 31(1): 24–33.

Hodkinson A. and Devarakonda, C. (2009) "Conceptions of inclusion and inclusive education: A critical examination of the perspectives and practices of teachers in India", *Research in Education*, 82(1): 85–99.

Jordan, A., Glenn, C. and McGhie-Richmond, D. (2010) "The Supporting Effective Teaching (SET) project: The relationship of inclusive teaching practices to teachers' beliefs about disability and ability, and about their roles as teachers", *Teaching and Teacher Education*, 26: 259–66.

Lamb, B. (2009, December) *Lamb Inquiry: Special Educational Needs and Parental Confidence*, Department of Children's Services and Families, DCSF–01143–2009.

Office of the United Nations High Commissioner for Human Rights [OHCHA] (2006) *Convention on the Rights of Persons with Disabilities*. Online. Available at: http://www.ohchr.org/english/law/pdf/disabilities-convention.pdf (accessed 30 June 2010).

O'Keeffe, D. (2011) "Program boosting indigenous university partnerships", *Education Review*, May: 6–7.

Pearce, M. and Forlin, C. (2005) "Challenges and potential solutions for enabling inclusion in secondary schools", *Australasian Journal of Special Education*, 29(2): 93–105.

Reid, A. (2011) "What sort of equity?", *Professional Educator*, 4: 3–4.

Reid, A., Cranston, N., Keating J. and Mulford, B. (2011) *Exploring the Public Purposes of Education in Australian Primary Schools*, Melbourne: Australian Government Primary Principals Association.

Rose, R. and Forlin, C. (2010) "Impact of training on change in practice for education assistants in a group of international private schools in Hong Kong", *International Journal of Inclusive Education*, 14(3): 309–23.

Rouse, M. (2008) "Developing inclusive practice", *Education in the North*, 16: 6–13.

Sharma, U., Forlin, C. and Loreman, T. (2008) "Impact of training on pre-service teachers' attitudes and concerns about inclusive education and sentiments about persons with disabilities", *Disability and Society*, 23(7): 773–85.

Spasovski, O. (2010) "Principles of the inclusive education and the role of teachers and in-school professional staff", *The Journal of Special Education and Rehabilitation*, 11(1/2): 67–86.

UNESCO, United Nations Educational, Scientific and Cultural Organization (2010) *EFA Global Monitoring Report – Reaching the Marginalized*, Oxford: Oxford University Press and UNESCO Publishing.

Voltz, D. L. and Collins, L. (2010) "Preparing Special Education administrators for inclusion in diverse, standards-based contexts: Beyond the Council for Exceptional Children and the Interstate School Leaders Licensure Consortium", *Teacher Education and Special Education: The Journal of the Teacher Education Division of the Council for Exceptional Children*, 33(1): 70–82.

World Health Organization (2011) *World Report on Disability*. Online. Available at: http://reliefweb.int/sites/reliefweb.int/files/resources/9789240685215_eng.pdf (accessed 20 February 2012).

Chapter 10

Inclusion for innovation

The potential for diversity in teacher education

Gwang-jo Kim and Johan Lindeberg

Keywords: learning-friendly environment, diversity, innovation, human rights

Chapter overview

This chapter aims to provide an overview of inclusive education to readers of diverse backgrounds – be they students, policy-makers, or individuals who have a particular interest and/or are engaged in this area of education. It draws substance from various programs and activities of UNESCO as well as existing international legal instruments and frameworks which not only promote education but also consider it as a fundamental human right. What follows will try to describe the important role of inclusion and the potential for diversity in education in general, and teacher education in particular. Subsequent sections will explain the concept of inclusive education, the value of inclusion and the need for teacher education for inclusion, and how to achieve it.

Introduction

Diversity is one of the challenges to ensuring that every human being can exercise his or her right to education. Diversity takes a completely negative and inappropriate turn when used within the context of an individual's race, sex, religious belief, social and economic status, as well as political affiliation. In some countries, diversity in any of the aforementioned contexts could result not just in that individual's inability to reclaim what is rightfully his or hers, but could also cost his or her own life.

Embracing diversity helps counter the possibility of a particular situation from deteriorating. An example is a classroom full of students from different ethnic and religious groups, or socio-economic backgrounds; when their differences are highlighted in a way that pushes them apart instead of drawing them closer, one can only surmise that tension amongst them will manifest at a certain point in time which, if left to simmer, will potentially turn into a dangerous confrontation. Learning to embrace and accept diversity is important to reverse the negative impact it may have on our society. This is, of course, easier said than done; in a world that thrives on negative news, there is a lot that needs to be done so that the world can become an ideal place to live in, where peace, security and harmony prevail. So where does one start? As in many other things, learning starts at home and in school. Learning to embrace diversity should also start at home and continue in school.

Why inclusive education?

The *2010 Education for All (EFA) Global Monitoring Report (GMR)* states that countries' failure to adequately address inequalities linked to wealth, gender, ethnicity, language, disability, and other markers for the disadvantaged is holding back the progress of achieving EFA. These indicators tell us that unless governments act to reduce disparities through effective policy reforms, the EFA promises due in 2015 will be broken. The report highlights key challenges, particularly with regard to the quality of learning, and mentions the need for education systems across the world to be inclusive. Some 75 million children, 55 per cent of whom are girls, remain out of school and with current trends millions more will remain so in 2015 (UNESCO, 2009). Worse, millions of children are finishing school without having acquired even the minimal literacy and numeracy skills and the learning gap and disparities in learning achievements between different groups remain very high (UNESCO, 2010).

The challenge of providing EFA requires attention to issues related both to equity in, and to quality of, education. Providing education is not just an issue of removing barriers for marginalized groups to access education; it is also about enhancing quality of the education delivered. Therefore, teachers play an important role as facilitators of this process; they have to remove barriers, find alternative ways around them or identify remedial actions required in order to safeguard access to learning for all children. Since teachers are expected to bear the problems that go with this responsibility they need to be appropriately equipped to meet the challenges in accomplishing this role. Through qualitative initial teacher training future teachers need to learn the appropriate knowledge and skills required to be able to successfully put the notion of inclusiveness into practice.

The right to education is not limited to equitable access to education but in extension, also about equitable access to quality learning outcomes. The right to education is not just the right to be in school, but also the right to learn (UNESCO, 2010). It is a basic human right and is considered indispensible for the realization of all other human rights as enshrined in a great number of international human right law documents, of varying legal nature, that define both the ends and the means of education.

The United Nations Committee on Economic, Social and Cultural Rights (*UNCESCR, The Right to Education (art. 13): 12/081999. E/C.12/1999/10. General Comments*) has identified four key dimensions of the right to education: availability, accessibility, acceptability, and adaptability. These four dimensions are part of the foundation of an inclusive education system. Unless education is available, accessible, acceptable, and adaptable there is no right to quality education for all.

The four dimensions of the right to education

1. *Availability* – functioning educational institutions and programs have to be available in sufficient quantity within the jurisdiction of the State party. What they require to function depends upon numerous factors, including the developmental context within which they operate; for example, all institutions and programs are likely to require buildings or other protection from the elements, sanitation facilities for both sexes, safe drinking water, trained teachers receiving domestically competitive salaries, teaching materials, and so on; while some will also require facilities such as a library, computer facilities and information technology;

2. *Accessibility* – educational institutions and programs have to be accessible to everyone, without discrimination, within the jurisdiction of the State party. Accessibility has three overlapping dimensions:

    a. Non-discrimination – education must be accessible to all, especially the most vulnerable groups, in law and fact, without discrimination on any of the prohibited grounds;

    b. Physical accessibility – education has to be within safe physical reach, either by attendance at some reasonably convenient geographic location (e.g. neighborhood school) or via modern technology (e.g. access to a "distance learning" program);

    c. Economic accessibility – education has to be affordable to all. This dimension of accessibility is subject to the differential wording of article 13(2) in relation to primary, secondary and higher education: whereas primary education shall be available "free to all", States parties are required to progressively introduce free secondary and higher education;

3. *Acceptability* – the form and substance of education, including curricula and teaching methods, have to be acceptable (e.g. relevant, culturally appropriate and of good quality) to students and, in appropriate cases, parents; this is subject to the educational objectives required by article 13(1) and such minimum educational standards as may be approved by the State (see art. 13(3–4));

4. *Adaptability* – education has to be flexible so it can adapt to the needs of changing societies and communities and respond to the needs of students within their diverse social and cultural settings.

Inclusive education has a prominent space on the political agenda having been recognized and reinforced in the *World Declaration on Education for All* (UNESCO, 1990), the *Salamanca Statement* and *Framework for Action on Special Needs Education* (UNESCO, 1994), and the *Dakar Framework for Action* (UNESCO, 2000). A rights-based approach to education aims to assure every person the right to quality education; it is the kind of education that promotes and protects the individual's right to dignity and optimal development.

To achieve EFA

EFA goal Number 6 clearly states that all activities should improve all aspects of the quality of education. This includes a strong focus on the well-being of the learner and the relevance of content and achievements. It also identifies the quality of learning processes and the learning environment as essential components. In order to realize the right to quality education for all learners, a comprehensive and holistic approach is required. Inclusive education is truly rights-based in its nature and will require all different aspects of the education system to be redesigned. Therefore, there is a need for the whole education system to reform if we realistically aim to achieve quality education for all. This is of particular importance for teacher education, in preparing teachers to encourage and facilitate inclusive learning to take place in the classroom.

It is recognized that teachers are the single most important education resource a country has. All education innovations and reforms depend on teachers to make them happen. Therefore, it is of utmost importance to make sure that teachers are equipped and ready to create and manage an inclusive learning environment of good quality. Teachers need adequate training and support but perhaps also need the system to challenge some of their attitudes towards diversity in the classroom (UNESCO, 2010).

To promote equitable economic, social, and political development

One of the most significant milestones in the history of the United Nations is the adoption in 1948 of the *Universal Declaration of Human Rights (UDHR)* which states that "recognition of the inherent dignity and of the equal and inalienable rights of all members of the human family is the foundation of freedom, justice, and peace in the world" (UDHR, para. Preamble). The UDHR further states that education should "promote understanding, tolerance and friendship among all nations, racial or religious groups and shall further the activities of the United Nations for the maintenance of peace" (UDHR, art. 26).

In today's era of globalization, more than 60 years after the adoption of the UDHR, we are living in a socially and culturally diverse world that makes the fundamental values described in the UDHR more relevant than ever.

People are the basis of innovation and human capital is the essence of innovation. They generate the ideas and knowledge that power innovation, and they apply this knowledge and the resulting technologies, products, and services in the workplace and as consumers (OECD Innovation Strategy, 2010). Disparities between different groups of people in a society impede social development and have implications for that society's economic development and the distribution of opportunities. To counter disparities and offer people equal opportunities, they need a wide variety of skills, as well as the capacity to learn, adapt, and/or retrain. Education can empower individuals but empowering people to innovate relies on relevant education and the development of wide-ranging skills that complement formal education. Education opens up opportunities and offers individuals increased freedom of choice and provides the most disadvantaged groups the vehicle for social and economical mobility.

Education systems, though, also create visible and invisible barriers for the most excluded and can reinforce discrimination in society. Financial disparities remain a major challenge and data tells us that even though most people are improving their financial situation the disparities are growing. The so-called wealth effect in education clearly shows that inequalities in wealth are a universal source for education marginalization as education poverty and inequality have a high cost for societies but also for the individuals affected. Inclusive education policies aiming to combat disparities and disadvantages can be a powerful tool in promoting non-discrimination and equality as well as realizing social mobility and challenging root causes for marginalization (UNESCO, 2010).

To promote social cohesion and inclusion

The principal criticism of globalization is that "not everyone has an equal 'stake' in the success of the new economic order" (Ball, 1998, p. 120), aggravating the inequities that exist not only between nations, but also within nations. As economic activities become increasingly knowledge-based, educational opportunities have become an even more important determinant in income distribution (Watkins, 2000). For this reason, countries need to fulfil, protect, and promote access to education for all without discrimination, and to make sure that education systems provide understanding and respect for all people, their cultures, civilizations, values, and ways of life. It is also important to remember that each individual is unique, and she or he is a member of a variety of ethnic, social, and cultural groups, possessing different personal characteristics and preferences; in other words, we all have multiple identities. Nobel laureate Amartya Sen cautions us that the focus on a single identity (notably religion, ethnicity, or nationality) is prone to conflict and violence, and the politics of global confrontation today is frequently seen as "a corollary of religious or cultural divisions" (Sen, 2005, n.p.). He argues that education should not only socialize learners in their own (or dominant) cultural ethos and values, but more importantly, it should help them develop the ability to reason about their decisions and lead the kind of life they have reasons to value.

What is inclusive education?

A simple definition of inclusive education is based on the right of all learners to a quality education that meets basic learning needs and enriches lives. Focusing particularly on vulnerable and marginalized groups, it seeks to develop the full potential of every individual with the ultimate goal of ending all forms of discrimination and fostering social cohesion (UNESCO, 2011). Inclusive education is a process that involves the transformation of the education system in order to accommodate all children regardless of their individual needs. It is concerned with identifying and removing the barriers to quality participation in learning for all learners and should also be seen as an ongoing process, constantly focusing on those excluded from accessing education as well as those in school but not learning.

Inclusive education recognizes the need for education systems to be inclusive of all learners as holders of a right to education. This implies that they not only have the right to access *to* education, but human rights must also be applied *in* education and promoted *through* education. Stated differently, participation in education is not an end in itself; it is a process which should empower individuals to develop self-esteem, confidence, the ability to apply knowledge and skills in diverse circumstances, and for a range of social, cultural, economic, and political purposes.

Inclusion should be seen as a process of addressing and responding to the diversity in the needs of all children, youths, and adults through increasing participation in learning, cultures, and communities, and reducing and eliminating exclusion within and from education. It involves changes and modifications in content, approaches, structures, and strategies, with a common vision that covers all children of the appropriate age range and a conviction that it is the responsibility of the regular system to educate all children (UNESCO, 2009a). Inclusive education has slowly evolved from being conceptualized as the integration of learners with disabilities into regular schools to being understood as a process of education system transformation to facilitate the education of all children, regardless of background and individual needs. Today, inclusive education is also seen as concerned with eliminating discrimination and exclusion stemming from bias and negative attitudes in society; that it is relevant to all aspects of the education system and is by no means limited to formal education alone (UNESCO, 2009b).

The human rights imperative of inclusive education also means that particular attention is given to the root causes of discrimination, inequality, and exclusion of vulnerable and marginalized groups. It focuses on identifying and removing barriers for participation in learning for all learners (Shaeffer, 2008). Since the International Conference of Education in 2008, the concept of inclusive education has also been broadened to encompass "general guiding principle to strengthen education for sustainable development, lifelong learning for all, and equal access of all levels of society to learning opportunities" (UNESCO, IBE, 2008, p. 18).

Inclusive education, therefore, is an approach that investigates how to transform education systems in order to remove barriers that prevent learners from participating fully in education. It also examines how the education delivered can be adapted to make it relevant to the local context; that it includes and treats all students with respect; and that it is flexible so that all can participate. Ultimately, inclusive education is about visualizing a school for all where diversity is respected, celebrated, and utilized for the benefit of all.

How to achieve inclusive education?

Access and quality are clearly interlinked and are mutually reinforcing; this was recognized already in the *Salamanca Statement* that reads:

Regular schools with inclusive orientation are the most effective means of combating discriminatory attitudes, creating welcoming communities, building an inclusive society and achieving education for all; moreover, they provide an effective education to a majority of the children and improve the efficiency and ultimately the cost effectiveness of the entire education system.

(UNESCO, 1994, p. ix)

Political will, determination and commitment

Earlier in this article, we questioned where to start in learning to embrace diversity in order to create a peaceful environment. Our reaction is that in order to meet our societies' challenges and counter marginalization and exclusion, governments need to develop education systems that embrace the values of individual diversity and utilize it to enhance the quality and relevance of the learning. They also have to make sure that education systems actively combat prevailing prejudices and educational exclusion, which lead to social alienation and exclusion. Such systems will contribute to the construction of peace, understanding, justice, and freedom within society as a whole. However, these values need to be reflected in practice in everything from constitutional guarantees to budget allocations. Respect for diversity should be reflected in the national legislation and policy frameworks through clear provisions against discrimination and exclusion.

Learner-oriented pedagogy and the role of teachers

Inclusive learning environments often entail challenging traditional concepts of teaching practices; they aim to utilize diversity and transform them into what have previously been seen as obstacles to a pedagogical resource. Welcoming diversity in the classroom opens up opportunities for the introduction of creative and innovative practices as traditional teaching practices might be seen as insufficient to appropriately cater to all children in the class. However, this also requires new mindsets of teachers, education personnel, parents, and children. An inclusive education system should be learning-friendly in its nature and the system adaptable to the diverse needs of individual learners. Today, most education systems and, therefore, schools are expecting children to adapt to the system, rather than the other way around, and the great embedded value of utilizing the diversity in the classroom is partly lost (UNESCO, 2006).

One important concept that everybody, teachers in particular, must acknowledge is that "all learners are different" and learners from diverse backgrounds and abilities are an everyday reality in every classroom. Whether or not this becomes a problem or a resource depends on the education system and ultimately the school and the teacher. Having a diverse group of learners in the classroom is likely to add value to the overall quality of the education of all students in the class (UNESCO, 2006).

An inclusive system should complement subject-based academic performance as sole indicators for learning achievements by moving towards including values, attitudes, and skills required to meet challenges of contemporary societies (UNESCO, 2009b). It implies moving from simply learning to know towards also learning to be, learning to do, and learning to live together (UNESCO, 1996). The successful transformation of current practices towards a more inclusive education system also demands that solutions are designed by all concerned stakeholders themselves. Local ownership based on an inclusive process that is not fueled by external prescriptions but rather by the local needs and ideas increases the chances of creating sustainable change (UNESCO, 2009).

Getting marginalized learners into school does not just increase their opportunities to learn because they are able to interact with other children. It also promotes their participation in family and community life. In addition, children and adults with whom they interact also benefit. They learn not just to respect diversity but to embrace it by celebrating tolerance and understanding and by doing so realizing that everyone is special. However, embracing diversity and welcoming it into the classrooms is not an easy task. Teachers often feel overworked and underpaid, and they may have to handle large classes including children with diverse backgrounds and abilities. This might lead to more work, although it does not have to be the case (UNESCO, 2006).

If education systems set out to manage the diversity among our children by recognizing their strengths and weaknesses, planning lessons accordingly, using teaching strategies and adapting our curriculum to fit each child's abilities and background, and, most importantly, knowing how to mobilize our teachers, parents, community members, and other professionals, it will help us provide a *good quality education for all children*. The great diversity found in every classroom can be transformed into a positive force that increases the quality of the learning and better equips children for the increasingly complex and dynamic society they live in.

References

Ball, S. J. (1998) "Big policies/small world: an introduction to international perspectives in education policy", *Comparative Education*, 34(2): 119–30.

OECD Innovation Strategy (2010) *Ministerial Report on the OECD Innovation Strategy: Innovation to Strengthen Growth and Address Global and Social Challenges*. Online. Available at: http://www.oecd.org/dataoecd/51/28/45326349.pdf (accessed 19 August 2011).

Sen, A. (2005) *Solution to Cultural Confusion is Freedom and Reason*. Online. Available at: http://news.ft.com/cms/s/92fa74de–6042–11da–a3a6–0000779e2340.html (accessed 19 August 2011).

Shaeffer, S. (2008) *Realizing Inclusive Education through Applying a Rights-Based Approach to Education [ED/BIE/ CONFINTED 48/Inf.2]*, Geneva: UNESCO IBE.

UNESCO (1990) *World Declaration on Education for All and Framework for Action to Meet Basic Learning Needs*, Thailand: Jomtien.

UNESCO (1994) *The Salamanca Statement and Framework for Action on Special Needs Education*, Paris: UNESCO.

UNESCO (1996) *The Treasure Within: Report to UNESCO of the International Commission on Education for the Twenty-First Century*, Paris: UNESCO.

UNESCO (2000) *The Dakar Framework for Action*, Senegal: Dakar.

UNESCO (2006) *Embracing Diversity: Creating Inclusive and Learning-Friendly Environments*, Bangkok: UNESCO.

UNESCO, IBE (2008) *Conclusions and Recommendations: 2008 International Conference on Education*, Geneva: UNESCO IBE.

UNESCO (2009) *Education for All: Global Monitoring Report 2009*, Paris: UNESCO.

UNESCO (2009a) *Policy Guidelines on Inclusion in Education*, Paris: UNESCO.

UNESCO (2009b) *Towards Inclusive Schools and Enhancing Learning*, Paris: UNESCO.

UNESCO (2010) *Education for All: Global Monitoring Report 2010: Reaching the Marginalized*, Paris: UNESCO.

UNESCO (2011) *Inclusive Education*. Online. Available at: http://www.unesco.org/en/inclusive–education/ (accessed 19 August 2011).

United Nations (1948) *The Universal Declaration of Human Rights*, Paris: United Nations.

Watkins, K. (2000) *The Oxfam Education Report*, Oxford: Oxfam.

Chapter 11

Seven essential components for teacher preparation programs for inclusion

Humberto Rodríguez

Keywords: teacher preparation for inclusion, inclusion, teacher education, new paradigms

Chapter overview[1]

Education for all with quality and equity has a high priority in Latin American countries. In this way, teachers have a central importance and should develop specific skills and vision to contribute to this goal (Robalino, 2005). Seven essential components for teacher preparation programs for inclusion are introduced. This contribution has been the result of intensive work training teachers in Monterrey, Mexico.

First of all, a brief global vision about education for all and inclusion is presented; the Mexican context is introduced and the origin of the experience, detailing the legal framework and the organization of the special education services, is outlined. Second, reflections on teacher education for inclusion are presented and a specific profile for the inclusive teacher is shared. Each essential component is explained, some of which are supported by diagrams. In the final part, some conclusions from training teachers in Mexico are outlined.

A global frame

Education is a fundamental right for every child and young person. This is already a global agreement. Every country hopes to develop a new school that is ethical and egalitarian, making possible a quality education for all without exceptions (Martínez and Buxarrais, 1998). Inclusive education has promoted new paradigms in schools, rethinking every concept about disability, and emphasizing support systems and interactions needed for the best learning, as each student presents individual conditions, needs and particular interests.

In this way, new roles and responsibilities in a collaboration between professionals, parents and the community have been tested. The goal is to eliminate all barriers in order to achieve learning (Lipski and Garther, 1998).

1 This chapter was originally written in Spanish.

Inclusion promotes quality and equity education for all, without any type of barrier or exclusion, including those who may be potentially marginalized due to disability, gender, emotional/behavioural problems, family background, ethnicity, giftedness, migrants, poverty, hearing or visual impairment, language delay, among others.

(UNESCO, 1994, p. 6)

This is a big challenge for all but it is our opportunity to advance dialogue and participation, making possible a well-being through providing quality education to all without exception.

The Mexican context

Not every education system in the world agrees, yet there is always an opportunity to improve and advance on the best results. Mexico is no exception to this. It has a lot of educational challenges, combined with complicated social and economic contexts.

Mexico has signed every international statement about inclusion, and has promoted significant changes in this regard. In my opinion, the most ground breaking change has been *The General Education Law* issued in 1993. This Federal Law recognized special education as a part of Basic Education and specifies its mission as follows:

Special Education is destined to individuals with temporary or permanent disabilities as well as those with outstanding aptitudes. It treats students in an appropriate manner according to their conditions and with social equity. For children with disabilities, education will support their inclusion into regular education through the application of methods, techniques and specific materials. For those individuals not able to be included in regular education classrooms, an educational program will be developed to respond to their individual learning needs. This will include the development of independent living and social skills supported by the use of programs and materials. This educational program includes orientation to parents and/or guardians as well as to teachers in basic education that receive students with special educational needs.

(United Mexican States, 1993, *General Education Law* Article 41)

As a consequence of this law every special education service has been transformed, two in particular: (1) The Services Support Units for Regular Education (USAER), a group of diverse professionals placed in regular schools; and (2) the Multiple Attention Centers (CAM), attending children with profound needs, promoting independence and inclusion in the workplace. Both start with the general curriculum as a core.

Another important feature of the Mexican context is that every educational program is responsible, by mandate of the Federal Department of Public Education (SEP), for including all teacher training. This way the schools for teachers (Escuelas Normales), which are public institutions of higher education, and also the private schools for teachers must implement the *Federal Programmes for Teachers*. The SEP has made important changes in all teacher education programs, promoting common and general assignments for all, and also including some subjects for familiarization with inclusion, e.g. *special needs education* and *adolescents at risk*.

Reflections on teacher education for inclusion

Inclusion requires a broad vision and specific competencies for all teachers. Teachers need to know that diversity is present in the classroom, and that they should attend to learners with a range of diverse needs. In this way, it is imperative to prepare teachers for inclusion in all curricular plans, for preservice and inservice teachers, with the following professional aptitudes (Rodríguez, 2010; Carver, 1998):

- Researcher. Always searches for explanations about their educative reality, has intellectual skills to propose diverse hypotheses, solve problems, generate innovation, and face challenges in the education field.
- Strategic. Is a professional with strong self-regulation, skills for planning, guiding and assessing, not only their self-intellectual resources about the learning of curricular issues but also in their performance as a teacher. Always has an attitude to learn and improve. Faces uncertainty with creativity.
- Resilient. Always moves towards the future, in spite of difficult situations, by making healthy adjustments against adversity (see Figure 11.1).

The knowledge, skills and attitudes for all inclusion teachers must emphasize that the purpose of all teacher interventions is the students' learning and teachers also

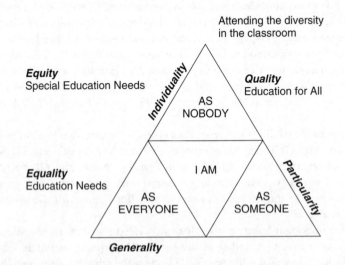

Figure 11.1 Preparing teachers for inclusion (Rodríguez, 2010)

need to have high expectations for all (inclusive vision), develop inclusive projects including diverse teaching strategies and support systems (inclusive practices), and participate in collective work (inclusive language) (Stainback and Stainback, 1999; Stromstd, 2003).

I identify three important educational aspects that every teacher needs to make present in inclusion: equality – promoting the same opportunities for all; quality – offering functional and meaningful learning; and equity – responding to the special educational needs of all children.

In this way, an inclusive teacher should be distinguished by the following three profiles:

1.   The inclusive teacher is a professional educator committed to his/her community, who recognizes individual differences and considers them in his/her educational intervention actions, participates in collective teaching because it is essential for collaboration and dialogue, and is creative to implement education by facing the challenges of diversity in specific educational project interventions (Giroux, 1990).
2.   The inclusive teacher, by their multi-tiered training, has holistic educational views with strong skills and experience in order to participate in diverse contexts.
3.   The inclusive teacher is accompanied in his/her early professional career by a mentor, under facilitation and cooperation models.

Seven essential components for teacher preparation programs

Teachers are the key for the success in inclusion (Barber, 2008). Next, I introduce seven essential components for teacher preparation programs. I present some explanations and characterizations that in my opinion are fundamental for inclusion. This is based on our experience with trainee teachers in Monterrey, Mexico.

First: High social and community content

The inclusive teacher is a professional in education with a strong commitment to his/her community. The teacher preparation program should include subjects with high social and community content because they need to be sensitive to the needs of students and their environment. I believe it is important to recognize the school as a point of encounter among different people. This promotes agreement between all the members of the community and creates meaningful relationships between the factors that impact upon students' learning by removing barriers and promoting high expectations and a positive environment characterized by continuous improvement and values. Dialogue, participation and collaboration allow full awareness to all as a community and thus ensure successful experiences in inclusion. For this reason teachers need to be involved in this.

Second: Quality, equality and equity

The inclusive teacher recognizes individual differences and implements learning strategies for all (Ferguson, 2008). The educational intervention is oriented to diversity and promotes learning strategies for all (equality), for many and for the individual (equity). These are other essential aspects in the teacher preparation programs. Quality, equality and equity concepts should be translated into specific actions during educative interventions.

In order to illustrate the individual differences in the classroom, I follow a tridimensional view. In this way, I use an equilateral triangle to explain this approach. All three sides are equal in length, and in the triangle's center I write "I am".

- On the base I write "I am like everyone" (equality).
- On one side I write "I am like someone else" and on the other "I am the only one" (equity).

Every inclusive teacher needs to move among these three realities in his/her classroom. It also allows co-teaching or concurrent participation. Inclusion promotes cooperation in the classroom. I believe this representation helps us understand the diversity concept as well.

In inclusive education, the school and classrooms are very dynamic and have a lot of interactions and roles. The exchange and experience enrich individuality. Diverse contexts indicate diverse relationships and interactions. Figure 11.1 has been the result of reflections crossing views from philosophy and psychology.

Third: Working collaboratively

Collaborative work among educators facilitates inclusion and it needs to be promoted by the *Teacher Preparation Programme* (UNESCO, 2005). In my opinion, inclusion is founded on a collective of teachers, a team sharing knowledge, making decisions, solving problems together and generating actions in order to improve the school and to increase the learning for all. Consequently, collaborative work is a source of dialogue, co-teaching and updating. In this way I would like to introduce the process of collaborative work

La Escuela Normal de Especialización de Monterrey, an institution of higher education that trains teachers in special education, promotes collaborative work in all faculties. Nowadays learning this way is invaluable and considered as a fundamental component for inclusive education. All preservice teachers should know and develop skills in this way because:

- The teacher learns when teaching and the students teach when they learn.
- Everyone takes on leadership tasks because we assume roles as protagonists.
- Outcome increases when we make synergy, identity is strengthened when we make joint decisions, shaping teams in the resolution of problems, allowing them to learn or re-learn social skills.

- The results begin when we work together because nobody will do it for us, whatever we must do, let's do it.
- The economic resources are a result of the collaborative work and not a condition.
- Heterogeneity provides a great richness.
- Accountability and recognition processes are boosted in the community.

The process is shaped in six important steps as follows (Casanova and Rodríguez, 2009):

1. Building a common vision. Who are we? Who do we want to be? What are our goals, expectations and interests?
2. Recognizing our reality. How are we? Why are we like this? We need to analyze our beliefs based on precise data and information.
3. Decision-making. How do we propose to improve our present? We need to build and establish an agreed method of participation for change.
4. Developing proposals. What are we doing to change the situation? Who is leading this? Everyone needs to know all the actions.
5. Evaluating our actions. How and how much have we advanced? Are our agreements functioning? What needs to be modified, strengthened or implemented? We need to make necessary adjustments.
6. Beginning anew. Which areas do we need to improve? What do we need to do? New actions for improvement.

Fourth: Dialogue

All programs for preservice teachers and service teachers must be based on the interpretative and critical paradigms. Allow encounters with others, and the collective and interpretive insight into environments and circumstances and the development of research activities are fundamental. The inclusive teacher has strong skills in action research methods. I strongly believe that this paradigm generates conditions for dialogue and collaboration. Dialogue needs a strong relationship and the essence of collaboration in order to recognize other's views. Recognizing that another person has their own worldview that leads them to explain, interpret and act from their personal background is important. Collaboration, thus, takes the value of the other person, their strengths, occupations and concerns, so that a final vision transforms from two ideas (you and me) to give a new focus (us). Dialogue and collaboration are key elements in inclusive education.

Fifth: Contextual professional practice

Contextual preparation, allowing preservice teachers to connect with a range of educational services, gives them an opportunity to identify diversity as an enriching element. It has three main steps: (1) re-signification, (2) approaching the schools by doing diverse activities, and (3) internship under the tutelage of a mentor.

For teachers to promote inclusive education, they should be trained in direct link with the educational services. I take as a reference the so-called contextual professional practice (Imbernón, 2002). This approach, in our experience, must be presented to all throughout the training process structure with multi-directional flow between theoretical ideas and experiences close to the educational field. Therefore, I propose three important stages:

(1) Re-significance of the future teachers' own school experience

This period of time is essential. Each future teacher should discuss their own experience as a student, analyze emotions and be aware of school and pedagogical theory made by teachers, allowing them to "see" those components that were previously "hidden", such as the school's culture, type, teachers, uses and customs that marked the dynamics of the school and its predominate values, characterizing their experiences from other angles and points of view. It certainly requires time to work individually and collectively, comparing similarities and differences in experiences. I propose that this time must be during the first and second semesters of teachers' training programs.

(2) Approach to various educational contexts

This consists of visiting previously selected schools and making observations and educational practices. This involves three stages:

- Plan of activities: after reviewing the educational context, it is important to develop tools, observation guides, questionnaires and interviews, make teams and prepare activities, among other things.
- Implementation of the plan.
- Presentation of experiences: this is done in the classroom in which all of the evidence and results are presented from the previous phase.

As a result of these activities, each preservice teacher compiles a portfolio and checks their intervention. They are accompanied at all times by an experienced teacher. This experience should certainly include diverse environments, contexts and educational services that characterize the education system.

(3) Professional practices in real environments

A long period of the teacher's training must be spent in a school under the tutelage of a teacher. This teacher must provide mentoring activities to enrich their teaching experience with the knowledge of a mentor who attends and promotes inclusive activities. Currently, the faculty has agreements with diverse educational centers. Partnerships between the training institution for teachers and schools are necessary. I also think this enriching experience enables the development of educational research

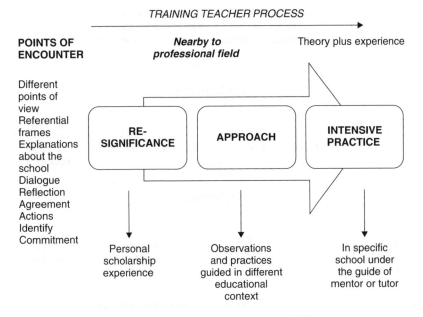

Figure 11.2 The teacher training process (Rodríguez, 2010)

in the specific teaching domain of the preservice teacher. The last two semesters are ideal for this important step. Figure 11.2 outlines the teacher training process.

Sixth: Cross-categorical/multi-tiered formation

Diversity needs a global and common vision; philosophy, values, legal framework, language and shared knowledge as learning theories, special educational needs, support systems and educational intervention (Smith, 2001). It also needs tutoring and curricular adjustments. Inclusive education must characterize all teacher training programs, offering skills and common benchmarks for everyone regardless of education level (e.g. primary, secondary or higher education). This versatile training enables various teachers, regardless of their field or level of training, to collaborate and participate in the diversity of educational contexts together. A collaboration intervention model is provided in Figure 11.3. The common references on inclusive education frameworks that must be present in all teacher training programs are:

• Common vision. The philosophy of inclusion, legal frameworks that enable an education for all with quality and equity, educational policy that promotes attention to diversity, the historical evolution since marginalization to inclusion, and conceptions among others are all fundamental aspects in educational programs.

developing an approach to better prepare the inclusive education teacher. In order to do this we:

- Work together with other institutions to build a collaboration network, connecting colleagues and diverse professionals, exchanging knowledge and making new friends.
- Promote educational research projects to develop innovation.
- Participate in diverse social and educative programs in each community.
- Infuse collaborative work in all teachers because it is the best way to attend to the diversity of our schools. In this sense, the mentoring process has a transcendent role.
- Choose the best student profile for teacher education.
- Enrich the teacher preparation programs with transversal competencies along the curricular plan.
- Increase all professional skills in term of alternative and augmentative communication systems such as Braille, Sign Language and Communication Board through a supplementary program.
- Make educational proposals to the Federal Education Department in order to improve the training of teachers in Mexico based on action research.
- Collaborate with academic centers to share knowledge.

References

Barber, M. (2008) *How the World's Best-Performing School Systems Come out on Top, No.41, PREAL Documentos,* New York: McKinsey and Company.

Carver, C. (1998) "Resilience and thriving: Issues, models and linkages", *Journal of Social Issues,* 54: 237–46.

Casanova, M. and Rodríguez, H. (2009) *La inclusión educativa, un horizonte de posibilidades [The Inclusive Education, A Horizon of Possibilities],* Madrid: Ed. La Muralla.

Domingo, J. (2004) "Asesoramiento al centro educativo [Advice to educational center]", México: SEP. Biblioteca para la actualización del maestro.

Ferguson, D. (2008) "International trends in inclusive education: The continuing challenge to teach each one and everyone", *European Journal of Special Education Needs,* 23: 109–20.

Giroux, H. A. (1990) *Los profesores como intelectuales. Hacia una pedagogías crítica del aprendizaje [Teachers as Intellectuals. Toward an Interpretative Pedagogic of Learning],* Barcelona: Paidós.

Imbernón, F. (2002) *La formación y el desarrollo profesional del profesorado [The Training and Profesional Development of Teachers],* Madrid: Graó.

Lipsky D. K. and Garther, A. (1998) "Factors for successful inclusion: Learning from the past, looking toward the future", in S. J. Vitello and D. E. Mithaug (eds), *Inclusive Schooling – National and International Perspectives,* Mahwah, NJ: Lawrence Erlbaum Associates, pp. 98–112.

Martínez, M. and Buxarrais, M. R. (1998) *La necesidad de educar en valores en la escuela [The Need of Educating Values in the School],* Spain: Aula de novación Educativa.

Nieto, J. Modelos de asesoramiento (2004) *En Asesoramiento al centro educativo en Jesús Domingo Segovia [Advice's Models],* México: SEP.

Robalino, M. (2005) *Protagonismo docente en el cambio educativo [Educational Leadship in Educational Change]*, Santiago: UNESCO.

Rodríguez, H (2010) *Teoría y práctica en la educación inclusiva [Theory and Practice in Inclusive Education]*, Spain: Adeo.

Smith, T. (2001) *Teaching Students with Special Needs in Inclusive Settings*, Upper Saddle River, NJ: Pearson.

Stainback, S. and Stainback W. (1999) *Aulas Inclusivas [Inclusive Classroom]*, Madrid: Narcea.

Stromstd, M. (2003) *Developing Inclusive Teacher Education*, London: Routledge Falmer.

UNESCO (1994) "Declaracion de Salamanca y marco de acción para las necesidades educativas especiales [*The Salamanca Statement and Framework for Action*]", Spain: Salamanca.

UNESCO (2005) "Protagonismo Docente en el cambio educativo [Educational Leadership in Educational Change]", Santiago: Revista PRELAC No.1.

United Mexican States (1993) *Ley General De Educacion [General Education Law]*. Online. Available at: http://www.sepbcs.gob.mx/legislacion/ley_general_educacion.html (accessed 3 November 2011).

Chapter 12

Gifted, talented or educationally disadvantaged?

The case for including 'giftedness' in teacher education programs

Wilma Vialle and Karen B. Rogers

Keywords: ability grouping, acceleration, selective schools, underachievement, dropout, labeling, heterogeneous, homogeneous, differentiation, twice-exceptional

Chapter overview

This chapter argues that the presumption that gifted education practices conflict with the principles of inclusion is erroneous. However, there are distinct educational disadvantages for gifted students in classrooms where teachers do not appropriately differentiate instruction to match the needs of those students. A critical role for teacher education for inclusion is debunking myths around giftedness and preparing preservice teachers to accept their responsibility for educating gifted students.

Introduction

The term 'gifted', for many, conjures up images of spectacle-clad, pale-faced individuals who embrace each school day with enthusiasm. In a recent survey, 200 teacher education students were asked to draw a gifted child and write five words associated with the word 'gifted'. Ninety-five per cent of the drawings depicted a smile, along with stereotypical glasses or light-bulbs. The words, too, were positive – the most common response was 'creative' (68 per cent) – with only a handful invoking 'nerd', 'geek', 'socially awkward', 'demanding', 'egotistical', 'irritating' and 'overachiever'. This snapshot suggests that preservice teachers look favourably on gifted children. But how do their attitudes affect their classroom behaviours and where do they think giftedness fits within what they have already been taught about inclusive classrooms?

Inclusion in Australian contexts is enacted in heterogeneous classrooms and comprehensive schools, but gifted education is viewed as promoting the separation of gifted students into selective high schools and gifted primary school classes (Vinson, 2002). The challenge for teacher educators, then, is to help preservice teachers reconcile the seeming contradictions between best practice according to the gifted movement and the principle of inclusion. The premise of this chapter is that these two views are not necessarily incompatible.

The tendency to polarise gifted education and inclusion reflects many of the binaries in the discourses around the education of gifted students, as reflected in professional bodies such as the NSW Teachers Federation. This organisation argues that placing gifted students in selective schools strips comprehensive schools of intellectual role models, leaving predominantly "non-academic, ambivalent students" (Vinson, 2002, p. 127). This view of the majority of students in the school system is highly presumptive. It also characterises gifted students as being academically motivated, an assumption that is also questionable.

The NSW Teachers Federation proposed dismantling selective streams in New South Wales, a call that was supported by a public inquiry into education, funded, not coincidentally, by the NSW Teachers Federation (Vinson, 2002). The Federation's position rests on the following principle:

> The pursuit of educational excellence for all, regardless of cultural, religious, racial or economic background, geographical location or special needs, has directly shaped Australia to be one of the most tolerant, socially cohesive, non-violent and multicultural societies in the world.
>
> (NSW Teachers Federation, 2010)

Proponents of gifted education have no argument with the aims of educational excellence for all. However, whether educational excellence routinely happens for gifted students in comprehensive schools is debatable.

Giftedness and achievement

In Australia, 'giftedness' is defined as potential, while 'talent' is defined as performance of that giftedness (Gagné, 2003). Giftedness does not translate automatically into academic attainment and underachievement by gifted students remains the most significant problem reported for this population (Morisano and Shore, 2010). The 'slump' in achievement begins as early as Year 4, but is definitely in place for many students by Year 5. As students move through the school system the problem is exacerbated and, by early high school, the problem exists at full force. Studies have speculated that the number of underachieving gifted students lies between 10 per cent (Wills and Munro, 2001) and 50 per cent (Seeley, 1993). The 2001 Senate Inquiry (Senate Employment, 2001) described the rampant underachievement witnessed in Australia's schools and suggested that immediate attention be paid to countering the phenomenon.

While individual and family factors are among the causes cited for scholastic under-performance, school factors also play a part. Gross (2010) observed that the "majority of gifted children have underachievement imposed upon them" by schools that do not allow them to work at their own pace (p. 33). Social difficulties tended to be more acute in the middle school years, perhaps because there are fewer outlets for finding like minds than later in school. Swiatek et al. (2000) found that many highly gifted students, particularly girls, tended to deny their giftedness in an attempt to 'fit in'. The asynchrony between a child's physical, social, emotional and cognitive development creates social stresses and challenges, which may move their focus away from trying to do well at school (Grobman, 2009). Peer relationships, too, are a critical school factor in underachievement (Henfield et al., 2008). In summary, some gifted students camouflage their abilities in order to fit in socially, leading them into patterns of underachievement.

School curricula and learning environment have also been 'blamed' for underachievement, particularly where there is required re-mastery of previously learned material; slow pace; where students feel under-challenged; or curriculum content does not match individual interests or abilities (Matthews and McBee, 2007). Other research has identified students' attitudes to school and motivational variables as critical for achievement (Hoekman et al., 2005). Colangelo et al. (2004a) noted that compared to high achievers, underachievers reported less satisfaction with school and had lower career aspirations.

Studies have suggested that underachievement extends beyond schooling (McCall et al., 1992). The longitudinal work of McCall and colleagues, for example, found that the underachieving pattern established in high school was still present 13 years post-school. Gifted students may represent as many as 20 per cent of high-school dropouts (Bridgeland et al., 2006). These students reported that the lack of challenge in school curricula was among the major reasons they left school early.

While the etiology of underachievement in gifted students is complex, school factors contribute to such outcomes. There is a significant challenge, then, for the teaching profession – and teacher education – to ensure that in a system of inclusion, students at the high end of the ability spectrum are appropriately challenged.

Teachers' attitudes and beliefs

At the beginning of this chapter, we reported the positive words attributed to giftedness by preservice teachers. The positive view in our data accords with other research, which has found moderately positive attitudes on the part of preservice teachers (Megay-Nespoli, 2001). However, this positive view is not universal, with some research demonstrating that peers, preservice teachers and teachers preferred students who were average, non-studious and athletic while the least-preferred students were brilliant, studious and non-athletic (Ziegler et al., 2010).

While positive attitudes toward gifted students should predispose teachers to acceptance of evidence-based strategies that support gifted students' development, this is not necessarily the case. Vialle (2010) explored teachers' attitudes to the education of gifted students prior to the implementation of a professional development program. The aim was to determine what participants knew and believed about giftedness to inform the development of their year-long professional development program. The participants were 150 teachers responsible for classes from Kindergarten to Year 12. Their teaching experience ranged from 1 to 20+ years with equivalent numbers of males and females. Participants completed the

Gagné–Nadeau 'Opinions about the gifted and their education' scale (Gagné, 1991) and additional open-ended questions.

The teachers overwhelmingly agreed that giftedness should be recognised and receive special provisions. While there was some support for special classes, a preference for mainstream classrooms was evident. Teachers were sensitive to elitism and labeling, with 60 to 70 per cent seeing these issues as drawbacks of special programs for the gifted. The teachers were most ambivalent about whole-year acceleration, despite the substantial literature base that supports academic acceleration (see Colangelo *et al.*, 2004b). Finally, the academic and social-emotional needs of gifted students were sometimes seen as being in competition. A typical comment was "They need to have their talents developed and maximised without compromising their development in other areas".

When asked "What do you think are the most pressing needs of gifted students?" teachers most frequently answered 'encouraged' (50 per cent), 'extended' (50 per cent), 'engaged' or 'motivated' (46 per cent), 'challenge' (22 per cent), 'be accepted for who they are' (22 per cent), 'have their needs met' (14 per cent), and 'achieve their potential' (14 per cent). A few teachers pointed to particular concerns: 'to feel normal, part of the regular group' (4 per cent), 'boredom' (4 per cent), 'under-achievement' (2 per cent), and 'under-trained staff' (2 per cent).

Evident in this research with practising teachers are some inconsistencies. The teachers were more accepting of ability grouping and acceleration when they pertained to sporting prowess ("If a Year 7 kid is good enough to play in the Senior Rugby side, he should be allowed to do so") than to academic abilities ("They should extend themselves in the mainstream classroom"). For some teachers there was a trade-off between students with other special needs and those who are gifted ("I'm far more concerned about the lower ability/special needs students"). Further, some teachers expressed the view that gifted needs should be overlooked when they conflicted with the needs of everybody else. Finally, academic needs were seen as less important than social-emotional needs.

Evidence-based practice

In 2007, Rogers reported an extensive 'best-evidence synthesis' of all the published research and general literature on educating gifted learners, dating from 1861. She crystallised this research into five evidence-based recommendations for gifted students. None of these recommendations is fully incompatible with the principles of inclusion.

1. Gifted and talented learners need daily challenge in their specific areas of talent.
2. Opportunities should be provided on a regular basis for gifted learners to be unique and to work independently in their areas of passion and talent.
3. Provide various forms of subject-based and grade-based acceleration to gifted learners as their educational needs require.

4.   Provide opportunities for gifted learners to socialise and to learn with like-ability peers.
5.   For specific curriculum areas, instructional delivery must be differentiated in pace, amount of review and practice, and organisation of content presentation.

(Rogers, 2007)

Of these five recommendations, ability grouping (Recommendation 4) is the area where there is the most potential conflict between the evidence from gifted education research and the principles of inclusion. Ability grouping is opposed by some educators who erroneously link it with tracking (Oakes, 1985). Ability grouping differs from tracking in two important respects, size and permanence. Unlike tracking, ability groups can range in size from two students to a whole class and can be formed and re-formed according to the purpose and content of the activity. Rogers' (2007) synthesis examined various forms of ability grouping, all of which offered gains in the academic and the affective areas. Rogers (2007) concluded:

> In summary, the evidence is clear that powerful academic effects and small to moderate affective effects are produced when gifted children are grouped with like-ability or like-performing peers and exposed to differentiated learning tasks and expectations.

(Rogers, 2007, p. 389)

Claims that ability grouping is elitist and benefits privileged classes are also misleading. In the absence of appropriate provisions for gifted students, it is the students from low socioeconomic (SES) or indigenous groups who are most likely to be disadvantaged. Zigler and Farber (1985) point out that wealthy parents can pursue other options for their gifted offspring that are not open to students from low SES groups. This contention is supported by evidence from a recent report, which drew attention to disturbing gaps in excellence achievement (Plucker *et al.*, 2010). Based on data gathered from across the United States, the authors demonstrate that although the achievement gap for race and SES may be closing generally, at the excellence end of the continuum it is actually widening. They conclude that "continuing to pretend that a nearly complete disregard of high achievement is permissible, especially among underperforming subgroups, is a formula for a mediocre K–12 education system and long-term economic decline" (Plucker *et al.*, 2010, p. 34).

Differentiating the curriculum

The research on academic achievement is extensive and what it confirms is that what the teacher does in the classroom makes a difference in students' academic outcomes. Hattie's (2009) meta-analysis of 800 meta-analytical studies (over 50,000 studies) on academic achievement concluded that about 30 per cent of the variance in academic achievement can be attributed to instructional quality – the teacher.

Thus far we have proposed that preservice and practising teachers generally hold positive attitudes toward gifted students and recognise the need for them to receive appropriate educational services. While they are not averse to some forms of ability grouping, they prefer gifted students to be retained in mainstream classes and most are educated in these heterogeneous classrooms. It would seem, then, that there should be no problems for gifted students in a system based on inclusion. Unfortunately, intent is not the same as action, and the evidence on underachievement and dropout suggests that gifted students are not receiving the attention they need.

For teachers to have the desired impact on gifted students' performance in heterogeneous classrooms, differentiation of the curriculum is essential (Tomlinson, 2008). Our use of the term 'differentiation' as it is applied here, refers to modifications that are made to the curriculum content, process, product and learning environment to match the learning needs of the individual. But, according to a national survey conducted in the United States, there is a lack of effective differentiation for gifted students in classrooms (Archambault *et al.*, 1993). Further, teachers are more likely to plan lessons directed at the whole class, even when they have indicated support for an inclusive classroom approach that responds to diverse learning needs (Morocco *et al.*, 1996). So, why don't teachers differentiate the curriculum for gifted students? The teachers surveyed by Vialle were aware of the need to differentiate and they were willing to do so, but they overwhelmingly reported that they were unsure how to go about the task. This supports some previous research (Callahan *et al.*, 2003). Undoubtedly, differentiation is hard, particularly in the contexts of the many competing demands that occupy teachers in today's classrooms.

This hard task is made impossible when preservice teachers and inservice teachers do not receive adequate training on the nature and needs of gifted students or strategies for differentiation. We would argue that this is the most significant challenge facing teacher educators in promoting inclusion for gifted students. Research suggests that teachers who have received substantial training are far more successful in differentiating their instruction for gifted students in heterogeneous classrooms (Westberg and Daoust, 2003). In Australia, though, the number of universities that offer any coursework on giftedness in preservice programs beyond a one-off lecture is small, although many offer postgraduate qualifications.

Potential pitfalls

A distinct challenge for teacher education is to debunk the 'one-size-fits-all' myth. Gifted students are not a homogeneous group; they vary as much from each other as they do from their non-gifted peers. There are different levels of giftedness, motivation, interest, patterns of strength, and so on. Consequently, there is no single approach that will fit the needs of all students. Planning for gifted learners needs to match their distinctive profiles. Twice-exceptional children – that is, students who are gifted and also possess a disability or condition that impacts on their learning – increase the complexity of the task for teachers, demanding understanding of both conditions and the unique way they interact.

Another issue is susceptibility to fads, particularly those that seem to offer a simple solution to the complex endeavour of teaching diverse learners in an inclusive classroom. One such fad has been the proliferation of Multiple Intelligences (MI) worksheets, masquerading as a differentiated curriculum for gifted students. There is much to commend MI theory and if well understood and used in a considered manner, it can be a useful tool. But it is not a differentiated program for gifted students just because it contains a variety of activities. A high degree of challenge is essential in a differentiated curriculum.

Conclusion

Gifted students share with all other students the need to be accepted for who they are, to be engaged and challenged in their learning every day, to move at their own pace, and interact with students of like ability. This demands teachers who have a positive attitude toward gifted students, understand their diverse needs, and can differentiate accordingly. Such skills are particularly pertinent in the context of inclusive classrooms. Without such skills, there is an increased likelihood that the outcome for the gifted child will be underachievement or disengagement from school.

It remains the challenge for teacher educators to help prepare teachers for the significant role they play in the talent development process. The first step is compulsory study of the nature and needs of gifted students in all teacher preparation programs. Specialist training for teaching gifted students is essential and needs to start in preservice teacher education programs. Research confirms that teachers who have systematic training in gifted education hold more positive attitudes towards gifted students and are more effective in meeting their needs (Westberg and Daoust, 2003). Where possible, such training should be linked to the practical experiences preservice teachers undertake in schools; the opportunity to observe and plan differentiated experiences for gifted students would assist their learning in this respect (Hudson et al., 2010).

Teaching is a complex but rewarding career; teaching teachers brings with it huge responsibilities amid competing demands. A system that is serious about inclusion must ensure that graduating teachers have an appropriate mind-set and skill-set that allows them to appreciate all the forms of diversity they will encounter in their classrooms. Such diversity includes students who are gifted.

References

Archambault, F., Westberg, K., Brown, S., Hallmark, B., Emmons, C. and Zhang, W. (1993) *Regular Classroom Practices with Gifted Students: Results of a National Survey of Classroom Teachers*, Storrs, CT: NRCGT.

Bridgeland, J. M., Dilulio, J. J. and Morison, K. B. (2006) *The Silent Epidemic: Perspectives of High School Dropouts*, Washington, DC: Civic Enterprises.

Callahan, C., Tomlinson, C., Moon, T., Brighton, C. and Hertberg, H. (2003) *Feasibility of High End Learning in the Middle Grades*, Charlottesville, VA: NRCGT.

Colangelo, N., Assouline, S. G. and Gross, M. U. M. (2004a) *A Nation Deceived: How Schools Hold Back America's Brightest Students*, Iowa City, IO: Belin-Blank Center for Gifted Education.

Colangelo, N., Kerr, B., Christensen, P. and Maxey, J. (2004b) "A comparison of gifted underachievers and gifted high achievers", in S. M. Moon (ed.), *Social Emotional Issues, Underachievement, and Counseling of Gifted and Talented Students*, Thousand Oaks, CA: Corwin Press, pp. 119–32.

Gagné, F. (1991) *Brief Presentation of Gagné and Nadeau's Attitude Scale: Opinions about the Gifted and Their Education*, Montréal: GIREDT Center, Université du Québec á Montréal.

Gagné, F. (2003) "Transforming gifts into talents: The DMGT as a developmental theory", in N. Colangelo and G. A. Davis (eds), *Handbook of Gifted Education*, 3rd edn, Boston, MA: Allyn & Bacon, pp. 60–74.

Grobman, J. (2009) "A psychodynamic psychotherapy approach to the emotional problems of exceptionally and profoundly gifted adolescents and adults", *Journal for the Education of the Gifted*, 33(1): 106–25.

Gross, M. U. M. (2010) *Miraca Gross, in Her Own Write: A Lifetime in Gifted Education*, Sydney: GERRIC, UNSW.

Hattie, J. (2009) *Visible Learning: A Synthesis of over 800 Meta-Analyses Relating to Achievement*, London: Routledge.

Henfield, M. S., Owens, D. and Moore, J. L. (2008) "Influences on young gifted African Americans' school success", *Elementary School Journal*, 108(5): 392–406.

Hoekman, K., McCormick, J. and Barnett, K. (2005) "The important role of optimism in motivational investigation of the education of gifted adolescents", *Gifted Child Quarterly*, 49(2): 99–110.

Hudson, P., Hudson, S., Lewis, K. and Watters, J. J. (2010) "Embedding gifted education in pre-service teacher education", *Australasian Journal of Gifted Education*, 19(2): 6–19.

Matthews, M. S. and McBee, M. T. (2007) "School factors and the underachievement of gifted students in a talent search summer program", *Gifted Child Quarterly*, 51(2): 167–81.

McCall, R. B., Evahn, C. and Kratzer, L. (1992) *High School Underachievers: What Do They Achieve as Adults?*, Newbury Park, CA: Sage.

Megay-Nespoli, K. (2001) "Beliefs and attitudes of novice teachers regarding instruction of academically talented learners", *Roeper Review*, 23: 178–82.

Morisano, D. and Shore, B. M. (2010) "Can personal goal setting tap the potential of the gifted underachiever?", *Roeper Review*, 32: 249–58.

Morocco, C., Riley, M., Gordon, S. and Howard, C. (1996) "The elusive individual in teachers' planning", in G. Brannigan (ed.), *The Enlightened Educator*, New York: McGraw-Hill, pp. 154–76.

NSW Teachers Federation (2010) "The future of public education: Reaffirming the primacy of comprehensive education". Online. Available at: http://www.nswtf.org.au/journal_extras/ac04fut.html (accessed 29 October 2010).

Oakes, J. (1985) *Keeping Track: How Schools Structure Inequality*, New Haven, CT: Yale University Press.

Plucker, J. A., Burroughs, N. and Song, R. (2010) *Mind the (Other) Gap! The Growing Excellence Gap in K-12 Education*, Bloomington, IN: Indiana University.

Rogers, K. B. (2007) "Lessons learned about educating the gifted and talented: A synthesis of the research on educational practice", *Gifted Child Quarterly*, 51: 382–96.

Seeley, K. (1993) "Gifted students at risk", in L. K. Silverman (ed.), *Counseling the Gifted and Talented*, Denver, CO: Love, pp. 263–75.

Senate Employment, Workplace Relations, Small Business and Education References Committee (2001) *The Education of Gifted Children*, Canberra: Commonwealth of Australia.

Swiatek, M. A., Lupkowski-Shoplik, A. and O'Donoghue, C. C. (2000) "Gender differences in EXPLORE scores of gifted third through sixth graders", *Journal of Educational Psychology*, 92: 718–23.

Tomlinson, C. A. (2008) "Differentiated instruction", in J. A. Plucker and C. M. Callahan (eds), *Critical Issues and Practices in Gifted Education*, Waco, TX: Prufrock Press, pp. 167–77.

Vialle, W. (2010) Evaluation of professional development in gifted education: A school-university partnership. Unpublished data held at the University of Wollongong, Australia.

Vinson, T. (2002) *Inquiry into the Provision of Public Education in NSW*, Annandale, NSW: Pluto Press Australia.

Westberg, K. L. and Daoust, M. E. (2003) *The Results of the Replication of the Classroom Practices Survey: Replication in Two States*, Storrs, CT: NRCGT.

Wills, L. and Munro, J. (2001) "Changing the teaching for underachieving able children", in D. Montgomery (ed.), *Able Underachievers*, London: Whurr Publishers, pp. 111–26.

Ziegler, A., Fidelman, M., Reutlinger, M., Neubauer, T. and Heilemann, M. (2010) "How desirable are gifted boys for girls, and gifted girls for boys?", *Australasian Journal of Gifted Education*, 19(2): 16–20.

Zigler, E. and Farber, E. A. (1985) "Commonalities between the intellectual extremes: Giftedness and mental retardation", in F. D. Horowitz and M. O'Brien (eds), *The Gifted and the Talented: Developmental Perspectives*, Washington, DC: APA, pp. 387–408.

Chapter 13

New dimensions of teacher education on the inclusivity of school guidance for regular schools in Hong Kong

Ming-tak Hue

Keywords: school guidance, inclusive counselling, inclusive strategies, behaviour management, labelling, inclusion in regular school

Chapter overview

Regular schools in Hong Kong are concerned about the growing enrolments of students with special educational needs (SEN) and how these students could be included in school guidance. Based upon the author's nine-year personal experience of conducting courses on school guidance in the context of inclusive education at a key training institution in Hong Kong and research findings of a case study into teachers' constructs of the inclusivity of school guidance (Hue, 2010), three dimensions of teacher professional training for the inclusivity of school guidance are identified: developing inclusive counselling practices; developing inclusive strategies for behaviour management; and dealing with the impacts of wider systems. This chapter gives insights into the professional needs of guidance teachers from regular schools and the promotion of the inclusivity of school guidance through teacher education.

Inclusive education

Under the ethos of inclusive education, in western countries such as the UK and the US students with SEN have the right to be educated in regular schools (Cigman, 2007). Hong Kong schools, like elsewhere, are searching for ways to put such an ethos into practice. At the same time teachers have been concerned about the growing number of students with SEN enrolled in regular schools and how these students can be supported effectively and included in the caring system of school guidance (Education Department, 2002; Forlin, 2010).

In the context of Hong Kong education, one of the issues on inclusive education is how students with SEN could be included in regular schools. For a long time students with severe special educational needs or multiple disabilities have been accommodated by special schools where intensive support services are offered. Since 2002, other students with SEN have been encouraged to enroll in regular schools.

These students have been assessed with at least one of the eight types of SEN, including hearing impairment, visual impairment, physical disability, intellectual disability, speech and language impairment, specific learning difficulties, attention deficit/hyperactivity disorder, and autistic spectrum disorders (Education Bureau, 2011). Hence regular schools face the challenge of fulfilling the diverse needs of students with SEN.

School guidance, known as 'pastoral care' in UK schools, plays a key role in fulfilling the diverse needs of all students (Best, 1999). It aims to promote the welfare of students, the whole personal growth of students and the development of various aspects of 'self' (Watkins, 2001). Since the policy on inclusive education was formulated in 2002, school guidance has become deeply involved in putting its ethos into practice. In particular it has supported the learning of students with SEN as well as various aspects of their personal growth, even though the policy does not make specific suggestion on what role school guidance should play in the implementation of inclusion.

In the Hong Kong context, teacher professional training on school guidance is offered at two levels: individual and department. The former aims to provide teachers with basic skills and fundamental knowledge about counselling therapies so that they are able to play a guidance role and offer effective guidance for individual students in need (Education and Manpower Bureau, 2004). At the departmental level, teachers are equipped with knowledge and skills for building the guidance team, which is also known as the counselling team, coordinating services offered by professional organizations, and developing programs aimed at enhancing the whole personal growth of all students.

In facing the growing number of students with SEN in regular schools, many teachers see developing an inclusive approach to school guidance as a new challenge. Research indicates that teachers' attitudes have the potential for shaping the promotion of inclusion (UNESCO, 2010). For example, Al-Zyoudi (2006) showed that teachers who had experience in working with students with SEN were more positive towards inclusion. Research also confirms that teachers who had additional training in inclusive education had more positive attitudes towards inclusion and more confidence using inclusive practices (Gwernan-Jones and Burden, 2010; Sharma et al., 2006). So far, as indicated by the literature, there is a close link between the discourses on inclusion and school guidance. Hence it is necessary to develop an inclusive approach to school guidance based upon the experience of the Hong Kong society. Thus, the concerns of local schools and teachers could be better addressed.

Dimensions of teacher professional training

In what follows, the directions for teacher professional training will be discussed based upon the author's nine-year working experience in this area. During this period, the author conducted professional training courses on school guidance, in the context of inclusive education, for in-service teachers. In addition to my personal experience of teacher education, the discussion is grounded upon the research findings from a case study into school guidance in a regular secondary school. In the case study, the research methods of interviews with guidance teachers, school social workers and students, textual analysis of school documents, and observation of how students with SEN were helped in counselling meetings were conducted. It has been found that most teachers who are working with students with SEN in regular schools considered themselves ignorant of SEN before the policy on inclusion was implemented in 2002. There was a period of time when they were overwhelmed with feelings of anxiety and stress about implementing the policy. Having received teacher professional training their learning led them to engage in an ongoing process of 'self-reflection', in which they became reflective of their beliefs about SEN and current practices of guidance. They gradually enhanced their knowledge of SEN and ability to help these students. Based on their experience, three directions which should be re-addressed in the current programs for teacher professional training are highlighted for the promotion of the inclusivity of school guidance, including "Developing inclusive counselling practices"; "Developing inclusive strategies for behaviour management"; and "Dealing with the impacts of wider systems".

Developing inclusive counselling practices

School guidance is used to dealing with diversity among students, but, as guidance teachers acknowledge, how it can be offered effectively in the context of SEN has not yet been fully articulated. To enhance the inclusivity of school guidance, the teachers hold a view that the diverse needs of students with SEN should be fulfilled. As well, the students' potentials, capabilities and talents should be explored as these could be used as resources to help the students make a change in terms of behaviour and emotion. When compared to the 'mainstream' students, the teachers find it more difficult to counsel those with SEN, as the latter group of students encounters a wide range of problems. As the teachers insist, each case of student with SEN is unique, and accordingly specific goals of guidance should be defined. With these goals, they can then identify appropriate intervention strategies.

When exploring effective ways of helping, most teachers acknowledge that some theoretical approaches to counselling are found more effective than others. For example, humanistic person-centred therapies for counselling students with SEN are usually adopted. With the use of these therapies, they are able to demonstrate their respect, warmth and acceptance, and then develop a positive interpersonal relationship with students. In doing this, basic counselling skills, such as careful observation, active listening, and addressing students' here-and-now feelings, are used. Due to the fact that most students with SEN experience emotional difficulties, and are less capable of expressing their feelings and thoughts verbally, the teachers find it necessary to simplify the language they use and constantly check with students about the meaning of their conversation so as to avoid ambiguity and misunderstanding. To ensure quality guidance, the teachers expect to further refine their skills of non-verbal communication and enhance their ability of interpreting the meaning underlying the body language of the students. They also expect to know more about alternative therapies, such as arts, music, play and pets, and seek possibilities of learning new skills for facilitating the process of counselling and helping students express their inner feelings and thoughts. For example, for students with an intellectual disability, some teachers have attempted to transform a counselling room into a play-room where games are provided. The students are invited to play there during playtime and lunch break. They then engage in play with these students and it is treated as part of the helping process, though it is not structured in a therapeutic form.

Furthermore, adoption of proactive approaches to school guidance is useful in the promotion of inclusivity. As teachers acknowledge, helping would be more effective if interventions can be identified and executed in advance. To do this, apart from encouraging classroom teachers to report suspected cases of SEN during school activities, such as the orientation day for new students, teachers should develop an ability to observe how students interact with others and how they engage in activities. Whenever suspected cases of students with SEN are identified, they have to contact their parents and the teachers who taught them in primary school in order to collect more information about the students and thus develop early intervention strategies.

Developing inclusive strategies for behaviour management

While facing a growing number of students with SEN, teachers find it necessary to develop inclusive strategies for behaviour management. In working with other teachers to support students with SEN who misbehave in the classroom and beyond, many guidance teachers face the challenge of ensuring that the collective values of discipline, for example, fairness, consistency and uniformity, can be maintained while the diverse needs of individual students are addressed. In practice, students with SEN are expected to take responsibility for their behaviour just as their non-SEN peers do. It is ensured that these students do not use their SEN classification as an excuse for misbehaviour, disruption or bullying as some of these students are used to doing. At the same time, the teachers try to step into the shoes of students by taking their point of view and showing them empathy in order to see the incidents from the students' perspective.

In some schools, various measures are set up within school organization so that behaviour management can be made more inclusive, and include some elements of guidance, such as empathic understanding, acceptance and congruence, in the process of discipline. For example, teacher assistants with counselling training or social workers are employed to specifically look after the students who are referred to them by classroom teachers, and help them improve their behaviourial problems. When first meeting the students, in general they try to calm them using basic counselling skills, and then review the incident of misbehaviour with them. After this an individual learning plan is tailored to the student's needs.

Dealing with the impacts of wider systems

By including students with SEN in school guidance, there is a need for teachers to become aware of the impacts of wider systems, which function beyond the school but affect individual students, and equip them with knowledge and skills to deal with its impacts upon individual students. As specified by the teachers, such wider systems include the labelling effects of SEN, the inflexibility of the current education system and the unexamined quality of services which the school bought from professional organizations. With regard to the labelling effect, the teachers realize that having been diagnosed and assessed as SEN, most of these students tend to associate their type of SEN with their academic identity, especially those who were assessed when at kindergarten or primary school. Being assessed as SEN is regarded by the teachers as 'a curse' which encourages students' poor academic identity. These students believe in the existence of this 'curse' and learn to use it as part of their academic identity. They realize that they will be unlikely to do well in examinations, and so tend to give up even before they have started.

Another wider system is related to the inflexibility of the existing curriculum design and the arrangements for public examinations which have impacts on the inclusivity of school guidance. For example, as teachers acknowledge, most students with SEN cannot cope well with learning due to their lower level of academic ability and the difficulties bought on by their SEN. They cannot catch up with the existing curriculum as non-SEN students do. However, they are required to cover the same curriculum and then sit the same examinations as the non-SEN students. Most students who predict that they will probably fail in the examination have difficulties finding meaning out of their schooling. To help these students cope with the impact of this wider system, many teachers feel powerless and constantly seek new inclusive strategies for dealing with the labelling effect and building the positive image of students' "self".

Regarding the wider system of professional organizations, many schools rely on offering services on improving students' reading and writing abilities and enhancing their social and communication skills. On the one hand, the teachers welcome having support from these professional parties as this takes away some of the burdensome workload of school guidance. On the other hand, they doubt the outcomes and effectiveness, as these services have never been evaluated. The guidance teachers describe this current situation as 'spending lots of money to buy supplements'. It is further explained by the use of a common Chinese saying, 'the beginning and the end are turned upside down'. They question whether they have fallen into a trap of 'spending money for the purpose of spending money; and doing for doing, rather than helping the kids'. To ensure the effectiveness of these outside services, ideally speaking, both teachers and parents should develop ways to get involved in the programs or the services delivered by the external professional parties, and the roles of guidance teachers therein should be more clearly defined, otherwise the positive impacts on students could be minimal.

Conclusion

Since 2004, many schools have been developing an inclusive approach to school guidance as a way to comply with the policy of inclusive education and fulfill the diverse needs of students with SEN. In the course of this development, many teachers develop their own knowledge of inclusivity, and seek further to develop the inclusivity of school guidance by adopting a 'self-reflection' approach. In supporting teachers to deal with this new challenge of education, an inclusive approach to school guidance could be addressed in four dimensions of teacher professional training programs: the development of inclusive guidance practices, the adoption of a proactive approach, the promotion of positive behaviour management, and collaboration with other professional organizations.

When examining the development of an inclusive approach to school guidance, it is suggested that the inclusive therapies of counselling are humanistic and person-centred. In addition to using basic counselling skills, the inclusive practices of school guidance include: building an inclusive interpersonal relationship with students, adopting alternative therapies for helping students, simplifying the language of counselling, using the non-verbal communication, and keeping the helping process flexible. Furthermore, a proactive approach to school guidance has great potential for promoting inclusivity. It means that school guidance should be offered not only to those students who have been diagnosed with specific types of SEN, but also to those students who are identified as suspected cases of SEN. As the teachers acknowledge, a proactive approach could be more effective in helping these students before their unidentified difficulties emerge as real problems. This is also regarded by the teachers as a more ideal time for school guidance intervention when various parties, such as parents and form tutors, can collaborate with school guidance as a team to care for these students.

Another dimension of the inclusivity of school guidance is the promotion of positive behaviour management. This study further confirms the findings of Hue's study (Hue, 2010) by showing that in the context of Hong Kong schools, discipline should be taken into account when school guidance is promoted. School discipline emphasizes the value of collectivism. It tries to treat all students as citizens in the school community so as to keep consistency, uniformity and order. It consists of the fervent belief in the virtues of order, self-discipline, uniformity and consistency. By comparison, school guidance sees each student as individual and unique. It has a belief in humanism and individualism. Guidance and discipline appear to oppose each other, as some studies have suggested (Chung, 1998; Tsang, 1986; Wong, 1994; Wong, 1997), but this is merely in a relative sense. With this cultural construct of school guidance in mind, when inclusivity is promoted it is necessary to consider how individual students with SEN could be included, not only in school guidance, but also in school discipline so that the personal and social aspects of students' 'self' could be promoted, and so that the students could be helped to be their better 'self' in the school community as citizens who have certain social and civic responsibilities to perform.

Moreover, the inclusivity of school guidance can hardly be developed without bringing in resources from professional organizations. Even though specialized services are currently bought by school guidance, the ideal form of this partnership has not yet been established. Most teachers, hence, are concerned about how these specialized services could be integrated with school guidance, and how the quality of these services and their outcomes could be effectively evaluated and assessed. To promote the inclusivity of school guidance, teacher education has to address the importance of building and strengthening the partnership between guidance teachers and experts from professional organizations, so that the latter could be better integrated into school guidance, rather than merely functioning as a service provider set apart from the school. Also, the partnership should be extended to other school participants, such as form tutors, students and parents, as a means of improving the effectiveness of the specialized service offered.

This study draws our attention to the fact that the development of an inclusive approach to school guidance should involve a change of practices and beliefs so as to promote the ethos of inclusion. Although this chapter lacks students' voices and the views of professional organizations, it has the potential for opening up debate about appropriate ways of promoting the inclusivity of school guidance and the self-esteem of the students with SEN. By addressing the three dimensions of teacher education as suggested above, it would make it more likely for teachers to discover inclusive strategies to fulfil the diverse needs of students with SEN, thus developing the school as a caring community.

References

Al-Zyoudi, M. (2006) "Teachers' attitudes towards inclusive education in Jordanian schools", *International Journal of Special Education*, 21(2): 55–62.

Best, R. (1999) "The impact of a decade of educational change on pastoral care and PSE: A survey of teacher perceptions", *Pastoral Care in Education*, 17(2): 3–13.

Chung, Y. B. (1998) *Teachers' and Students' Perceptions on the Co-Operation of Discipline and Guidance*. M.Ed. Faculty of Education, University of Hong Kong.

Cigman, R. (ed.) (2007) *Included or Excluded? The Challenge of the Mainstream for Some SEN Children*, New York: Routledge.

Education and Manpower Bureau (2004) "Student guidance in secondary schools: What is school guidance?" Online. Available at: http://sg.emb.gov.hk/login_frame.asp?lang=1 (accessed 28 October 2010).

Education Bureau (2011) "Special Education". Online. Available at: http://www.edb.gov.hk/index.aspx?nodeID=7389and langno=1 (accessed 19 September 2011).

Education Department (2002) "Understanding and helping students with special educational needs: A guide to teaching". Online. Available at: http://www.edb.gov.hk/Utility Manager/Publication/upload/sen_guide_e.pdf (accessed 1 November 2011).

Forlin, C. (2010) "Developing and implementing quality inclusive education in Hong Kong: Implication for teacher education", *Journal of Research in Special Educational Needs*, 10(3): 41–8.

Gwernan-Jones, R. and Burden, R. (2010) "Are they just lazy? Student teachers' attitudes about dyslexia", *Dyslexia*, 16(1): 66–86.

Hue, M. T. (2010) *Report on a Case-Study of Fulfilling the Diverse Needs of Students with SEN in a Regular School in Hong Kong*. Unpublished report submitted to the Department of Special Eduction and Counselling, the Hong Kong Institute of Education, Hong Kong.

Sharma, U., Forlin, C., Loreman, T. and Earle, C. (2006) "Pre-service teachers' attitudes, concerns and sentiments about inclusive education: An international comparison of novice pre-service teachers", *International Journal of Special Education*, 21(2): 80–93.

Tsang, S. Y. A. (1986) *Schooling and Pastoral Care in Hong Kong*. Ph.D. University of Keele.

UNESCO (2010) "EFA Global Monitoring Report 2010: Reaching the marginalized". Online. Available at: http://www.unesco.org/new/en/education/themes/leading–the–international–agenda/efareport/reports/2010–marginalization/ (accessed 13 October 2011).

Watkins, C. (2001) "Comprehensive guidance programme in an international context", *Professional School Counsellor*, 4(4): 262–71

Wong, A. M. H. (1994) *Collaborative Management in School Discipline in Some Secondary Schools*. M.Ed. Faculty of Education, University of Hong Kong.

Wong, C. Y. F. (1997) *Teachers' Perception of the Relationship between Discipline and Guidance – A Case Study*. M.Ed. Faculty of Education, University of Hong Kong.

Chapter 14

Gender and achievement in the UK and Hong Kong

Becky Francis, Pattie Yuk-yee Luk-Fong and Christine Skelton

Keywords: gender, achievement, attainment, boys, girls, social class, ethnicity, Hong Kong, UK, England

Chapter overview

Gender and achievement is a controversial issue. While second-wave feminists attended to the underachievement of girls, in recent years an international concern has developed in relation to the apparent underachievement of boys, to the extent that many commentators have identified the fervor in media and policy surrounding this issue as a moral panic. The debate around boys' underachievement was initiated in the early 1990s in the UK and in Australia, but is now well established in other countries too. Moreover, it has been shown to influence the understandings of student teachers, and teachers in the classroom, raising clear issues for teacher educators. Feminist researchers have argued that many of the concerns about boys are misplaced, and the tenor of the debate retrogressive. The overwhelming focus on attainment at the expense of other issues (such as identity and power) in these debates perpetuates ignorance and lack of concern for the ongoing reproduction of gender inequality by educational institutions.

This debate has not been taken up seriously in the Hong Kong education arena. However, concerns about the issue among some parents and teachers evoke the 'panic' experienced elsewhere (University of HK Faculty of Education Alumni Association, 2005). In this chapter, we seek to analyse the figures on gender and achievement in England and Hong Kong, and to unpick some of the assumptions and explanations underpinning commentary on boys' underachievement in both countries, in order to provide a more balanced account of the field.

Education achievement patterns in England and Hong Kong

In England, messages from the Department for Education (DfE) have tended to perpetuate the view that boys are underperforming in comparison with girls across the curriculum (see analysis in Skelton *et al.*, 2007). However, of the three subject areas presented as 'key' in the English compulsory curriculum – mathematics, science and literacy/English – there is no significant gender gap for mathematics and science. Throughout the compulsory education stages, boys and girls in England perform fairly evenly in mathematics and science, with boys as a group outperforming girls in higher level mathematics. The most substantial gap is in English, where girls as a group significantly outperform boys.

Table 14.1 shows the percentage of pupils gaining the important A*–C grades in the key subjects of English, mathematics and science at GCSE, the exams taken at the end of compulsory schooling in England at the age of 16.

The 'gender gap' is actually only significant in language/literacy but it is the size of this gender gap that skews results so that policy makers and commentators make claims about 'girls outperforming boys' across the board (Francis and Skelton, 2005). OECD PISA data shows that this pattern of girls substantially outperforming boys in their national first language is reflected internationally. The disproportionate underachievement among boys in literacy is likely to impact on their achievement in other curriculum areas: One will struggle with exams in many curriculum areas if one's literacy is weak.

Some of these trends also apply in Hong Kong. McCall and Beach (2000) show that elementary school girls do better at Chinese, English and general performance and boys do better at mathematics – also, that parents and teachers are more sensitive to the underachievement status of boys. Likewise in terms of gender and science achievement, Hong Kong boys' and girls' science scores in scientific literacy do not differ overall as measured by OECD PISA (although there are some gender trends regarding question areas).

The data from the Hong Kong Certificate of Education Examination (HKCEE) illustrates gender performance patterns occurring at the exit of secondary school, at 16, similar to those in England.

Girls outperform boys in both compulsory subjects in the HKCEE: Chinese language and English language. Boys outperform girls at mathematics. However, more girls than boys also meet the minimum entry requirements for the Hong Kong Advanced Level Examination (HKALE): 47 per cent and 36 per cent respectively in 2009 (HKALE: The university entrance examination for the eight University Grant Committee funded universities in Hong Kong).

Furthermore, the most popular HKCEE subjects for boys other than the compulsory subjects of Chinese, English and mathematics are the more 'prestigious' science subjects like physics, chemistry and biology, whilst girls choose humanities

Table 14.1 Percentages of pupils achieving A*–C at GCSE in key subjects, 2009

	English	Mathematics	Science
Boys	57%	58%	61%
Girls	71%	59%	64%

Adapted from: Department for Education, 2010.

Table 14.2 Percentages by gender of students gaining C–A (4–5*) grades in the ten most popular subjects in HKCEE, 2009

	Male	Female	Total
English Language	12.4%	22.3%	17.3%
Chinese Language	11.7%	22.4%	16.9%
Mathematics	30.9%	25.7%	28.3%
Economics	22.7%	22.1%	22.4%
Biology	32.4%	31.9%	32.2%
Physics	31.7%	24.5%	28.9%
Chemistry	31.7%	29.9%	31.0%
Geography	20.6%	22.4%	21.6%
Chinese History	15.8%	18.6%	17.4%
Principle of Accounts	22.1%	22.9%	22.6%

Adapted from: HKEAA 2009b.

subjects such as geography and Chinese history (Wong *et al.*, 2002; see Francis, 2006 for UK patterns).

Achievement at the HKALE shows a similar pattern to the HKCEE. Use of English and Chinese language and culture are the only compulsory subjects, and women perform better at both (HKEAA, 2009) (HKEAA: Hong Kong Examination and Assessment Authority). Most men take the science stream while women's choices of subjects are more spread out across subjects (HKEAA, 2009). In terms of attainment, at this level gendered trends are clear: Men significantly outperform women at pure mathematics and science subjects while women consistently outperform boys at Chinese and English languages.

Although in England we see somewhat less gender discrepancy in achievement in science and mathematics (both in terms of subject uptake, and attainment – though it continues to be the case that more young men than women take mathematics and physics post-16), the gendered trends remain in subject preference. For example,

Table 14.3 Percentages by gender of students gaining C–A (4–5*) grades in the ten most popular subjects in HKALE, 2009

	Male	Female	Total
Use of English	10.7%	16.6%	13.9%
Chinese Language and Culture	16.9%	28.2%	22.9%
Chemistry	24.4%	19.3%	22.1%
Physics	25.9%	16.4%	22.7%
Economics	26.4%	18.8%	21.9%
Pure Mathematics	26.2%	17.5%	23.6%
Biology	18.4%	19.3%	18.9%
Geography	22.5%	21.6%	21.9%
Mathematics and Statistics	18.9%	17.8%	18.3%
Principle of Accounts	26.9%	20.6%	22.8%

Adapted from: HKEAA 2009a.

at undergraduate level young women tend towards the humanities, social sciences and healthcare, and young men towards engineering, IT, business and sciences (with the exception of biology) (Francis, 2006). In Hong Kong, the gender divide in subjects perhaps can be explained by the system of education in which students are assigned to either a stereotypically male (science) stream or stereotypical female (arts) stream at secondary four (tenth grade) (see Wong *et al.*, 2002). It would seem that the binarised subject choice routes maintained until now in the Hong Kong system exacerbate gender stereotypical choices and gender segregation, and further accentuates boys outperforming girls at 'prestigious' subjects such as science and mathematics and girls outperforming boys at languages and humanities subjects.

In Hong Kong, too, boys' underachievement at language puts them at a great disadvantage in learning other subjects. An aggregating circumstance in Hong Kong is that the preferred medium of instruction is English, which is not the first language of most students. Many underachieving boys are struggling with not only literacy in two languages, but also learning and understanding all other subjects in the more unfamiliar language. This demands attention to the reasons for boys' (global) under-performance in literacy, and the gender constructions underpinning this pattern.

Intersection of gender, class and race

As feminist researchers in the UK and elsewhere have been quick to point out, other factors than gender are stronger predictors of educational achievement. For example, in the UK, taken on their own, both ethnicity and (especially) social class have a stronger impact on attainment (although it is also the case that within every social group there is a gender gap in literacy which favors girls). The impact of social class on achievement is particularly acute in the UK, as illustrated by the OECD PISA studies. Table 14.4 illustrates this point in the case of England, using the indicator of free school meals (FSM) as a proxy for relative poverty (we acknowledge that free school meals is an unsatisfactory indicator of social class, and even of poverty, yet it is the only indicative record maintained by schools in England).

Table 14.4 shows a gender gap for both pupils receiving FSM and those not taking FSM (non-FSM) (a gap of nine percentage points for FSM pupils; ten

Table 14.4 Achievements at Key Stage 4 GCSE qualifications in 2006, by free school meals (FSM) and gender

GCSE	5 or more A*–C Eligible pupils			5 or more A*–C % Achieving		
	Boys	Girls	Total	Boys	Girls	Total
Non-FSM	261,971	252,545	514,516	56.2	66.0	61.0
FSM	39,498	38,589	78,087	28.7	37.4	33.0

Adapted from: DfES, 2007.

for non–FSM pupils). But the gap it reveals for FSM is far wider. The figures show that nearly double the proportion of girls and boys not taking FSM (more affluent pupils) achieve five or more GCSE A*–C grades than their counterparts taking FSM. And this includes a gap of 19 percentage points between boys not taking FSM (56 per cent) and girls taking FSM (37 per cent): This gap illustrates how (indicatively) middle-class boys tend to outperform girls from low-income families. So Table 14.4 illustrates two points. First, how in England the social class gap dwarfs the gender gap for achievement. And following from this, how nonsensical it is to discuss gender as an isolated factor in relation to achievement.

Gender and 'race' interact with social class in sometimes unpredictable ways: Social class and gender have a less significant impact on the achievement of some ethnic groups than others. The complexity at stake once ethnicity and family income (as indicated by FSM) are taken into account with gender in patterns of achievement is demonstrated by Table 14.5, which focuses on the case of England.

Even for the most substantial pupil groups (given that the numbers for some ethnic groups are very small), Table 14.5 shows the diversity of achievement patterning by ethnicity, social class and gender. The trend to smaller social class gaps for achievement in minority ethnic groups (see Archer and Francis, 2007) is illustrated by these figures. Similarly, in comparison to the huge social class gap for the White British majority, of 35 percentage points between White British girls gaining 5 A*–C (non-FSM 66 per cent, FSM 31 per cent), and of 32 percentage points for White British boys (non-FSM 56 per cent; FSM 24 per cent) (we use capital letters for 'White' and 'Black' to indicate the social constructedness of these categories: That these are titles alluding to 'race', and highlighting the odd mixture of 'race', ethnicity and national categories that are applied in official British contexts (Archer and Francis, 2007)). Pupils of Indian heritage, and the smaller group of pupils of Chinese heritage, continue to outperform other groups: Although girls in these ethnic groups are outperforming boys, boys from these groups outperform nearly all other groups of girls (including the majority group of White British girls). Mirza (2008) has alerted researchers to dangers in this kind of analysis of 'achieving' and 'underachieving' ethnic groups, arguing that such approaches set up groups as discrete and in competition, pathologising particular groups (such as Black boys) and creating 'model minorities' (such as pupils of Indian and Chinese heritage).

Rather than high-achieving minority ethnic groups in Britain being 'celebrated', their attainment tends to be problematised by teachers as 'achieved in the wrong way'. In spite of their high attainment, teachers question their methods of achievement, with suggestions it is produced by inauthentic and even problematic means of parental pressure and/or hyper-diligence (Archer and Francis, 2007). We would suggest that use of the term 'model minorities', even in a critical sense, risks ignoring the pathologisation and ongoing racism which such 'achieving' minority ethnic pupils continue to experience. Nevertheless, Mirza's critique alerts us to the dangers of such analyses in potentially reifying difference, and stereotyping certain groups as either 'underachieving' or 'achieving'. Hence a tension emerges between a need to analyse patterns of achievement in order to identify (and potentially address)

Table 14.5 Achievements at Key Stage 2 (for English) in 2006 by ethnicity, free school meals (FSM) and gender

Key Stage 2 English	Non-FSM						FSM					
	Eligible pupils			% achieving			Eligible pupils			% achieving		
	Boys	Girls	Total	Boys	Girls	Total	Boys	Girls	Total	Boys	Girls	Total
White	**208,080**	**198,748**	**406,828**	**79**	**88**	**83**	**34,258**	**32,742**	**67,000**	**52**	**66**	**59**
White British	201,597	192,597	394,194	79	88	83	32,280	30,936	63,216	52	66	59
Irish	798	790	1,588	85	92	88	236	202	438	54	66	59
Traveller of Irish Heritage	53	53	106	30	32	31	128	108	236	20	30	25
Gypsy/Roma	212	188	400	38	44	41	184	178	362	19	38	28
Any other White background	5,420	5,120	10,540	75	82	78	1,430	1,318	2,748	55	65	60
Mixed	**6,817**	**6,670**	**13,487**	**81**	**90**	**85**	**2,313**	**2,250**	**4,563**	**61**	**77**	**69**
White and Black Caribbean	2,221	2,229	4,450	77	87	82	1,030	992	2,022	58	76	67
White and Black African	637	621	1,258	80	90	85	213	274	487	67	72	70
White and Asian	1,497	1,442	2,939	86	92	89	326	315	641	62	77	69
Any other mixed background	2,462	2,378	4,840	83	90	86	744	669	1,413	64	79	71
Asian	**15,798**	**14,779**	**30,577**	**75**	**84**	**79**	**5,571**	**5,405**	**10,976**	**62**	**74**	**68**
Indian	5,892	5,528	11,420	83	90	86	680	718	1,398	69	80	75
Pakistani	5,989	5,456	11,445	68	79	73	2,844	2,653	5,497	57	70	63
Bangladeshi	2,021	1,973	3,994	73	81	77	1,577	1,593	3,170	68	78	73
Any other Asian background	1,896	1,822	3,718	76	83	79	470	441	911	64	71	68
Black	**7,788**	**7,646**	**15,434**	**72**	**85**	**78**	**4,529**	**4,480**	**9,009**	**56**	**70**	**63**
Black Caribbean	3,211	3,096	6,307	69	84	76	1,214	1,203	2,417	55	75	65
Black African	3,694	3,806	7,500	74	85	79	2,869	2,849	5,718	56	67	62
Any other Black background	883	744	1,627	72	85	78	446	428	874	57	73	65
Chinese	890	917	1,807	83	90	86	119	89	208	76	90	82
Any other ethnic group	**1,853**	**1,655**	**3,508**	**69**	**78**	**73**	**1,070**	**1,010**	**2,080**	**57**	**66**	**62**
All pupils	**245,446**	**234,421**	**479,867**	**78**	**88**	**83**	**48,701**	**46,755**	**95,456**	**54**	**68**	**61**

Adapted from: DfES, 2006.

inequalities; and the danger of exacerbating inequalities by doing so. Analysis of the figures provides an important means by which to explode the myths surrounding issues like gender achievement (such as boys' or Black underachievement). In the British case such analysis plays a vital role in highlighting the impact of social class on educational achievement. However, it is vital that such analyses are attuned to the intersection of multiple social indices; and also articulate acknowledgement that patterns identified are *only* patterns. Many individual pupils continue to buck the trends; hence it is vital that patterns do not lead to the projection of particular expectations and stereotyping onto pupils.

Illustrating the importance of such statistical analysis, it has been shown that, among groups of girls taking FSM, the largest group – White British girls – have virtually the lowest achievement figure at 31 per cent (excluding the 102 girls of traveller/gypsy/Roma background). Hence this substantial group of girls are attaining below the achievement of virtually all groups of boys not taking FSM, illustrating again the significance of social class for the White majority of pupils in England. Clearly this shows how the discourse of boys' underachievement per-petuated in Britain over the past 15 years ignores and masks the needs of many girls. Further, the tables also illuminate the particular under-attainment of working-class White British boys and those of Caribbean heritage.

This analysis has revealed the complexity in achievement patterns, and the importance of considering multiple factors of identity.

Gender-neutral educational policy in a masculinist society

In Hong Kong it is claimed that a gender-neutral policy is applied in education policy (Cheung and Holroyd, 2009). A meritocratic approach is adopted for the education of all children, i.e. most educational policies are made without a gender perspective. However, Hong Kong policy makers are determined advocates in maintaining high academic standards for all students, and are very proud of the high rankings in the OECD PISA results (in which Hong Kong's 15-year-old students fare better than their counterparts in the UK at all tested subjects).

In Hong Kong, there are no official classifications of social classes, or indices of poverty/wealth (Lai, 2001). Hong Kong is a relatively 'racially' homogeneous society, with Chinese accounting for 95 per cent of the population (Census and Statistics Department, 2007) (although Hong Kong is evidently ethnically mixed, notably, for example, between Hakka and Han Chinese). Figures concerning gen-der achievement for children in poverty or of different ethnicity are not available from the Hong Kong Examination Authority database despite increasing public and media attention to these in recent years. There are meagre survey data from non-government organisations (NGOs), in which children in poverty are depicted in deficit terms (Hong Kong Boys and Girls Association, 2009); the assumption being that given the resources the children can succeed in school. In the debate about ethnic minority groups (e.g. newly arrived children from Mainland China,

Pakistan or India) researchers have found that many teachers have stereotypes of ethnic minority students, irrespective of cultural background, as being 'useless', 'misbehaving', 'impolite', and 'having difficulty adjusting to local curriculum' (Ku *et al.*, 2005; Heung, 2006). A meritocratic discourse prevails in which both teachers and students perceive success as ethnic minority students' personal responsibility (Chee, 2010).

The OECD PISA study further sheds light on the relationship between immigration status and academic performance in Hong Kong. The performance of immigrant students who were born outside Hong Kong is significantly poorer than that of local-born students in reading, mathematics and science. Interestingly however, the performance of students of second-generation immigrants is on par with local-born students.

Culture evidently has a role to play in educational achievement, both in terms of institutional expectations of pupils (and of particular pupil groups), and in pupils' approaches to learning. It has been argued that the high regard for education in the Confucian cultural heritage and consequent parental discipline to secure their children's achievement comprises crucial aspects in the relatively high achievement of Hong Kong Chinese; although researchers have been skeptical as to the extent of homogeneity of attitudes. However, the strongly patriarchal aspect of Confucian culture and traditions has further implications which underpin the ostensibly gender-neutral educational policy: The gender stereotypical curriculum and streaming, as well as the gender-biased parental discipline and expectations. Thus, even though Hong Kong has always focused on academic achievement of students as a homogeneous group, parents and teachers are notably more concerned about boys' underachievement.

Conclusion

By analysing the figures on gender and achievement in England and Hong Kong, this paper has attempted to unpick some of the global 'myths' about 'boys' underachievement'. Assumptions that boys underachieve in all subjects are not substantiated. In both the UK and in Hong Kong, there is a substantial gender gap (favouring girls) in attainment in language and literacy. There has been a narrowing of gaps between boys and girls in the traditionally masculine subjects of mathematics and science, particularly in England (since the introduction of the National Curriculum in the late 1980s). However, gendered trends reflecting the relationship between gender and knowledge and resulting associations between masculinity/femininity and particular subject areas mean that gender differentiated patterns remain in subject preference and uptake. In Hong Kong, the gender divide in arts and science streams remains acute with more boys pursuing prestigious subjects like science and mathematics and girls outperforming in languages and humanities. While there is a clear need to address attainment gaps, eradicating the gender divide in subject uptake is also crucial – especially as this later impacts gender (in)equity in access to high-income employment and other life chances.

Approaches to gender and achievement vary in different countries for historical and cultural reasons. The United Kingdom has a long history of investigating these issues. It is time for Hong Kong to think about gender-sensitive education policy and make substantial effort to do research in this area. United Kingdom research shows that it is schools where gender constructions are less accentuated and where work is done to reduce constructions of gender difference that are most effective in reducing the gender gap for achievement (Warrington *et al.*, 2000; Skelton *et al.*, 2007). This is because particular constructions of gender are shown to impact on student achievement.

Analysis of achievement patterns in the UK also demonstrates the need to go beyond gender in assessing achievement patterns, to include ethnicity and social class. Crucially, such analysis in the UK shows, for example, that middle-class white boys continue to outperform working class white girls, even in literacy/English. Such examples belie popular assumptions that all boys are underachieving, or that all girls are achieving. But also, they remind us of the importance of other aspects of social identity as impacting achievement. Our identification above of a lack of recorded data for ethnicity and social class in Hong Kong, then, is important, suggesting an urgent need for such data to be collected and analysed – although in doing so, caution must be exercised to avoid stereotyping groups as 'model minority', 'achieving' or 'non-achieving minority', and so on. While such data is vital for understanding the ways in which our education system facilitates or constrains particular social groups, and clarifying trends as we have sought to do in this chapter, it is important to understand the subjectivities and learning processes of individual students, and to avoid projecting trends to stereotype particular pupils. These complexities need careful articulation to student teachers, yet it is vital that teacher educators engage this important work in order to dig below the moral panic of 'boys' underachievement' and enable new teachers to deliver gender-equitable practices for their pupils.

References

Archer, L. and Francis, B. (2007) *Understanding Minority Ethnic Achievement*, London: Routledge.

Census and Statistics Department (2007) *Hong Kong 2006 Population By-Census*, Hong Kong: Census and Statistics Department.

Chee, W. C. (2010) "When the cultural model of success fails: Mainland Chinese teenage immigrants in Hong Kong", *Taiwan Journal of Anthropology*, 8(2): 85–110.

Cheung, F. M. and Holroyd, E. (2009) *Mainstreaming Gender in Hong Kong Society*, Hong Kong: Chinese University Press.

Department for Education (2010) "DfE: GCSE and equivalent attainment by pupil characteristics in England 2009/10", *Statistical First Release*. Online. Available at: http://www.education.gov.uk/researchandstatistics/datasets/a00196609/gcse-and-equivalent-attainment-by-pupil-characteri (accessed 22 February 2012).

Department for Education and Skills (2006) "Additional information: Combination tables showing achievements at Key Stages 1 and 2, GCSE and Equivalent and of Level 3

Qualifications in 2006 by ethnicity and English as a first language, free school meals, special educational needs and gender", *National Curriculum Assessment, GCSE and Equivalent Attainment and Post-16 Attainment by Pupil Characteristics in England 2005/06 (Provisional)*. Online. Available at: http://www.education.gov.uk/rsgateway/DB/SFR/s000693/index.shtml (accessed 22 February 2012).

Department for Education and Skills (2007) "National Curriculum Assessments, GCSE and Equivalent Attainment and Post-16 Attainment by Pupil Characteristics in England 2005/06 (Revised)", *National Statistics – First Release*. Online. Available at http://www.education.gov.uk/rsgateway/DB/SFR/s000708/sfr04-2007v2.pdf (accessed 22 February 2012).

Francis, B. (2006) "Troubling trajectories: Gendered 'choices' and pathways from school to work", in C. Leathwood and B. Francis (eds), *Gender and Lifelong Learning*, London: Routledge, pp. 57–69.

Francis, B. and Skelton, C. (2005) *Reassessing Gender and Achievement*, London: Routledge.

Heung, V. (2006) "Recognizing the emotional and behavioral needs of ethnic minority students in Hong Kong", *Preventing School Failure*, 50(2): 29–36.

Hong Kong Boys and Girls Association (2009) 基層家庭兒童生活需要調查 [*Survey Report on the Needs for Living of Hong Kong Poor Families*], Hong Kong: Hong Kong Boys and Girls Association.

Hong Kong Examination and Assessment Authority (2009) *Examination Report HKALE 2009*, Hong Kong: HKEAA.

Hong Kong Examinations and Assessment Authority (2009a) "Table 5c: 2009 HKALE performance of candidates in each subject", *2009 HKALE Exam Report*. Online. Available at: http://www.hkeaa.edu.hk/DocLibrary/HKALE/Release_of_Results/Exam_Report/Examination_Statistics/alexamstat09_5.pdf (accessed 22 February 2012).

Hong Kong Examinations and Assessment Authority (2009b) "Table 5c: 2009 HKCEE performance of candidates in each subject", *2009 HKCEE Exam Report*. Online. Available at: http://www.hkeaa.edu.hk/DocLibrary/HKCEE/Release_of_Results/Exam_Report/Examination_Statistics/ceexamstat09_5.pdf (accessed 22 February 2012).

Ku, H., Chan, K. and Sanduh, K. K. (2005) *A Research Report on the Education of South Asian Ethnic Minority Groups in Hong Kong (Research Report No. 11)*, Hong Kong: Department of Applied Social Sciences, The Hong Kong Polytechnic University and Unison Hong Kong.

Lai, M. (2001) "Hong Kong students' attitudes towards Cantonese, Putonghua and English after the change of sovereignty", *Journal of Multilingual and Multicultural Development*, 22(2): 112–33.

McCall, R. B. and Beach, S. R. (2000) "The nature and correlates of underachievement among elementary schoolchildren in Hong Kong", *Child Development*, 71(3): 785–801.

Mirza, H. (2008) "Race, gender and educational desire", document presented at the Inaugural Lecture, Institute of Education, London, November.

Skelton, C., Francis, B. and Valkanova, Y. (2007) *Breaking Down the Stereotypes: Gender and Achievement in Schools*, Manchester: Equal Opportunities Commission.

University of Hong Kong, Faculty of Education (2005) "Why boys fail and what can we do?", document presented at Alumni Association Event, University of Hong Kong, October.

Warrington, M., Younger, M. and Williams, J. (2000) "Student attitude, image and the gender gap", *British Educational Research Journal*, 26(1): 393–407.

Wong, K., Lam, Y. R. and Ho, L. (2002) "The effects of schooling on gender differences", *British Educational Research Journal*, 28(6): 827–43.

Chapter 15

Conceptualizing social inclusion within teacher education

Cathy Little and David Evans

Keywords: autism, social inclusion, teacher education, teacher attitudes

Chapter overview

Greater numbers of students with disabilities are being educated in mainstream settings, enrolled in regular classes, placed with 'regular' students, and with teachers who often have limited experience or knowledge about their specific disability. The decision for placement of these students in regular classes, with little consideration for their unique social needs, unwittingly acts as a catalyst for their social isolation. Little, if any, consideration is given to these students' specialized social needs when they are placed in regular education classrooms. Little attention is given to preparing these students for the social integration that is assumed will take place. Teachers with limited knowledge of disability struggle to successfully include these students socially into their classes. This chapter will examine the role of teachers in the facilitation of socially inclusive opportunities for students. An initial discussion of the term 'social inclusion' will be followed by an exploration of constructs impacting upon teachers' attitudes toward the social aspects of disability. The chapter concludes with a discussion of the implications of social inclusion for teacher training programs.

Inclusion

Changing attitudes toward disability have resulted as part of a sweeping change in social justice and human rights issues. In the United States the *Individuals with Disabilities Education Improvement Act* (IDEA, 2004), passed in 2004, legally mandates prescribed educational services for students with disabilities. In 1994 the *Salamanca Statement* (UNESCO, 1994) called on all governments to adopt an inclusive education policy by enrolling all students in regular schools.

In Australia, for example, the *Disability Discrimination Act* (1992) and the *Disability Standards for Education* (2005) set out to eliminate discrimination against a person on the grounds of disability and reinforce the right to education of students with a disability "on the same basis as" students without a disability (Commonwealth

Attorney General's Department, 2005, pp. 15–18). Although the *Disability Discrimination Act* does not specify the setting where students with a disability should be educated, there is an expectation that regular classroom teachers would be able to meet the diverse needs of all students.

Inclusion of children with disabilities into mainstream educational settings is a well-debated and discussed topic (Lingard and Mills, 2007). Inclusion in education advocates that students with special needs can and should be educated alongside their normally developing peers with appropriate support services, rather than being placed in special education classrooms or schools (Mesibov and Shea, 1996). General education teachers, therefore, are finding more children with disabilities being enrolled in their classes than they have previously. Weiss (2008) argues that while most teachers welcome these learners into their classroom, some experience trepidation, unsure about their level of skill required to help such students, what support systems they have at their disposal and what will be the impact of this student on others in the class.

However, in discussing successful inclusive practice, the measure of success appears to be placed on students' placement and/or achievement of academic outcomes. The nature of some disabilities (e.g. autism) is primarily a social disorder. Success for students on the autism spectrum, therefore, needs to also include their social achievements or social competence.

Autism and social disability

Placement in a regular class for students with an autistic spectrum disorder (ASD), especially those diagnosed with Asperger Syndrome, may result in 'exclusion' because the student's individual needs, in particular their social needs, are not being addressed by the classroom, the school or the teacher. "Teachers and schools working with children with Asperger Syndrome may not be aware of how to provide the best inclusive environment" (Bullard, 2004, p. 176).

Asperger Syndrome is a variant of ASD located on the spectrum of autistic disorders. Most students diagnosed with Asperger Syndrome will display a qualitative impairment in social interaction accompanied by an inability to develop friendships, impaired use of non-verbal behaviour such as eye gaze and facial expression and subtle impairments in communication (Jordan, 2008). For example, a student with Asperger Syndrome may display fluent speech, but have difficulty with conversation skills, sometimes showing a perseverative interest in one topic and making literal interpretations of comments made to them. Students who have been diagnosed with Asperger Syndrome have "particular difficulties in communicating with their peers and developing appropriate relationships with others at school" (Carrington and Graham, 1999, p. 5). Students with Asperger Syndrome often exhibit a high verbal intelligence score, yet have profound difficulties in the pragmatics of social communication.

Roberts (2004) stresses "an essential component in the development of a positive school climate and the success of the student with autism generally, is the development of social skills" (p. 14). In order to function successfully as part of the school, students with autism need to develop appropriate social behaviours. Simply including or placing students with autism in the general classroom does not automatically lead to better socialization outcomes for them (Cooper *et al.*, 1999). If we expect students with autism to demonstrate appropriate social behaviours or social competence in specific social situations, then explicit teaching of such skills will most probably be required. Sainsbury (2000, p. 19) states:

> The essential social problem in autistic spectrum conditions is not one of avoidance of, or lack of interest in, interacting with others, but inability to grasp the tacit rules that govern social interaction intuitively, or to "read" the facial expression, tone of voice and body language of others.

Social inclusion

Social competence is defined as a person displaying behaviours which "when used must be effective in achieving his or her social goals and the selection of these behaviours must be appropriate for the context" (Brown *et al.*, 2008, p. 4). When considering a student's social competence, of particular interest is how students are successfully included in regards to their social needs, a notion of 'social inclusion', and how this is perceived and defined by teachers and students. Is social inclusion merely a conceptual construct, part of the broader theoretical framework of inclusion? Or, is social inclusion an operational, observable practice that teachers can facilitate as part of the learning process for students with disabilities in regular classrooms?

In recent years there has been more emphasis on the notion of social inclusion, referring to a student being included beyond academic and classroom activities. It involves active levels of social involvement with teachers and peers. Koster *et al.* (2009) state that the concept of social inclusion includes aspects of friendship, acceptance, interaction, relationships, social status and bullying.

Moving beyond this superficial definition of social inclusion as merely equity of representation, this paper utilizes a level of definition that recognizes equity of recognition. This definition views social inclusion as a dynamic process of recognition of individuals and groups for who and what they are (Raffo and Gunter, 2008).

The placement of students with disabilities in regular education settings is the result of a process made in accordance with a number of guiding constructs. Figure 15.1 introduces social inclusion as an element of the broader construct of inclusion, and shows the environments into which the principles of inclusion are realized. One of the fundamental environments that shape the impact of social inclusion is the environment in which the child receives their education program.

The research of Chamberlain *et al.* (2007) recognizes that the social inclusion of students with an ASD in regular classes is successful when supported by "the active efforts of parents and teachers to make dramatic improvements in the social

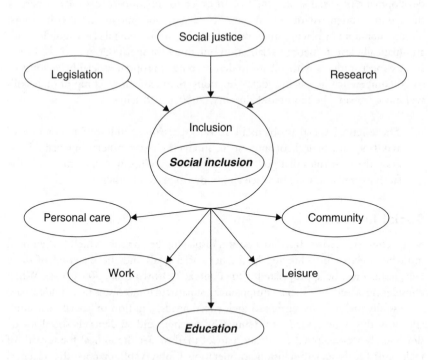

Figure 15.1 Social inclusion as an element of the broader construct of inclusion, and the environments into which the principles of inclusion are
realized

networking of children with autism" (p. 239). By promoting social inclusion teachers can assist with the formation of equal relationships with enhanced social engagement for students.

It is not enough to simply place students in regular classes and 'hope' that they
learn to socialize. Siperstein and Parker (2008) in their discussion around the practice
of 'mainstreaming' stated that "simply moving children with disabilities from segregated special education schools and classrooms to the regular education environment did not ensure their social integration" (p. 120). Teachers must be responsible
for the provision of an environment that facilitates socially inclusive opportunities.
"In order to give opportunities for students to develop their social competence,
more is needed than simply interacting with others" (Roe, 2008, p. 151).

Factors impacting teacher attitudes

A powerful predictor of successful inclusion of students with a disability is the attitude of the general education teacher (Ainscow, 2007). While legislation can dic-
tate and enforce the provision of equal educational opportunity it cannot enforce

acceptance. Teacher education programs have a unique place in the fostering of positive attitudes toward students with disabilities; enhancing understanding, promoting awareness of individual need, and instructing how to accommodate for diversity within the classroom (Alderman and Green, 2011).

One factor influencing the effective implementation of inclusive practice is teachers' attitudes. There is substantial research examining how teacher attitudes directly influence students' attitudes and behaviour, and the subsequent success of a program encompassing the principles of inclusion (e.g. Ainscow, 2007; Avramidis *et al.*, 2000). Although it appears that teachers tend to support the concept of inclusion as a social and educational principle, their validation at an operational level, and their demonstration of inclusive principles appears to be strongly related to their perceptions of students' disabilities. It could be argued that these reluctant views are shaped by the surface level, social behaviour or social competence of students. In fact, problem behaviour is often the primary barrier to inclusion and social integration in the general education classroom (Alderman and Green, 2011).

Research further highlights teachers' concerns about lack of knowledge, lack of support systems and overriding legislative policy as obstacles to the inclusion process (e.g. Robertson *et al.*, 2003). Westwood and Graham (2003) reported that for some general education teachers, having a student with special educational needs in their class was a major difficulty due to a "lack of appropriate teaching resources, problem behaviours exhibited by some students and a lack of appropriate professional training" (p. 3).

The connection between the success of inclusion of students with disabilities and teachers' attitudes towards inclusion is dynamic. With new knowledge teachers are better able to facilitate the successful inclusion of students; this success leads to confirmation and deepening of other elements of professional knowledge. Other aspects to be considered at this operational level include: teachers' knowledge of Asperger Syndrome; their professional pedagogy and personal skills and experience; opportunities for professional development; the provision of systems support; and, the element of collaboration. As shown in Figure 15.2, these elements have a two-way effect in that they both inform and affect the teacher, and in return are molded and developed by the teacher in response to new and changing beliefs and attitudes.

It would be remiss to not address the attributes of the student when discussing teacher attitude. As preservice educators, one must recognize and acknowledge the attributes that students bring to the classroom that can significantly impact upon teacher attitudes. As illustrated in Figure 15.2, characteristics such as attributes of family involvement and support, peer interaction and relationships, curriculum needs and personal strengths, can contribute to the development of either positive or negative attitudes of a teacher toward a particular student.

Boutot (2007) analyzed the characteristics of students deemed both popular and unpopular by their peers. She found a close correlation between the characteristics of unpopular students and those associated with an ASD, and suggested that teachers may need to explicitly teach skills that strengthen, or eliminate behaviours that jeopardize the acceptance of students with Asperger Syndrome.

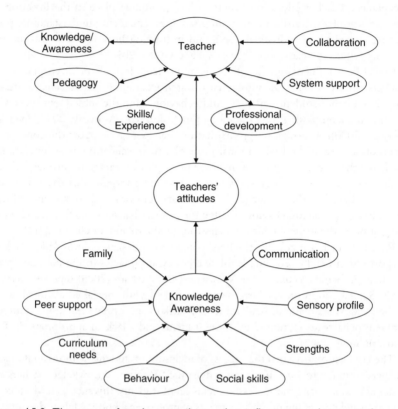

Figure 15.2 The range of student attributes that influence teacher attitudes

Implications for teacher education

Siperstein and Parker (2008) state that, "Today, children with disabilities are more likely to be physically included and have access to general education curriculum than they have ever been; however, little ground has been gained with regard to social integration" (p. 121). Contemporary preservice teacher education programs emphasize social constructivist pedagogy, promoting the value of designing learning experiences that emphasize the social nature of learning. Current teaching practices in regular classrooms are dominated by the social constructivist model, promoting the value of social activity in learning and the contributions that learners can make to their own learning (McInerney and McInerney, 2010).

The adoption of a social constructivist model within classrooms and schools draws heavily on the social competence of students. With its emphasis on social skills combined with appropriate communication modes, encapsulated in an expected behavioural set, social learning environments allow students to actively engage with their learning. However, this is not a one-size-fits-all model. When teaching students with social disabilities, or students on the autism spectrum, a social learning model of education may exclude students who have difficulty engaging socially. Educators must consider the idiosyncratic nature of ASD in order to provide a quality education environment.

Figure 15.2 illustrates a range of attributes students bring to the classroom. Of these attributes, four are labeled as the 'core competencies' of ASD. These core competencies demonstrated by marked impairments in reciprocal social interaction and communication and by repetitive and restricted interests and behaviours and unusual sensory experiences, combine uniquely to shape each individual and can thus have a marked impact upon the teacher and the formation of their attitudes. An awareness of individual student characteristics needs to be reflected across all curriculum and methods courses within teacher preservice education courses and embedded within coursework and professional experience placements.

The concern for students with an ASD, especially those diagnosed with Asperger Syndrome, is that due to the very nature of their disability, placement in a regular class may result in 'exclusion' because the student's individual needs are not being met by the classroom, the school or the teacher. Knowledge of effective teaching practices, such as the use of visual supports, structured routines, advanced organizers, use of timers to limit perseveration, using social stories to model positive behaviours, teaching peers how to act appropriately with the student with Asperger Syndrome are all documented as successful practices for meeting the needs of students with an ASD (Bullard, 2004). These effective teaching practices need to be considered by future teachers when designing learning environments that demand high levels of social behaviour to be part of a learning experience or activity.

Recent studies have demonstrated that the role of the partner in interactions is especially significant (Humphrey and Symes, 2011; Locke et al., 2010). A primary goal in regular schools is to provide opportunities for students with Asperger Syndrome to interact with typical age peers, and "General education classroom students can facilitate the successful inclusion of students with special needs by making them feel welcome in the classroom and making friendships with them" (Mastropieri and Scruggs, 2000, p. 245). Preparing students to engage in learning experiences that require social engagement not only provides a strong learning environment, but can assist students with Asperger Syndrome to be included socially.

The generalization of skills across situations can be developed through a structured plan for teaching socialization. Socialization is a skill that is as important as communicating, reading and writing and needs to be included in students' learning programs. Students with Asperger Syndrome typically do not learn to socialize through observing and imitating others. Students with Asperger's Syndrome lack an awareness of the needs of others in relation to themselves. Specific social skills need to be taught. Explicit instruction is required to increase the student's awareness of the ways in which people behave and how to interact with others. Social skills training should not be restricted, however, to the classroom. Alongside structured programs that teach specific behavioural routines, informal social interactions and behaviours suitable for the playground must be taught.

It is imperative that educators acknowledge the 'value' of this learning as an extremely demanding and stressful task which is of prime value to the student with Asperger's. The learning of social skills requires a prolonged and systematic effort for these students, but it has lifelong implications. Research has shown that social skills are related to long-term adjustment and prognosis for both individuals with and without an ASD (Boutot, 2007).

It is a common assumption that people with an ASD do not seek or are not interested in social interactions. For a lot of students on the spectrum this is a false assumption. Many students with an ASD want friendships and relationships but are not sure how to go about obtaining them. Bauminger and Kasari (2000) suggest that children with high functioning autism seem aware of their social situations and desire social engagement with others, but may lack the skill and opportunity to do so.

A student with Asperger Syndrome may exhibit a sensory disorder, and demonstrate extreme reactions, modulation difficulties and overreactions to sensory stimuli (Cumine et al., 2010). Environmental screeners can assist in assessing environments and allow for identification of sensory triggers. Awareness of hypersensitivity and hyposensitivity should be part of a preservice teacher education program that supports the inclusion of students with diverse learning needs. Teachers need to know how to reduce sensory overload for students and minimize input if possible. Simple measures may include the positioning of a student's desk to reduce the level of light, noise, or outside distractions, or allowing a student to listen to their iPod when doing deskwork, as general classroom noise levels can be distracting.

Many classroom activities assume a requisite level of language, communication and social interaction. A large majority of children with Asperger Syndrome present with what appears to be appropriate expressive language skills which to the neuro-typical (non-autistic) person may equate to the belief that the child possesses good communication skills. When students with Asperger Syndrome demonstrate atypical social behaviour and use language in an unfamiliar manner, they may often be misunderstood and attitudes towards them adversely influenced. The impact of this for preservice teacher education programs is the need for teachers to think flexibly in terms of how they engage their students and how they expect them to respond. For example, does an in-class report have to be presented verbally? If so, what training and preparation is required to equip the student? Or, would a suitable alternative for a student with a language difficulty be to write their report, or create a visual representation?

Conclusion

The inclusion of a student with a disability in a regular class can often present the class teacher with a challenge to their existing beliefs and pedagogy. This can lead to a feeling of uncertainty in regards to instruction and management, arising as a result of the student's unique learning and behavioural style. An individual student's impact in the classroom is shaped by numerous elements.

Preservice teacher education programs need to consider the need of all students at all points. Research has revealed that educating students with an ASD requires an understanding of the unique cognitive, social, sensory and behavioural deficits that characterize ASD (Roberts, 2004). Sainsbury (2000) writes that the single most social relationship for a schoolchild with an ASD is their relationship with the teacher. She adds that good experiences with thoughtful teachers make an overwhelming difference to her life. Good teachers are those with a broad knowledge base of Asperger Syndrome, with good organization skills, and the ability to plan creatively. In order to meet the social and emotional needs of students, teachers need to have an understanding of these individual needs and as stated by Roe (2008): "Create contexts that promote social inclusion alongside academic achievement" (p. 147). This is the responsibility of all teachers; it is the responsibility of all personnel preparing teachers for tomorrow.

References

Ainscow, M. (2007) "Taking an inclusive turn", *Journal of Research in Special Educational Needs*, 7(1): 3–7.

Alderman, G. L. and Green, S. K. (2011) "Social powers and effective classroom management: Enhancing teacher–student relationships", *Intervention in School and Clinic*, 47: 39–44.

Avramidis, E., Bayliss, P. and Burden, R. (2000) "A survey into mainstream teachers' attitudes towards the inclusion of children with special educational needs in the ordinary school in one local education authority", *Educational Psychology*, 20(2): 191–211.

Bauminger, N. and Kasari, C. (2000) "Loneliness and friendship in high-functioning children with autism", *Child Development*, 71: 447–56.

Boutot, E. A. (2007) "Fitting in: Tips for promoting acceptance and friendships for students with autism spectrum disorders in inclusive classrooms", *Intervention in School and Clinic*, 42(3): 156–61.

Brown, W. H., Odom, S. L. and McConnell, S. R. (2008) *Social Competence of Young Children: Risk, Disability and Intervention*, Baltimore, MD: Paul H. Brookes.

Bullard, H. R. (2004) "Ensure the successful inclusion of a child with Asperger syndrome in the general education classroom", *Intervention in School and Clinic*, 39(3): 176–80.

Carrington, S. and Graham, L. (1999) "Asperger's syndrome: Learner characteristics and teaching strategies", *Special Education Perspectives*, 5(2): 15–23.

Chamberlain, B., Kasari, C. and Rotheram-Fuller, E. (2007) "Involvement or isolation? The social networks of children with autism in regular classrooms", *Journal of Autism and Developmental Disorders*, 37: 230–42.

Commonwealth Attorney General's Department (2005) *Disability Standards for Education*, Canberra: Australian Government.

Cooper, M., Griffith, K. and Filer, J. (1999) "School intervention for inclusion of students with autism", *Focus on Autism and Other Developmental Disabilities*, 14(2): 110–15.

Cumine, V., Dunlop, J. and Stevenson, G. (2010) *Asperger Syndrome: A Practical Guide for Teachers*, London: Routledge.

Humphrey, N. and Symes, W. (2011) "Peer interaction patterns among adolescents with autistic spectrum disorders (ASDs) in mainstream school settings", *Autism*, 15: 394–419.

IDEA (2004) *Individuals with Disabilities Education Improvement Act of 2004*. Online. Available at: http://idea.ed.gov/explore/home (accessed 19 August 2011).

Jordan, R. (2008) "Autistic Spectrum Disorders: A challenge and a model for inclusion in education", *British Journal of Special Education*, 35(1): 11–15.

Koster, M., Nakken, H., Pijl, S. and van Houten, E. (2009) "Being part of the peer group: A literature study focusing on the social dimension of inclusion in education", *International Journal of Inclusive Education*, 13(2): 117–40.

Lingard, B. and Mills, M. (2007) "Pedagogies making a difference: Issues of social justice and inclusion", *International Journal of Inclusive Education*, 11(3): 233–44.

Locke, J., Ishijima, E. H., Kasari, C. and London, N. (2010) "Loneliness, friendship quality and the social networks of adolescents with high-functioning autism in an inclusive school setting", *Journal of Research in Special Educational Needs*, 10(2): 74–81.

Mastropieri, M. and Scruggs, T. (2000) *The Inclusive Classroom: Strategies for Effective Instruction*, 2nd edn, Upper Saddle River, NJ: Prentice-Hall.

McInerney, D. and McInerney, V. (2010) *Educational Psychology: Constructing Learning*, Frenchs Forest, NSW: Pearson Australia.

Mesibov, G. B. and Shea, V. (1996) "Full inclusion and students with autism", *Journal of Autism and Developmental Disorders*, 26(3): 337–46.

Raffo, C. and Gunter, H. (2008) "Leading schools to promote social inclusion: Developing a conceptual framework for analysing research, policy and practice", *Journal of Education Policy*, 23(4): 397–414.

Roberts, J. (2004) *A Review of Research Relevant to the Education of Students with Disabilities, and In Particular Autism, in Segregated and Inclusive Educational Settings*, Sydney: AANSW.

Robertson, K., Chamberlain, B. and Kasari, C. (2003) "General education teachers' relationships with included students with autism", *Journal of Autism and Developmental Disorders*, 33(2): 123–29.

Roe, J. (2008) "Social inclusion: Meeting the socio-emotional needs of children with vision needs", *British Journal of Visual Impairment*, 26: 147–58.

Sainsbury, C. (2000) *Martian in the Playground: Understanding the Schoolchild with Asperger's Syndrome*, London: The Book Factory.

Siperstein, G. and Parker, R. (2008) "Toward an understanding of social integration: A special issue", *Exceptionality*, 16: 119–24.

UNESCO (1994) "The Salamanca statement and framework for action on special needs education", *World Conference On Special Needs Education: Access And Quality*, Salamanca, Spain, June. Online. Available at: http://www.unesco.org/education/pdf/SALAMA_E.PDF (accessed 19 August 2011).

Weiss, M. J. (2008) *Practical Solutions for Educating Young Children with High-Functioning Autism and Asperger Syndrome*, Shawnee Mission, KS: UAS: Autism Asperger Publishing Company.

Westwood, P. and Graham, L. (2003) "Inclusion of students with special needs: Benefits and obstacles perceived by teachers in New South Wales and South Australia", *Australian Journal of Learning Disabilities*, 8(1): 3–15.

Chapter 16

Professional development for teachers of students with autism spectrum disorders in Hong Kong

Fuk-chuen Ho

Keywords: professional development, autism spectrum disorders, collaboration

Chapter overview

The principle of educating students with special educational needs in the least restrictive settings renders a rapid growth of the population of students with autism spectrum disorders (ASD) in ordinary schools in the last decade. This change has caused a concern to teachers in ordinary schools. To equip teachers in ordinary schools with the knowledge and skills in dealing with students with special educational needs, different tiers of professional development programs have been developed. The problem is that these programs are mainly short-term and direct top-down transmission in nature. The lack of opportunity to try out the newly acquired knowledge and skills in real environments cannot give sufficient confidence to teachers to work with students with ASD independently. This chapter discusses the effectiveness of a current professional development (PD) program for teachers of students with ASD in Hong Kong SAR. A collaborative mode of PD is recommended that can assist teachers to gain hands-on experience in a field-based training program.

Introduction

ASD is a developmental disability which affects the normal functioning of the brain. In recent years, more children are being diagnosed with ASD. Over the last few decades there has been a major rise in the rate of ASD with around 6,500 families in Hong Kong with members with ASD (Health and Welfare Bureau, 1994, p. 12). The reports of the prevalence rate indicate that approximately 1 in 110 individuals are diagnosed (Center for Disease Control and Prevention (CDC), 2009). This could be due to a broadening of the conceptualization of ASD as a spectrum disorder. In addition, there is recognition that ASD can co-occur in individuals with other disorders.

The increase in the number of individuals with ASD has caused the rise in enrollment of this group of students in ordinary school settings and this has resulted in a corresponding demand for appropriate instructional programs to be provided. Teachers, therefore, need to understand the complexities that ASD encompasses. The core deficits of students with ASD have resulted in mounting pressure on teachers to design effective teaching programs for their special needs.

Services for students with ASD in Hong Kong

In Hong Kong, children with ASD first received increased attention and services in the 1980s. The shift from a social and health perspective to an education one was initiated by the Education Department (now the Education Bureau, EDB) in 1983. Most children with ASD were initially placed in special schools for children with mild or moderate intellectual disabilities. In 1987, the service was delivered in the form of a Resource Teaching Program (RTP). The ultimate goal of the RTP was to train and enable the children to participate fully in their own class. The role of the resource teachers was to give extra help in behaviour management and training in communication and social skills (Rehabilitation Division, Health and Welfare Branch, 1996). In the school year 2008/2009, all the 31 special schools for children with mild/moderate-grade intellectual disability operated the RTP.

In recent years, one of the major trends characterizing special education has been a growing awareness of the rights of all children. The Government of the Hong Kong Special Administrative Region launched an integration scheme in 1997. Children with mild-grade intellectual disability, hearing impairment, visual impairment, physical disability and ASD with average intelligence would be educated in as ordinary a setting as possible.

The student population in Hong Kong has become more diverse in schools in the past decade. The presence of the diversity in classrooms is a challenge to schools as well as an opportunity for them to reform the curriculum and instruction. Meeting the diverse needs of students requires a change of the landscape of teacher education. The reality of schooling under the system that students with special needs should be educated in ordinary school settings compels teacher training institutions to educate their program's participants in more authentic settings. Teachers are required to strengthen their knowledge and skills for effectively working with all students. It was indicated in the inclusive education report by Dowson et al. (2003) that in Hong Kong many teachers consider that the most problematic category of children with disabilities to deal with was those with ASD. Their perception about children with ASD was not surprising. Children with ASD manifest themselves in many facets of behavioural idiosyncrasies and developmental delays. In particular, they often have limited verbal and communicative behaviours and abnormal social relationships.

Jennett et al. (2003) noted that there is a need for adequate training for all teachers who work with students having ASD. The good teacher is a significant factor in improving the chances for success for all students. There is a need to develop and retain highly qualified teachers. Teacher quality encompasses many factors. Lewis et al. (1999) noted that teachers' content knowledge and teaching practices are two important subsets of good teacher quality.

The current practice of PD for teachers of students with special needs in Hong Kong works towards the accomplishment of these subsets of quality. In general, most Hong Kong teachers possess a basic degree. Teachers, however, may not have specialized professional training in the area of special education. To fulfill the requirement, it is important for teachers to attend programs that can provide them with the opportunity to acquire a good knowledge of children with ASD as well as the instructional strategies for supporting them.

PD program for teachers of students with ASD in Hong Kong

Before 2004, the special education training for teachers of special or ordinary schools was conducted in the form of a one-year full-time and one-year part-time program of study (i.e. The Course for Teachers of Children with Special Educational Needs, TCSEN). The program aimed to develop theoretical concepts and practical teaching techniques for teachers working with children who have special educational needs and to provide them with the necessary knowledge and skills for effective teaching. The program required participants to complete a study of four core courses, three specialized courses, three elective courses as well as a six-week field experience practice in the first year and an action research project in the second year. Program participants could opt for their desired specialized and elective courses for their main focus of study. More importantly, participants were required to try out the learned skills in their six-week field practice and focus on an area for action research. The EDB funded schools to recruit supply teachers to substitute the program participants to carry out regular teaching duty in schools. The delivery of this full-time mode of study, however, was so expensive that the government found it difficult to support in the long-term. In addition, there has been a demanding need for a massive number of teachers in ordinary schools seeking special needs training since the implementation of integrated education in 1997.

As the intensive mode of TCSEN is no longer feasible to provide for this large number of training places for teachers it was replaced by a part-time PD program for teachers (Catering for Diverse Learning Needs, PDP (CDLN)) in 2004. This program offers two levels of training to cater for the different needs of teachers. Level 1 consists of 30 hours of training on a basic understanding of learning diversity and classroom practice, and supporting students with special educational needs. Level 2 is a 90-hour program which provides more in-depth thematic studies and action research.

In addition to this regular PDP (CDLN), the EDB has commissioned the Hong Kong Institute of Education to run a five-year scheme of PD for teachers of students with special educational needs. Schools are funded by the EDB to release their teachers to attend the one-week basic, three-week advanced or two-week thematic full-time program. The basic and advanced programs are similar to the Level 1 and Level 2 of PDP (CDLN) respectively. The thematic programs consist of 60 hours of study. Participants can choose a theme on ASD, AD/HD, Intellectual Disability, etc. for an in-depth study.

Teachers who have a particular interest in ASD can enroll for the 30-hour ASD elective course in the advanced program and two 30-hour courses in the thematic program. With an inspection of the course content on ASD, the information is very comprehensive. The courses on ASD aim to assist program participants to acquire the knowledge and skills to develop comprehensive approaches to support the development of students with ASD so that these students can better adjust to school life. The program content includes analyzing the common features, and differences in behaviours of different sub-groups of students within the autism spectrum, from childhood to adulthood; reviewing the cognitive, communicative, social, and sensory integration deficits associated with ASD, and the behaviours that reflect these developmental difficulties; examining other factors influencing the behaviour of students with ASD (e.g. environment, health, stress and anxiety); evaluating current intervention practices (e.g. TEACCH, visual strategies, social stories, sensory integration), and insights provided by adults with ASD; identifying key features of effective interventions; conducting functional assessments and Applied Behavioural Analysis to address the essential developmental needs, and the needs arising from other factors influencing the behaviour of individual students; and exploring related provisions and support services to optimize students' potential of adjustment in school life.

A difficulty of the current PD program at their basic and advanced levels is of its multicategorical nature. A relatively in-depth study of a particular category of disability is offered at the thematic level. The training hours for a specific category of disability are quite limited. Scheuermann *et al.* (2003) queried whether non-categorical or multicategorical programs can provide instruction in the range of specialized skills needed by teachers of students with ASD. Scheuermann *et al.* doubted that teachers who qualified as generic special education teachers were adequately qualified to support students with ASD.

Another difficulty is that the content is delivered in the form of lectures and seminars within a very short period of time. The usual practice is that a three-hour lecture is used to cover one curricular item. This kind of delivery is economical, direct and efficient. The core problem of the current program, however, is its short-term and top-down transmission model which does not provide teachers with the opportunity to acquire hands-on experiences and make reflection through the try-out of newly acquired knowledge.

It is, therefore, important to strengthen the training programs which can provide evidence-based guidelines for teachers to cater for the needs of students with lower incidence needs in different settings.

A new mode of PD for teachers of students with ASD in Hong Kong

The traditional approaches which focus on short-term direct transmission PD programs are increasingly regarded as relatively ineffective (Darling-Hammond and Baratz-Snowden, 2007). Lewis *et al.* (1999) found that teachers who were involved in frequent cooperative planning and collaboration with their peers more often reported feelings of confidence and being well prepared to work in a modern classroom. Collaborative learning is at the core of communities of practice involving co-construction of meaning and mutual relationships through a shared enterprise.

In recent years, collaboration has been the focus of study across disciplines. In particular, learning communities are increasingly used for the co-construction of knowledge. It is important for PD courses to have collaborative activities, which provide opportunities for teachers to reflectively share their practice, revisit beliefs on teaching and learning, and co-construct knowledge. The expectation of collaborative practices in teachers' PDs is to acquire the knowledge through social interaction. In addition to the programs offered by the tertiary institutions, learning community has been another form of training for teachers in the area of inclusive and special education settings. A professional learning community is characterized by Eaker (2002) that "decisions are research-based with collaborative teams of teachers seeking out best practices" (p. 20).

Experience and expertise sharing among teachers themselves is an important form of PD. This practice is persuasive and valuable for its practicability as the experience and expertise are developed in real environments. These proposed activities, however, have limits. Teaching materials are selected based on self-perception and self-judgment and may not be theoretically sound or consider whether they are of interest to most trainees. An example is when a trainer from a special school adopts the behavioural approach to explain the social behaviour of children with ASD. Other principles, such as the theory of mind and central coherence, are excluded in the professional exchange with partner schools. The trainer's preference dominates the selection of teaching materials. Viewpoints of different perspectives are not taken. As such, university academics should also be asked to participate in these learning communities.

In 2007, the Hong Kong Special Schools Council and the Hong Kong Institute of Education initiated a Quality Education Fund (QEF) joint project using a collaborative mode of PD. The project aimed to deliver a field-based mode of training for teachers in special schools. Institute lecturers participated in the joint project to strengthen the theoretical learning input. The model of Professional Development Schools (PDS) (see Darling-Hammond, 1994) was adopted in this joint project. The major goals of PDS are to: (1) provide field-based settings for teachers; (2) engage inservice teachers in continuous PD; (3) promote and conduct inquiry to advance knowledge; and (4) provide exemplary education for students.

The university academics and supporting teachers worked together as consultants and advisors. Accordingly, 12 courses and a compilation of teaching materials were provided to 101 inservice special school teachers who appreciated the program and gave very positive feedback (Ho and Mansukhani, 2010). A major difficulty, however, identified in this joint project was the collaboration between the institute lecturers and the expert teachers of supporting schools. The tradition in teacher training in Hong Kong is that university trainers design the delivery materials. Schools play a very minimal role in this aspect. The courses in the project, though, were based on the strengths and uniqueness of schools to design the learning content and activities. A conflicting example is when supporting expert teachers adopted sensory integration to explain the social and behavioural difficulties of students with ASD, the institute lecturers wanted to introduce other approaches to give teachers a balanced view of the different approaches. In addition, the opportunity for experience sharing among trainees was not sufficient. Project evaluation depended on the views of trainees; thus, the training program's effectiveness was difficult to evaluate. Considering these issues, it is recommended that the future PDP should consider the following framework for the design of training programs.

Theoretical framework

The training program should be guided by an approach that heavily emphasizes the existing good practices of effective teacher development. In this proposed new model teachers should be provided with the opportunity to construct knowledge by exploration and questioning in the hope that the new knowledge can be readily incorporated into their existing teaching practices. The proposed program will include the following characteristics.

Collaboration

Through the activities of sharing and discussion and reflection, teachers become more active in the learning process. Some models of PD highlight the importance of the availability of a supporting network for teachers to share viewpoints and solve problems. Trainees in this program will work in school clusters. Each school cluster will have three parties of personnel: lecturers of teacher training institutions, expert teachers of supporting schools, and teachers of participating schools. Lecturers of the teacher training institution and teachers of supporting schools will be the trainers, whereas teachers of participating schools will be the trainees. There will be two levels of collaboration. At the trainer level, the institute lecturers and expert teachers will work closely together to design the teaching materials and monitor the trainees' learning progress. At the trainee level, teachers of participating schools will work with one another to share their experiences in the try-out teaching.

The principles of co-teaching will be incorporated in the partnership between institute lecturers and expert teachers of supporting schools as well as the collaboration among trainees. Friend and Bursuck (2009) propose six approaches to co-teaching: (1) One teach, one observe: one teacher leads the large group instruction, whereas the other collects the data on students' academic, behavioural, or social performance; (2) Station teaching: students are divided into three groups. Students rotate from station to station. Two stations are for teaching, and the third is for independent work; (3) Parallel teaching: the class is split into two groups; (4) Alternative teaching: one teacher works with most students, whereas the other teacher works with a small group for remediation, enrichment, and so on; (5) Team teaching: both teachers lead the large group instruction; and (6) One teach, one assist: one teacher leads the instruction, whereas the other teacher circulates among the students. In particular, team teaching would be encouraged. It is hoped that both lecturers and expert teachers would play equal parts in teaching in the program delivery.

Job relevance

Tate (2009) suggests that teachers consider PD relevant when the learning activities are related to their daily responsibilities. In this proposed new approach, both the institute lecturer and expert teachers will design the program materials. A common learning theme in each school cluster will be adopted. This project proposes that one school cluster focuses on studying the language of ASD disorders, whereas the other school cluster focuses on social problems. Thus, trainees with similar interests can easily identify relevant ideas or materials through observation and discussion. In addition, program trainees will be required to try out the new learning content in their daily teaching. As peer observation will be arranged, trainees will have greater opportunities to share ideas and materials.

Reflection

The National Staff Development Council (2009) recommended reflection as an effective follow-up activity in PD. A post-conference meeting will be arranged for each peer observation. Participants of school clusters will be given the opportunity to receive constructive comments and reflect on their own teaching activities. Every trainee will also be required to submit a reflection report after the program.

Incorporation of new knowledge into the existing content

Researchers (e.g. Bransford *et al.*, 2000) have suggested that recognizing teachers as professionals allows them to become more competent in new content. Trainers must understand the specific learning needs of the trainees because trainees' motivation will be enhanced when their needs and professional knowledge are considered throughout the program.

This proposed new project will adopt a school-based approach of PD. Lecturers and expert teachers will assist the trainees in identifying the strengths and weaknesses of their existing teaching programs. Suggestions to improve teaching will be built upon their current practices.

Conclusion

As the financial resource implication for the offer of full-time programs for teachers of students with special educational needs became exhaustive, there was a need to initiate new ideas into the existing PD programs using a direct short-term transmission model. Collaboration with expert teachers of local schools to equip program participants with hands-on experience is proposed as an additional component in the PD program. A collaborative mode of PD, emphasizing collaboration, job relevance, reflection and incorporation of new knowledge into existing content has been proposed.

Asking teachers to team teach, however, and to serve as models of practice and mentors for others has the potential to raise anxiety and create dissonance with the prevailing identity expectations for teachers as isolated, self-made experts. This anxiety and dissonance may focus teachers on their new roles more than on the details of their own classroom performance. As more PD programs emphasize the need to create spaces for teachers to interact, team teach, and educate each other, more research is needed that explores how these interactions impact teachers' roles, and the way teachers negotiate identities and construct knowledge.

Another important issue which deserves further exploration is the guarantee of occurrence of professional dialogue during the team communications. Good and Brophy (2008) point out that communication is broader than teachers simply sharing information. They refer to a "sense of community amongst teachers . . . based on information obtained in carefully planned and coordinated discussion with other teachers" (p. 444). While dialogue by itself may be insufficient, it is nevertheless a central component of professional support. Creating a strong professional dialogue is central to building a foundation for teacher empowerment; a direct vehicle to achieving empowerment is engagement in collaborative PD within schools.

References

Bransford, J., Brown, A. and Cocking, R. (2000) *How People Learn: Brain, Mind, and Experience and School*, Washington, DC: National Academy Press.
Center for Disease Control and Prevention (2009) *Autism Spectrum Disorders (ASDs): Data and Statistics: Prevalence*. Online. Available at: http://www.cdc.gov/ncbddd/autism/data.html (accessed 19 August 2011).
Darling-Hammond, L. (1994) "Developing professional development schools: Early lessons, challenges and promise", in L. Darling-Hammond (ed.), *Professional Development Schools: Schools for Developing a Profession*, New York: Teachers College Press, pp. 1–27.
Darling-Hammond, L. and Baratz-Snowden, J. (2007) "A good teacher in every classroom: Preparing the highly qualified teachers our children deserve", *Educational Horizons*, 85: 122–32.
Dowson, C., Heung, V., Ho, F. C., Hong, A., Hui, P., Luk, P. et al. (2003) *Case Studies of Four Integrated Schools in Hong Kong*, Hong Kong: Hong Kong Institute of Education.
Eaker, R. (2002) "Cultural shift: Transforming schools into professional learning communities", in R. Eaker, R. R. DuFour and R. DuFour (eds), *Getting Started: Reculturing Schools to Become Professional Learning Communities*, Bloominton, IN: National Educational Service, pp. 9–29.
Friend, M. and Bursuck, W. D. (2009) *Including Students with Special Needs: A Practical Guide for Classroom Teachers*, Columbus, OH: Merrill.
Good, T. L. and Brophy, J. E. (2008) *Looking in Classrooms*, 10th edn, New York: Pearson.
Health and Welfare Bureau (1994) *Report by the Working Group on Services for Autistic Persons*, Hong Kong: Health and Welfare Bureau, Government of Hong Kong.

Ho, F. C. and Mansukhani, R. (2010) "A collaborative mode of professional development for teachers of special schools in Hong Kong", *Hong Kong Special Education Forum*, 12: 37–48.

Jennett, H. K., Harris, S. L. and Mesibov, G. B. (2003) "Commitment to philosophy, teacher efficacy, and burnout among teachers of children with autism", *Journal of Autism and Developmental Disorders*, 33(6): 583–93.

Lewis, L., Parsad, B., Carey, N., Bartfai, N., Farris, E., Westat *et al.* (1999) *Teacher Quality: A Report on the Preparation and Qualifications of Public School Teachers*, Washington, DC: US Dept. of Education, Office of Educational Research and Improvement.

National Staff Development Council (2009) *NSDC Standards: Learning.* Online. Available at: http://www.nsdc.org/standards/learning.cfm (accessed 19 August 2011).

Rehabilitation Division, Health and Welfare Branch (1996) *Hong Kong Review of Rehabilitation Programme Plan*, Hong Kong: Health and Welfare Branch.

Scheuermann, B., Webber, J., Boutat, E. A. and Goodwin, M. (2003) "Problems with personnel preparation in autism spectrum disorders", *Focus on Autism and Other Developmental Disabilities*, 18: 197–206.

Tate, M. L. (2009) "Workshops: Extend learning beyond your presentation with these brain-friendly strategies", *Journal of Staff Development*, 30: 44–6.

Chapter 17

The role of educators in facilitating resiliency that assists normalization for young people with disabilities

Nur Aishah Hanun, Wayne Hammond and Kamarulzaman Kamaruddin

Keywords: resiliency, normalization, young people with disabilities, strength-based intervention

Chapter overview

Children and youths with disabilities face long-term difficulties which can function as risk factors impacting upon their development. Compounded by challenges from the environment, these young people can become highly vulnerable to adversity. Research has shown that when faced with difficulties, many experience low self-esteem and loss of empowerment leading to negative behaviours. In addition, sensory integration disorder (SID), which is known to be a common diagnostic feature in many disabilities including autism, AD/HD, and learning difficulties, was found to adversely impact upon their abilities to adapt to changes in their surroundings. These disadvantages pose as risk factors for resiliency, which is needed for successful inclusion within school settings. The Youth Resiliency Framework offers a simple tool for teachers and other professionals to evaluate these areas of concern. This chapter also offers research findings of proven coping skills used by youths with disabilities to triumph over adversity that teachers can adopt to help other children and youths with disabilities to better weather difficulties.

Introduction

The concept of normalization and deinstitutionaliation was first introduced by the Scandinavian countries in the 1960s (Winzer, 1996). This concept refers to the philosophical belief that all exceptional individuals, regardless of their type and level of disability, deserve to have access to education and living environments to be as close to normal as possible. This notion also advocates that the environment is arranged so that life and the surroundings of the individual are as close to the norm and least restrictive as possible (Ysseldyke and Algozzine, 1984).

Inclusive education for children and youths with disabilities emerged from the concept of normalization. While initially focusing on learners with disabilities, inclusion has now come to have a much broader definition which means including all learners who may be potentially marginalized (Forlin and Chambers, 2011). Inclusion, thus, manifests itself in the various efforts by schools to prepare their students for positive engagement as independent and contributing members of their community.

Teachers and parents who interact directly with children and youths with disabilities have a very important role to facilitate this normalization process. These young people often attend regular schools or other private institutions that have normally undergone various assessments resulting in individual educational plans that serve to guide teachers and parents. Even with these measures in place, research has shown that youths with disabilities often face adverse situations in educational settings.

Challenges faced by many children and youths with disabilities may come from difficulties with coping with academic demands in school, peer rejection to advances for friendship and acceptance, peer pressure leading to risky behaviours such as smoking and drugs, untimely and insensitive responses by teachers and parents, and finally, stigmatization of the self due to repeated negative responses experienced.

Resiliency is now known to be a major element in navigating life's adversities. Research has shown that individuals with a resilient mindset can weather adversity more positively and successfully than those without it. The ability to overcome and be in a better state of mind after an adversity characterizes the resilient individual. Commonly based on the availability of protective factors and other internal psychological strengths, adults have the capacity to use these elements to facilitate the development of the resiliency of children and youths in their care.

Resiliency and youths with disabilities

Children and youths with learning disabilities have been found by Spekman et al. (1993) to be particularly vulnerable to stress. They may also experience continuous challenges and negative life events leading to feelings of being less competent than peers in areas of social, academic, and behavioural functioning (Smith, 2003). With regards to schooling, they become members of what Steele (1995) described as the ability-stigmatized group.

Mather and Ofiesh (2006) have established that young people with disabilities who encounter difficulties in school often experience a negative cycle – a sense of helplessness and low self-esteem when teachers are not sympathetic and cannot comprehend their difficulties. Teasing and other negative feedback from peers would also exacerbate or worsen their vulnerability to low self-esteem, and subsequently contribute to feelings typical to the effects of stigma – incompetence and inadequacy in which they try to hide their poor skills to protect themselves from further emotional disruptions (Mather and Ofiesh, 2006). Thus in the effort to facilitate the normalization of children and youths with disabilities, the issue of stigma and low self-esteem are among the pertinent elements that need to be adequately addressed when preparing teachers for inclusion.

In addition, SID, which is known to be a diagnostic feature in many disabilities including autism, AD/HD, and learning difficulties, appears to impact negatively upon the resiliency of these young people with disabilities. Already weighed down by what Margalit (2004) described as a unique social–information processing pattern resulting in a deficiency in solving or dealing with social problems, SID compounds their socializing skills even further. Research done by Hanun *et al.* (2011) has shown that sensory processing impairments potentially compromise crucial areas of resiliency development including empowerment, self-control, and self-concept.

Clearly, children and youths with disabilities have to contend with many long-term and debilitating life conditions not faced by the majority of the population. Congruent to research findings by Goldstein and Brooks (2006), Mather and Ofiesh (2006), Margalit (2004), and Spekman *et al.* (1993), among others, facilitating a resilient mindset is crucial in efforts to facilitate normalization for children and youths with disabilities.

In addition to continuously having to overcome their disabilities, the growth and development of children with disabilities are often strongly influenced by many negative factors within and outside of their immediate environment. These negative elements may include dysfunctional families, physical or mental abuse, and the stigma of being different. Stigma has also been shown to be a major hindrance against positive resiliency (Hanun *et al.*, 2011). Thus in the effort to facilitate a successful inclusion process within schools, these risk factors must be adequately addressed.

A resiliency framework for evaluation and intervention

Resiliency Canada presents the developmental strengths frameworks as a viable model to understanding the key components that contribute to the resiliency development and well-being of children, youths, and adults in our communities. The resiliency factors/developmental strengths represent fundamental elements found to be essential for all children/youths to cope effectively with life's challenges and to become productive, responsible adults in society. Based on this research, and the literature on resiliency and youth development, the 31 Developmental Strengths Framework identifies the protective factors that encourage and enhance the well-being and development of all youths in our communities.

The child/youth resiliency framework developed by Resiliency Canada (Donnon and Hammond, 2007) is grounded in research on child and adolescent development in resiliency, risk prevention, and protective factors. This framework contains two main dimensions: the internal and the external protective factors. The internal protective factors consist of self-concept, self-control, empowerment, social and cultural sensitivity. The external protective factors consist of family, peers, community, commitment to learning and school culture. Additionally, subdomains can further be seen in Figure 17.1. Surveys of more than 65,000 youths in grades 3 to 12 in communities across the cities of Canada consistently show the importance of resiliency to refrain from risk and promote positive behaviours. The more

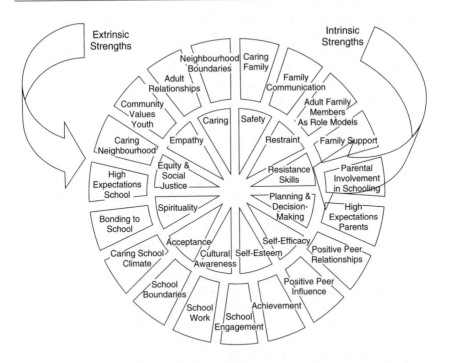

Figure 17.1 Child and Youth Resiliency Framework. Adapted from Resiliency Initiatives

resiliency factors or developmental strengths young people have, the more likely they are to make healthier choices and avoid risk-taking behaviours.

This resiliency framework offers teachers, counselors, parents, and other professionals working with children and youths with disabilities a crucial guideline as to the areas of concern that they need to look at in their efforts to instill sufficient resiliency such that these young people can function as near to the societal norms as possible. Measurements of strengths or challenges which can be further validated through interviews (learning about their stories) can be attained to aid in formulating a profile for intervention purposes. Children and youths with disabilities are often placed in community or private institutions and care centres, various types of educational settings and occasionally visit or are housed in hospitals or health clinics.

Teachers and other professionals who are in direct contact with children or youths with disabilities can facilitate or scaffold suitable coping skills that will enable them to function in society with minimal help and to overcome the stigma of being different. To reach this goal, one option is to use the framework to evaluate resiliency areas for strengths and challenges of the youths, and then systematically plan and implement interventions geared towards facilitating positive adaptation skills that lead to successful navigation within inclusive educational settings and better chances of normalization within their community.

Research done by Hanun *et al.* (2011) offers some insight about possible coping skills that children and youths with disabilities have used successfully to navigate adversity. The young people in their study were with mild cognitive impairment, compounded by other disabilities such as physical deformities, Down's syndrome, and Asperger's syndrome. Among the strategies used were diary writing, metacognitive thinking, positive self-talk, getting adult help, and fighting back.

Diary writing

Writing on paper or other visual media has been documented by researchers as having therapeutic effects for persons experiencing emotional distress (Bell, 2003). Children and youths with disabilities can be encouraged to write their experiences and feelings on paper. Younger children can be encouraged to draw. Venting out their fears, anger, and other hidden concerns may help the teacher, counselor, parents, or other concerned adults find ways to further assist directly or obtain help from other suitable professionals.

Research done by Cohn (2005) also explains this finding, stating that writing one's feelings and thoughts can contribute to healing emotional pain. In addition, it has the physiological effect of increasing the body's immune system. Parallel to this, a study by Heydt (2004) showed that writing down emotional pain can serve as a catharsis and help solve problems by making thoughts visible and assist with setting goals to achieve success to overcome the adversity.

Positive self-talk

Self-talk is a form of intrapersonal communication within the self that involves talking to oneself, and is found to be an important part of building one's self-esteem (DeVito, 2007). For example, findings by Hanun *et al.* (2011) clearly demonstrated that positive self-talk had assisted the youths with disabilities facing hostile situations to triumph over degrading statements and insensitive treatment made towards them. Research findings by psychologist Martin Seligman (1990) support this finding, stating that "our thoughts are not merely reactions to events; they change what ensues" (p. 9). According to Wood (2010), self-talk could help us manage our emotions, and that it can also become a self-fulfilling prophecy.

Children and youths with disabilities can be taught to talk to themselves positively about the disturbing situation when adversity strikes. Modeling the process is one option. Group sessions can also be done to facilitate learning and sharing experiences in itself could be therapeutic for them.

Metacognitive thinking

Different from positive self-talk, metacognitive thinking happens mostly within the internal thoughts of the individual. Additionally, metacognition often involves reframing the situation, thinking about your thoughts and helping to change perceptions and consequently how a problem is approached and solved. Teachers can model this skill by speaking aloud when thinking through a problem or negative situation. This reinforces the metacognitive thinking skills and the thought process involved. For children and youths with disabilities, repeated explanations may be needed about important points and reasons for thinking in certain ways.

Getting adult help and fighting back

Resiliency is about triumphing over difficult situations. And when children and youths with disabilities face adversity that they feel they cannot manage, they must believe that they can find help nearby and if in school, teachers must provide for that need. Succumbing to bullying that often occurs to disabled people should not be an option. Feeling terrified of any situation, no matter how trivial it may be to the teacher or parent, should not be endured by the bearer alone. Especially for those with SID, they must be taught to find help and feel secure in the environment.

Research has shown that how these young people negotiate adversity is a critical element towards resiliency. No matter what their limitation may be, teachers have the potential to facilitate resiliency among children and youths with disabilities for long-term and sustained successful life trajectories. Understanding the resiliency framework could help in this endeavour.

Additionally, the interdependency between the internal and external resiliency factors is explicitly described by DuBois and Hirsch (2000). What this means for teachers and parents is that for the internal factors to be strong, the external factors must provide the optimum environment for them. The external resiliency factors should scaffold the challenged internal resiliency factors for youths with disabilities. Thus family members, friends, teachers, and other members of the community should be aware that they have an impact upon the degree of resiliency of young children and youths with (or without) disabilities in their community.

Role of resiliency factors in youth development

From time to time, most children and youths experience considerable stress, hardship, and misfortune as a result of various personal and/or situational experiences. While some of these children or youths may develop serious and long-term educational, psychological, and social problems, a greater number grow up to lead healthy and productive lives in adulthood.

As such, the developmental strengths that contribute to resiliency exist within the individual and through the situational and relational experiences related to family, peers, school, and community. In particular, the additive effects of both intrinsic and extrinsic strengths have shown that youths are able to cope with adversity more effectively than those that experience few of the developmental strengths.

Importance of resiliency and at-risk behaviours

Figure 17.2 shows how important resiliency factors/strengths are to youths (N = 6,000) in helping them to refrain from risk-taking behaviours. Resiliency Canada's research consistently demonstrates that youths with higher resiliency factors and developmental strengths are less likely to be involved in a number of risk-taking activities. The average number of 14 risk-taking behaviours from all youths surveyed are grouped by six strength categories (0–5, 6–10, 11–15, 16–20, 21–25, and 26–30). There are 18 general questions used that measure risk-taking behaviours such as substance abuse (alcohol, tobacco, and illegal drugs), antisocial behaviour, violence, school problems, and gambling.

Importance of resiliency and constructive behaviours

Figure 17.3 shows how important resiliency factors/strengths are to youths (N = 6,000) in helping them to engage in positive and constructive behaviours. Resiliency Canada's research consistently demonstrates that youths with higher resiliency factors and developmental strengths are more likely to be involved in a number of positive and constructive activities. The average number of 14 positive behaviours from all youths surveyed are grouped by six strength categories (0–5, 6–10, 11–15, 16–20, 21–25, and 26–30). There are 14 general questions used that measure the constructive indicators (succeeds in school, values diversity, helps others, maintains good health, volunteerism, exhibits leadership, resists danger, delays gratification, and overcomes adversity).

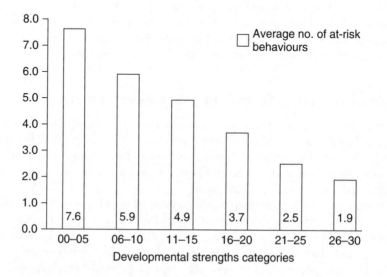

Figure 17.2 Degree of resilience and engagement in at-risk behaviours

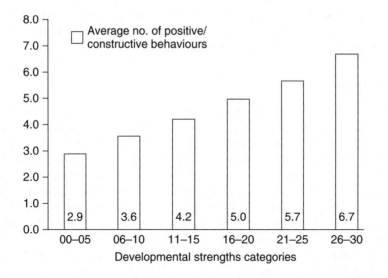

Figure 17.3 Degree of resilience and engagement in pro-social behaviours

Strength-based perspective reduces negative impact of stigma and labeling

Children and youths with disabilities often experience negative labeling and stig-matization by others. Not being within the physiological norm, children and youths with disabilities are often vulnerable to stigma and labeling. Research done by Hanun *et al.* (2011) found that these negative incidences can come from any segment of the external environment – family, peers, teachers, and the community. Their research also found that it harms the self-esteem, self-concept, and empower-ment of the recipients – important components of resiliency. In the development of a positive sense of self, the opinions of people who are deemed as significant or important are the ones that have the greater potential to affect the self-concept (Crocker and Quinn, 2003).

Numerous research has found that stigma and labeling inflicts low self-esteem and harms the self-concept of those affected (Marsh *et al.*, 2002; Martz, 2004; Mather and Ofiesh, 2006). Stigmatized disabled individuals also tend to experience the devaluation of character that can lead to feelings of isolation, estrangement and ostracization from the community, purposelessness, and especially if not working, a lack of self-worth (Martz, 2004; Davey and Keya, 2009).

The essence of a strength-based perspective is to perceive the individual as one who has good qualities and consciously aim to foster that positive feature. This standpoint is the opposite of the common deficit perspective which focuses on what is wrong or 'bad' in the person and then strive to reduce or eliminate that negative quality. As a function of their disabilities, this approach to fostering resiliency among these young people is even more crucial. Teachers and concerned members of the community can use the strategies mentioned above to assist the affected young people to navigate and overcome such adversities.

Conclusion

Within the process of normalization, youths with disabilities must learn how to successfully negotiate and triumph over life's adversities. This skill is crucial to afford them some degree of independence and subsequently enable these young people to assimilate and live as normal a life as possible among other members of their community. Intrinsic sources of risk factors which compound upon other environmental risk factors that are impacting upon young people with disabilities must be properly understood and adequately addressed during efforts to facilitate resiliency and normalization. A strength-based perspective as opposed to a deficit perspective should underlie all efforts to foster resiliency. The focus of care should be about collaboratively creating an "ecology of protective factors" around youths with disabilities that makes it increasingly difficult for the negative aspects and adversity of stigmatization to survive. The endeavor to facilitate resiliency among youths with disabilities would result in benefits for the community, the youths, and their families. Ultimately, understanding the resiliency processes whilst garnering all available resources would be fundamental in assisting young people with disabilities towards normalization and a better life trajectory in the future.

References

Bell, T. R. (2003) "Dear diary: The benefits of writing about your feelings". Online. Available at: http://www.healthandage.com/Dear-Diary-The-Benefits-of-Writing-about-Your-Feelings (accessed 15 October 2003).

Cohn, J. (2005) "Things I need to say: Keep a journal to keep in touch with who you are inside", *Current Health*, 1: 22–5.

Crocker, J. and Quinn, D. M. (2003) "Social stigma and the self: Meanings, situations, and self-esteem", in T. F. Heatherton, R. E. Kleck, M. R. Hebl and J. G. Hull (eds), *The Social Psychology of Stigma*, New York: Guilford Press, pp. 153–83.

Davey, G. and Keya, M. (2009) "Stigmatisation of people with mental illness in Bangladesh", *Mental Health Practice*, 13(3): 30–3.

DeVito, J. A. (2007) *The Interpersonal Communication Book*, 11th edn, New York: Pearson Education.

Donnon, T. and Hammond, W. (2007) "A psychometric assessment of the self-reported youth resiliency: Assessing developmental strengths questionnaire", *Psychological Reports*, 100: 963–78.

DuBois, D. L. and Hirsch, B. J. (2000) "Self-esteem in early adolescence: From stock to character to marquee attraction", *Journal of Early Adolescence*, 20(1): 5–11.

Forlin, C. and Chambers, D. (2011) "Teacher preparation for inclusive education: Increasing knowledge but raising concerns", *Asia-Pacific Journal of Teacher Education*, 39(1): 17–32.

Goldstein, S. and Brooks, R. B. (2006) *Handbook of Resilience in Children*, New York: Springer.

Hanun, N. A., Hammond, W. A. and Kamarulzaman, K. (2011) *Stigma and Protective Factors: A Study of Resilience among Youths with Disabilities*. MEd. Sultan Idris Education University, Malaysia.

Heydt, S. (2004) "Dear Diary: Don't Be Alarmed . . . I'm a Boy", *Gifted Child Today*, 27(3): 16–25.

Margalit, M. (2004) "Second-generation research on resilience–social–emotional aspects of children with learning disabilities", *Learning Disabilities Research and Practice*, 19(1): 45–8.

Marsh, H. W., Ellis, L. A. and Craven, R. G. (2002) "How do preschool children feel about themselves? Unraveling measurement and multidimensional self-concept structure", *Developmental Psychology*, 38: 376–93.

Martz, E. (2004) "A philosophical perspective to confront disability stigmatization and promote adaptation to disability", *Journal of Loss and Trauma*, 9: 139–58.

Mather, N. and Ofiesh, N. (2006) "Resilience and the child with learning disabilities", in S. Goldstein and R. B. Brooks (eds), *Handbook of Resilience in Children*, New York: Springer, pp. 239–56.

Seligman, M. (1990) *Learned Optimism: How to Change Your Mind and Your Life*, New York: Simon and Schuster/Pocket Books.

Smith, S. L. (2003) "What do parents of children with learning disabilities, ADHD, and related disorders deal with?", *LDA Newsbrief*, 38(4): 3–8, 16.

Spekman, H. J., Herman, K. L. and Vogel, S. A. (1993) "Risk and resilience in individuals with learning disabilities: A challenge to the field", *Learning Disabilities Research and Practice*, 8: 59–65.

Steele, C. M. (1995) "Stereotype threat and intellectual test performance of African Americans", *Journal of Personality and Social Psychology*, 69: 797–811.

Wood, J. T. (2010) *Interpersonal Communication: Everyday Encounters*, 6th edn, Boston, MA: Wadsworth, Engage Learning.

Winzer, M. (1996) *Children with Exceptionalities in Canadian Classrooms*, Ontario, Canada: Allyn and Bacon.

Ysseldyke, J. E. and Algozzine, B. (1984) *Introduction to Special Education*, Boston, MA: Houghton Mifflin Company.

Part III

Future directions

What is needed now?

Chapter 18

Future directions

What is needed now for effective inclusive teacher education?

Chris Forlin

Keywords: inclusion, teacher education, equity, accountability, standards, outcomes

Chapter overview

This chapter investigates the changed situation regarding future directions for preparing teachers for inclusion. A summary of the altered role for teachers and the expectations for them in regard to inclusive education are addressed. Two conflicting spheres of influence are raised whereby equity and accountability are considered as opposing pressures in preparing teachers for inclusion. An *Inclusive Wheel* is proffered as a metaphor for the interactive nature of many aspects of inclusion that need to be addressed simultaneously if teacher education is to be effective and to move forward.

Where are we now?

In recent years enormous transitions in ideas, expectations, and opportunities have occurred regarding the education of students with non-regular needs. Previously, students with specialized needs have been educated in segregated facilities, often categorically aligned so that they could be educated with peers having similar needs. Over the past 40 years there has been an evolution from segregated to inclusive placements, which has resulted in complex and often difficult changes in the way schools operate and in the expectations for teachers. Inclusive education, while initially focusing on providing for students with disabilities in mainstream schools, now encompasses a much broader designation that refers to all children who may have been historically marginalized from meaningful education, who come from varied multi-cultural and multi-diverse backgrounds, or who are at risk of not achieving to their potential (Forlin, 2010). This changed way of thinking has impacted more than anything on the task of teachers.

In many of the countries who have been involved with inclusion for some time, the expectations regarding implementing this effectively has made teaching very exigent, resulting in a teaching profession that is somewhat disillusioned and despondent with students also becoming disenfranchised with schooling, either dropping out or making life extremely disagreeable for their teachers (Rose and

Jones, 2007). In countries who are only recently embracing inclusion, many learners are receiving free education for the first time, resulting in the need to provide education for large numbers; frequently without a strongly developed infrastructure, and with teachers who are poorly trained and ill-equipped to deal with the students' diverse needs (Du Toit and Forlin, 2009).

Where are we headed?

Government and educational systems would seem currently to be in a dilemma regarding how to proceed with inclusion. There are two conflicting spheres of influence that they are trying to address which are in constant flux with each other. Both of these require sensitive and difficult decisions which rely heavily on the role of teachers to implement.

Focus on equity

The first sphere of influence is the international focus on equity. Many systems have tended to adopt a social justice and ethics-based approach to ensuring support for all learners, espousing the rights-based international Conventions to ensure equity of access and opportunity. These systems have developed policy and in some regions legislation that guarantees the right to education for all children. In some systems this process is embedded within a parent's right to select the type of school placement for their child, for example, in Ireland (Watson, 2009). In these instances, schools are legally obliged to accept all children and teachers are required to teach them.

In other systems, while they might espouse an inclusive educational approach in policy, this is not entrenched in law and parents do not have the final say in where their children are educated, as schools may refuse to accept some children for an inclusive schooling approach. Many school systems grapple with this distinction and even though they are increasingly being challenged to adopt a more inclusive approach, pressure from within schools themselves, teaching unions, and communities, often impact on the inclusivity of individual schools.

Accountability

The competing second sphere of influence is the increasing pressure placed on schools and school systems for accountability in improving the academic outcomes for students and ensuring that they achieve state, national, or federal standards. In the UK, for example, the national standards agenda has been a major force in shaping the direction taken by schools, although it has not necessarily been found to prevent an inclusive approach being adopted (Ainscow et al., 2006).

Within highly competitive systems schools have found great difficulty in balancing the inclusion of students with high support needs with the need for students to attain predetermined standards in literacy, numeracy, and science. A regime of target setting has resulted in an accountability culture that has raised tensions for schools (Ainscow et al., 2006). As schools endeavour to become more inclusive they are still required to achieve inflexible standards. In many instances teachers are judged on the results of their students, so there is little incentive for them to spend additional time with students who are unlikely to achieve good results. In addition, a willingness to offer places to students who demand higher levels of support may be compromised, thus limiting the options for students with special educational needs (SEN) to attend a school of their choice. Yet a review of research undertaken by Jordan *et al.* (2010) concluded that:

> Despite competing professional demands and variable resources, some teachers are able to cope with both high achievement standards and inclusive practices by espousing a belief system and adopting a series of instructional practices that are effective for all their students.
>
> (Jordan *et al.*, 2010, p. 264)

Considerable kudos is given to success in internationally comparable assessment scores and high stakes tests such as PISA. Even national assessments which are benchmarked to standards cause schools to become very focused on measurement and comparative results. According to a recent Australian report it is suggested that while there are many possible purposes for education in schools, very few are given priority when there are such high expectations for national testing (Reid *et al.*, 2011). The report further suggests that the government's commitment to choice and the promotion of independent competitive schools that compete within education markets is contradictory to goals of equity and the public purposes of education.

To ensure that schools are meeting the expectations of governments a range of monitoring approaches have been implemented. The enormous variation in accountability for the education of students is, nevertheless, apparent in many systems (e.g. House of Representatives Standing Committee on Education and Vocational Training, 2007; Lamb, 2009), with differences in procedures varying between and within countries and districts.

In many regions systemwide accountability is formalized through the use of external school inspectors whose role is to directly review provision for students with SEN. In the UK, for example, their *Framework for School Inspection* (Ofsted, 2009) recommends that school inspections should focus on three essential elements. In order to better meet the needs of parents of children with SEN, schools should provide parents with appropriate information to enable them to make informed decisions about the effectiveness of the schools they want their children to attend, or are already attending. In addition, the government should, through their accountability framework, ensure that minimum standards are being met. Third, school inspectors should assist in promoting the improvement of schools and the education system as a whole.

In order to achieve successful evaluation and ensure culpability at all levels, the *Lamb Report* (2009) made many recommendations based around school accountability for the education of students with SEN. One of these was directly related to the need for training in SEN and disability to be given to a wide range of people involved in all aspects of education for potentially vulnerable learners. This included recommendations (R) for training for the following groups: leaders in children's services (R4), all school improvement partners working with mainstream schools (R33), all inspectors (R34), members of independent appeals panels (R43), and tribunal chairs (R44). The *Lamb Report* suggested that it was important to maintain the same level of accountability for all students as less rigorous standards of accountability for different groups of children would convey a message to parents, schools, local authorities and others, that outcomes for these children have a lower priority than for others (Lamb, 2009, Item 24).

How can we achieve better teacher education for inclusion?

Given these two conflicting spheres of influence of supporting equity while achieving accountability, how can diverse regions around the globe ensure that teachers are appropriately prepared to establish and enact an inclusive educational approach that meets these ideals and ensures sustainability, has the support of all stakeholders, and provides a positive outcome for all involved? While this may already sound a difficult task to accomplish, it is further complicated in many instances by a lack of a suitable road map, conflicting expectations and demands regarding other innovations, and insufficient attention to the broad range of issues that need to be addressed. These combine to make implementation of inclusion highly challenging and even problematic for many education systems.

To implement an inclusive education system that will ensure equity and equal opportunities for all children and youths requires a range of initiatives to support the enactment of the philosophy. Legislation reinforced by appropriate policy is required not only to ensure equity of access but also to provide guidance to schools regarding their responsibility towards all learners. The development of effective inclusive schools requires a school to have the capacity for continuous problem-solving or response to intervention; application of universal curricula; effective child-focused pedagogies; alternative assessments; diverse outcomes; well-developed support structures; suitably trained teachers; accepting attitudes; multi-agency approaches; and above all, a school requires the flexibility to be able to make changes as needed to best meet the shifting diversity of their student population. Underpinning all of these is the key importance of the teacher whose role it is to implement such changes. These changes, though, are not limited to the role of teachers, but must also include all school staff in preparing them effectively for working in and embracing an inclusive school philosophy.

Even when good policy does exist, the translation of this into good practice that is sustainable and culturally and contextually appropriate is often underestimated for effective inclusion to occur. Being able to understand what this involves by viewing good practice examples is critical for governments and policy-makers. Based on collaboration between two key international organizations working in the field of inclusive education: the United Nations Educational, Scientific and Cultural Organization (UNESCO) and the European Agency for Development in Special Needs Education, a web resource was developed in 2010 for international and European policy-makers working to develop equity and equal opportunities within education systems globally. The examples of policy and practice illustrate the UNESCO *Policy Guidelines on Inclusion in Education* in a concrete way (see: http://www.inclu-sive–education–in–action.org/iea/).

There is an enormous amount written now about inclusion and there are plenty of websites, books, and research published about many aspects, as any search of the internet will acknowledge. There is still, though, limited research and exploration of preparation models needed for teachers to become inclusive practitioners. In particular, models of support that consider theory, research, and most importantly the practicality of implementation, are limited.

The Inclusive Wheel

This chapter presents an *Inclusive Wheel* as a metaphor for considering important aspects of inclusion that need to be addressed for the process to be successful (see Figure 18.1). The conceptualization of the development of inclusion in the

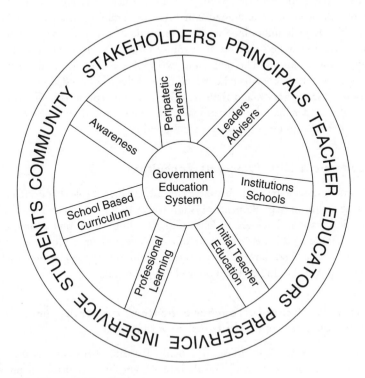

Figure 18.1 The Inclusive Wheel

Inclusive Wheel is grounded in the theory and research about inclusion and in partic-ular addresses the practical challenges faced by schooling systems, teachers, parents, and other stakeholders, as they attempt to support this approach. The focus in this discussion is those aspects of the wheel that are related to teacher preparation and the need for ongoing training and support.

The *Inclusive Wheel* uses a simple view of a wheel in motion to reflect the pro-cess of establishing and maintaining inclusive education as it advances forward. Its centrality is the driving force of the government or educational system. This initi-ates the development of the wheel and forms the foundation upon which all other elements are attached. In order to move forward, the wheel requires all aspects of inclusion to be addressed and these are represented by the spokes that join to the central hub. In turn these are surrounded on the rim by the range of stakeholders who will be affected by this process as the wheel gains momentum and rolls for-ward. For the wheel to move it must be balanced and secure and the spokes must be well aligned and firmly joined to both the central core and the rim. As it moves it will come into increasing contact with various stakeholders.

In the *Inclusive Wheel* there are seven spokes. Each of the spokes represents one aspect of inclusion that needs sufficient preparation for effective implementation. These symbolize the issues that governments, education systems, and schools will need to consider and plan for. As the wheel is circular these are not in any given order but all need to be addressed concurrently. Training of all stakeholders to become inclusive is undoubtedly a vital element of this process. Each of these groups forms a separate spoke on the *Inclusive Wheel* as each is critically important for supporting inclusion. The remaining two spokes focus on the students them-selves, through the school-based curriculum, and the links needed with the com-munity to raise awareness and facilitate a broader conception of inclusion that is considerably wider than the educational arena. There are, thus, five levels of staff training that need to occur involving the following.

1. Leaders/advisors: Principals, consultants

There is considerable research that identifies the significant role that principals play in leading inclusion (e.g. Harpell and Andrews, 2010). To facilitate this effectively requires leaders who have an in-depth understanding of the philosophy, exhibit positive attitudes and beliefs, are aware of the needs of their staff in implementing inclusive practices, and can take a proactive position to empower others to achieve. Greater emphasis should be placed on leadership training.

2. Institutions/schools: Teacher educators: University lectur-ers, teacher training institutions, or agencies

In regard to training for inclusion, the focus has mainly been on preparing prin-cipals, teachers, and other staff, and there has been little emphasis on preparing teacher educators to undertake this training. Yet these are vital players in providing this. Regions should revisit the role of teacher educators to ensure that their training needs are also being met. In Vietnam, for example, before they implemented training for teachers, a nationwide program was implemented to upskill all teacher educators so that they had the necessary skills, curriculum, and pedagogical knowledge to train teachers for inclusion (Forlin and Dinh, 2010). A similar model may be appropriate in many other regions.

3. Initial Teacher Education (ITE): Teachers in training, preservice undergraduate or postgraduate students

ITE would seem to be a critical time for preparing teachers to cater for diversity. Nonetheless, while many regions are now providing compulsory preparation in this essential area, there are many others who either choose to ignore this in lieu of other discipline demands, or who suggest that this is embedded within all of their practices (Forlin, 2010). There is, needless to say, a dearth of research on the efficacy of courses for preparing teachers for inclusion, and new graduates continue to suggest that they are inadequately prepared for the real world of schools and classrooms. This must be rectified if teachers are going to gain the most benefit from their training.

4. Professional learning: Teachers in practice; inservice teachers

For teachers who are already working in schools it is similarly critical that they are provided with access to relevant and evidence-based professional learning. Teachers must have the necessary skills and expertise to develop appropriate curriculum and implement effective pedagogies to meet all students' needs. The *Lamb Inquiry* suggests that all schools should plan to have at least one teacher who has expertise in the major areas of SEN to ensure appropriate identification and effective interventions can be developed. In many regions a specialist teacher is employed to take on this role (e.g. SENCO in the UK). An appropriate specialist model needs to be much more widespread if all regions are to meet the needs of all learners.

5. Peripatetic/parents: Other school staff, education assistants, visiting teachers, administrators, parents

Not only do principals and teachers need to be effectively prepared for inclusion, but likewise there are many other staff, parents, and the students themselves who require training about inclusion. Teachers have to work with a wide range of stakeholders; and this requires specific training in collaborative skills. In the UK, for example, the *Every Child Matters* legislation proposes that the involvement of children and parents should be fundamental to achieving appropriate outcomes and that this should occur through a multi-agency approach. Even so, throughout much of the Asia–Pacific region this approach has not been adopted. Parents traditionally avoid contact with schools; there is a lack of infrastructure to support a multi-agency approach; and almost no involvement of the children themselves in any decision making (Forlin, 2008). Greater emphasis is needed in this area.

Effective teacher education for inclusion in a global world

In the business world few employers would expect staff to initiate a new process without prior basic training in its development and implementation. Yet in teaching, new processes are constantly being initiated in a top-down decision without appropriate training for those who are to apply them. Not surprisingly then, this can cause angst and difficulty for schools. Teachers continue to voice that they are unprepared for inclusion; however, the foundation of an effective inclusive practice relies almost entirely upon the readiness of staff to implement it.

Support for better preparation of inclusive teachers has become a major focus in many regions, although strategies to improve this have not necessarily been implemented universally (Causton-Theoharis et al., 2007). In the UK, for example, there are already many new procedures put in place for ensuring that teachers are better prepared to cater for the needs of all learners. Building on the 'Quality First Teaching' philosophy, resources for SEN and disability for ITE and for teacher induction have been developed. Further, the recent Inclusion Development Programme is being disseminated throughout the UK. It is expected that these will significantly raise the awareness of new teachers about learners with SEN and disability and will enhance the capacity of schools to identify, assess, and provide for all children (Lamb, 2009).

The diversity of global situations is so extreme that it is impossible to provide a single response as to how teachers can be better prepared for inclusion. In many regions rapid industrial growth has resulted in a technological world where access to further training is expected in an 'anywhere, anytime, anyway' mode. In these situations, the use of the internet to obtain information is part of life for many people. To cater for this, service providers are increasingly offering online modulized courses where materials can be provided through the establishment of virtual learning communities (e.g. Bartolo, 2010).

In many regions where education systems are well established and functioning effectively, a systemic approach has been taken to prepare teachers. Regardless, this still has the potential for enormous variation between the range of providers employed to administer the training. For example, in Hong Kong a five-year system directed training program in skills for supporting students with SEN has seen considerable funding dedicated to this and intensive courses providing teaching relief to enable teachers to participate (Forlin and Sin, 2010). It is estimated that approximately 25 per cent of all teachers will have received basic training about inclusion by 2012 (G. Lai, personal communication, March 12, 2012). In the UK and Australia, conversely, funding for training has been mainly devolved to schools. A large number of credited local trainers have thus emerged within a competitive market for highly sought after, and in some instances quite lucrative, training roles. Only some of this training is accredited and the availability varies widely (Lamb, 2009).

Conclusion

To ensure support for the changing role of teachers, a public and community awareness program is also important and should be developed concomitantly with teacher training. People fear what they do not know, and this is often the case with inclusion. If support is to be gained from stakeholders they need to have an understanding about the proposed process and an opportunity to raise questions and to discuss expected outcomes. An inclusive education system cannot work in isolation. While education can take a leading role, it needs to be supported by the development of a more inclusive society if it is to be maintained and sustainable in the long term. Future directions for inclusive teacher education, therefore, must be founded on a critical evaluation of current practices as they apply within discrete jurisdictions. Teacher training provides three spokes of the *Inclusive Wheel* and is unmistakably critical to the success of inclusion. It cannot, however, enable an effective inclusive approach if the other four spokes are not similarly and concurrently addressed. Careful consideration should be given to models of training that best meet the needs of teachers for the type of inclusive education to be offered.

Good teacher preparation and ongoing professional learning must be undertaken by highly skilled educators who have not only the theoretical knowledge and the practical skills, but also a very clear understanding of the rapidly changing role of teachers and the challenges they face with implementing an inclusive pedagogy. Knowledgeable, empathetic, and effective teacher educators are required to support teachers to become inclusive practitioners. Suitable training or education is, therefore, required at all levels, ranging from teacher educators, to school leaders, teachers, and paraprofessionals. The education of other stakeholders such as parents and the community are also essential to facilitate a smooth transition to an effectual inclusive approach to education. If we are to develop and maintain quality education for all students, then innovative, relevant, and evidence-based inclusive teacher education is fundamental to move the inclusive wheel in the right direction.

References

Ainscow, M., Booth, T. and Dyson, A. (2006) "Inclusion and the standards agenda: Negotiating policy pressures in England", *International Journal of Inclusive Education*, 10(4–5): 295–308.

Bartolo, P. (2010) "Teacher education online: Towards inclusive virtual learning communities", in C. Forlin (ed.), *Teacher Education for Inclusion: Changing Paradigms and Innovative Approaches*, London: Routledge, pp. 120–9.

Causton-Theoharis, J. N., Theoharis, G. T. and Trezek, B. J. (2007) "Teaching pre-service teachers to design inclusive instruction: A lesson planning template", *International Journal of Inclusive Education*, iFirst Article, pp. 1–19.

Du Toit, P. and Forlin, C. (2009) "Cultural transformation for inclusion: What is needed? A South African Perspective", *School Psychology International*, 30(6): 644–66.

Forlin, C. (2008) "Education reform for inclusion in Asia: What about teacher education?", in C. Forlin and M.-G. J. Lian (eds), *Reform, Inclusion and Teacher Education: Towards a New Era of Special Education in the Asia-Pacific Region*, London: Routledge, pp. 61–73.

Forlin, C. (2010) "Teacher education for inclusion", in R. Rose (ed.), *Confronting Obstacles to Inclusion: International Responses to Developing Inclusive Schools*, London: Routledge, pp. 155–70.

Forlin, C. and Dinh, N. T. (2010) "A national strategy for supporting teacher educators to prepare teachers for inclusion", in C. Forlin (ed.), *Teacher Education for Inclusion: Changing Paradigms and Innovative Approaches*, London: Routledge, pp. 34–44.

Forlin, C. and Sin, K. (2010) "Developing support for inclusion: A professional learning approach for teachers in Hong Kong", *Journal of Whole Schooling*, 6(1): 7–26.

Harpell, J. V. and Andrews, J. J. W. (2010) "Administrative leadership in the age of inclusion: Promoting best practices and teacher empowerment", *The Journal of Educational Thought*, 44(2): 189–210.

House of Representatives Standing Committee on Education and Vocational Training (2007) *Top of the Class: Report on the Inquiry into Teacher Education*, Canberra: The Parliament of the Commonwealth of Australia.

Jordan, A., Glenn, C. and McGhie-Richmond, D. (2010) "The Supporting Effective Teaching (SET) project: The relationship of inclusive teaching practices to teachers' beliefs about disability and ability, and about their roles as teachers", *Teaching and Teacher Education*, 26: 259–66.

Lamb, B. (2009, December) *Lamb Inquiry: Special Educational Needs and Parental Confidence*, Department of Children's Services and Families, DCSF–01143–2009.

Ofsted (2009) *The Framework for School Inspection: The Framework for School Inspection in England under Section 5 of the Education Act 2005, from September 2009*, London: Ofsted.

Reid, A., Cranston, N., Keating, J. and Mulford, B. (2011) *Exploring the Public Purposes of Education in Australian Primary Schools*, Melbourne: Australian Government Primary Principals Association.

Rose, R. and Jones, K. (2007) "The efficacy of a volunteer mentoring scheme in supporting young people at risk", *Journal of Emotional and Behavioural Difficulties*, 12(1): 3-14.

Watson, S. F. (2009) "Barriers to inclusive education in Ireland: The case for pupils with a diagnosis of intellectual and/or pervasive developmental disabilities", *British Journal of Learning Disabilities*, 37: 277–84.

Chapter 19

Interregional discussions around inclusive curriculum and teachers in light of the 48th International Conference on Education

Renato Opertti, Jayne Brady and Leana Duncombe

Keywords: inclusive curriculum, inclusive policy, UNESCO, international conference on education, personalisation, competency-based approaches

Chapter overview

"Curriculum is without a doubt one major area that can foster development of inclusive education or, in the worst case, can be a barrier for inclusion" (Halinen and Savolainen, 2009, p. 2). The consensus around the 48th UNESCO International Conference on Education (ICE) reflected a key role for both teachers and curriculum in moving towards inclusive education systems, as well as the importance of equipping teachers with the appropriate skills and materials to teach diverse learners. This chapter aims to elaborate upon the interregional discussions which have emerged around inclusive curricula and teachers, in light of the 48th UNESCO International Conference on Education (ICE), with a view to democratising learning opportunities. The overall objective of this chapter is to provide a means of furthering debate and investigation around the future direction of teacher education for inclusion.

Key conceptual understandings in light of the 48th ICE

At the beginning of the twenty-first century, UNESCO defined inclusive education as "a process of addressing and responding to the diversity of needs of all learners through increasing participation in learning, cultures and communities, and reducing exclusion within and from education" (UNESCO, 2009a, p. 8). This definition moves away from traditional understandings of inclusive education as the sum of piecemeal initiatives and efforts in favour of specific groups or targeted categories, towards an understanding of inclusive education as a means to provide quality lifelong learning opportunities for all learners, where equity and quality go hand in hand.

A broadened concept of inclusive education is a process of strengthening the capacity of an education system to reach out to all learners. In particular, this process implies learning how to engage with and value diversity, and how diversity between individuals and groups can foster learning, as well as strengthen education systems, communities and societies towards the attainment of more inclusive and cohesive societies.

Teachers, amongst other stakeholders, have been seen to play a key role in this process. In line with this, teacher education should equip teachers with "the appropriate skills and materials to teach diverse student populations and meet the diverse learning needs of different categories of learners through methods such as professional development at the school level, preservice training about inclusion, and instruction attentive to the development and strengths of the individual learner" (UNESCO-IBE, 2008).

Equally, an inclusive curriculum has been identified as a crucial tool for inclusion and the central means by which the principle of inclusion could be put into action within an education system (UNESCO, 2009a). The outcomes of the 48th UNESCO International Conference on Education (ICE) also describe the key characteristics of an inclusive curriculum, i.e. flexible, relevant and adjustable to the diverse characteristics and needs of lifelong learners.

Inclusive curriculum and teachers

UNESCO-IBE perceives the curriculum as a mirror of the complex interfaces of society, politics and education within political and policy discussions and agreements of a variety of stakeholders (Braslavsky, 1999). Thus, an inclusive curriculum reflects the kind of inclusive society to which we aspire, i.e. one which ensures more equitable distribution of opportunities and the elimination of poverty and marginality.

Amongst these diverse stakeholders, teachers play a key role and have a direct impact on how new curricula are implemented, as well as how knowledge, skills, attitudes and values are shared and assessed. The curriculum has thus been defined "as a dense and flexible contract between politics/society and teachers" (Braslavsky, 1999, p. 10). From this perspective, the curriculum can be seen as both a policy and technical issue involving multiple stakeholders from inside and outside the education system, as well as a continuous and dynamic development of learning processes and outcomes.

In providing some concrete examples of an inclusive curriculum, the ICE outcomes recommend inclusive learning environments which encourage the active role and the participation of learners, effective and flexible curriculum frameworks that accommodate local contexts and diversify pedagogical practices, stronger links between schools and society, as well as the use of information and communication technologies in classrooms. These recommendations clearly reflect growing expectations with regard to teachers' roles, particularly in connection with issues of diversity and inclusion; teachers are now expected to have much broader roles, taking into account the individual development of children and young people, the management of learning processes in the classroom, the development of the entire school as a "learning community" and connection with the local community and the wider world (OECD, 2005).

As such, an inclusive curricular perspective of teachers implies a considerable reconceptualisation of teachers' attitudes, role and competencies, and therefore has important implications for the future direction of teacher education for inclusion. An understanding of this reconceptualisation must be developed by the teachers themselves and by other educational stakeholders if it is to be reflected in the education system as a whole. Some of the core dimensions of an inclusive curriculum and the implications for teachers and teacher education are outlined below.

Interregional discussions around inclusive curriculum

In general terms, the role of the curriculum can be seen around five key dimensions: (a) a definition of the outcomes and guiding principles for education; (b) an operationalisation of pedagogical and administrative action plans at the core of the education system; (c) a means to ensure the coherence and consistency of educational and administrative action plans and those of educational activities in relation to the intended educational aims and purposes; (d) a way to facilitate the development and training of people within their context; and (e) an adaptation of the education system in relation to an educational project, as well as with respect to society and the world (Jonnaert *et al.*, 2009).

An inclusive curriculum aims to strongly support an understanding of student diversities as enhancing and democratising learning opportunities around all five of these dimensions. It combines the density and strength of core universal concepts for addressing and guaranteeing their individual right to education. These include, for example, the value of diversity, the right to lifelong learning, comprehensive citizenship education, and the provision of options, flexibility and consideration for all learners within schools and classrooms.

It implies curricular provisions, settings, processes and content share common frameworks which at the same time provide tailored approaches towards the personal needs of all learners. Indeed, an inclusive curriculum does not imply a breaking-up of the education system nor the curriculum into smaller independent sub-units without any linkages between them. As articulated by Blanco:

> The key element of inclusion is not the individualisation but the diversification of the educational provision and the personalisation of common learning experiences . . . This implies advancing towards universal design, where the teaching–learning process and the curriculum consider from the very beginning the diversity of needs of all students, instead of planning on the basis of an average student and then carry out individualised actions to respond to the needs of specific students or groups who were not taken into consideration by an education proposal based on a logic of homogeneity instead of diversity.
>
> (Blanco, 2009, p. 14)

In more specific terms, interregional discourse around an inclusive curriculum has tended to concentrate on four main concerns, namely: the focus of the curriculum;

the purpose of the curriculum; the relationship between national, local and school interests; and the question of how to effectively support the development of the curriculum. Of particular relevance to teachers and teacher education are issues regarding the purposes of an inclusive curriculum, understanding and supporting the learning process of every student and supporting the development of an inclusive curriculum.

The purposes of an inclusive curriculum

One main concern in discussions around inclusive curriculum has focused on the fundamental purposes underlying an inclusive curriculum, namely as a tool for inclusion in the education system as a whole. Indeed, the national vision of the curriculum and its expression in an appropriate framework informs critical decisions with respect to other levels and dimensions of the system. As such, defining the purposes of an inclusive curriculum has been seen across many regions as a key foundation for educational concerns and reforms, in terms of policies, curriculum philosophy and content, classroom methodology and teacher education and professional development (UNESCO-IBE, 2009a). For example, in the Arab States curriculum development in the area of social studies has been central to all aspects of educational reform, in order to reflect the new political and social realities of the region (World Bank, 2008).

It has also supported the diversification of teaching methods and learning materials to address the cultural, social and individual diversities of all learners, while incorporating the multiple levels (i.e. global, national, local and school levels) and dimensions involved in the process. In Finland, the purposes of an inclusive curriculum have been to provide a common learning process and an empowering pedagogical tool for teachers to ensure that the opportunities provided for learning are relevant to all learners within the community of a class or school (Halinen, 2010).

Understanding and supporting the learning process of every student

Another main concern raised has been the importance of understanding and supporting the learning process of every student. This implies developing curriculum frameworks that understand how learners learn in different ways and have different needs with regard to curricular goals, contents, time, methods, materials, learning environments, as well as supports, and assessment, amongst other things. In particular, this means increasing participation in the learning processes – not just who gets to be included, but how – and re-assessing what is recognised as achievement in a learning community. It also means that teachers need to take into account the learners' own thinking about what to do next, as well as their own professional ideas and judgements based upon the learner to help them participate freely and actively in class.

In China, for example, the new school-based curriculum reform is attempting to better stimulate the active engagement of learners through collaboration and peer coaching, while encouraging students to address and resolve problems through open discussion with teachers. It also aims to develop more democratic relationships between teachers and students, with teachers playing a more facilitative role. The reform also provides for alternative assessment criteria and techniques in the traditional exam-oriented system (UNESCO-IBE, 2010).

Indeed, this conceptualisation implies that learners are at the centre of all considerations of teaching and learning processes, and attention must be paid to the individuality of learners and their participation and progress as learners. A key challenge has proved to be how to focus on enriching and extending what is ordinarily available to everyone through specialised teaching and learning supports. In the case of Scotland, Florian (2010) provides evidence that the effective deployment of additional resources that traditionally accompany learners identified as having 'special educational needs' support the learning of everyone, and specialists and regular teachers are encouraged to develop creative, new, collaborative and flexible ways of working that support all learners.

It is also seen as important to understand, identify and remove barriers to participation and learning within school communities. Across many regions, the way the formal education systems are structured has been shown to be a huge barrier to participation and learning within school communities. Indeed, a strong hierarchical separation between primary and secondary education, between lower and upper secondary education, and between general and technical disciplines creates interruptions and discontinuities in learning (UNESCO-IBE, 2009b).

Equally, assessment standards and techniques have been perceived as a key barrier to inclusion. Inclusive curriculums should aim to be responsive to learners' needs, therefore assessment should be performed and measured along these same inclusive values. Although many countries use national summative assessment methods, evidence suggests that this approach may not explain learning processes to learners, nor encourage them to improve and progress within the educational system. In the Latin American context, Magendzo has recommended a formative and diagnostic approach, noting that, "from failure there is no learning" (UNESCO-IBE, 2009b). In China, there have been reforms aimed at taking students' well-being and healthy development into account in assessments, instead of just academic credits alone.

Supporting the development of the curriculum

A final, overarching concern that emerges from the international discourse on inclusive curriculum is the importance of understanding how the curriculum interacts with other elements of the education system, and how, as a consequence, an inclusive curriculum must be supported and empowered by education systems as a whole, for example in terms of curricular approaches, as well as teachers and teacher education.

According to Roegiers (2010), greater attention should be given to curriculum engineering as providing the bases and foundations of curriculum design, and more specifically, as guiding the selection of curricular approaches which can make positive and lasting differences in learning processes and outcomes. Within this vision, curricular approaches emerge as a cross-cutting dimension to syllabi development, and also encompass teaching pedagogies and assessment, which have been traditionally addressed outside the domain of curriculum.

Equally, across all regions, research findings show that the key factor for good learning outcomes is not only what is taught but how it is taught. For example, the quality of teaching can have a much more significant role in determining the learning outcomes of students than other often mentioned challenges for quality, like class size or class heterogeneity (Halinen and Savolainen, 2009). As a result, in China, the Netherlands and South Africa, amongst other countries, effective professional development now aims at educating teachers to develop curricula as well as knowledge, skills and teaching approaches for diverse learners, e.g. using individual learning plans to support students' welfare and development, building teacher communities and leaders, as well as creating links back to research and other policies in terms of feedback and evaluation (UNESCO-IBE, 2010).

Indeed, it has been recommended that teachers should feel supported as well as challenged in relation to their responsibility to keep exploring and developing effective ways of enhancing the learning of all students. In particular, teachers need to be recognised, engaged and supported to be professional curriculum co-developers, whose confidence, competencies, knowledge and positive attitudes can invaluably reinforce the principles of inclusion and inclusive curricula (Opertti et al., 2009).

However, in several regions, teachers are not free to creatively adapt the curriculum based on local or individual needs due to a strict curriculum that dictates everything from the content of teaching and learning up to the everyday work in the classrooms. In some contexts, such creativity is even directly forbidden and differentiation from the expected is sanctioned by inspectors, even if it seems evident that the national level curriculum does not fit well with the local culture and conditions (Halinen and Savolainen, 2009).

At the same time, in most regions of the world many teachers are still undertrained, under-paid and work in difficult conditions. There have been numerous calls for governments to value and support the teaching profession through teacher education for inclusion and improve their working conditions (UNESCO, 2009b). Many of the new expectations and recommendations about inclusive teachers have not necessarily been considered in the principles of curricular reform, e.g. in school curricular content and timings, which has put pressure on teachers, as well as on their relationship with learners.

Moreover, even in regions where teachers are trained, there is often a mismatch between the basic and secondary curriculum and teacher education curricula. In most countries, preparation of a national curriculum is the task of the Ministry of Education, whereas the responsibility for designing teacher education curricula may be left with academic institutions or different departments. One example can be found in the current emphasis on wider competencies in curriculum, but the continuing focus on subject-based knowledge in teacher education curricula.

As a result, the competency-based approach may contrast considerably with how teachers have been trained in terms of subject knowledge and the definition of learning outcomes (Halinen and Savolainen, 2009).

Along these lines, teacher education needs to be more forward thinking and focus on preparing teachers to cater for multicultural and diverse school populations (Forlin, 2010). For example, the OECD have recommended that "teacher profiles need to encompass strong subjective matter knowledge, pedagogical skills, the capacity to work effectively with a wide range of students and colleagues, to contribute to the school and profession and the capacities to continue developing" (OECD, 2005). These profiles should guide both pre- and inservice training, as well as continuous professional development.

Forging the agenda around teacher education from an inclusive curricular perspective

In summary, the understanding of an inclusive curriculum as addressing the expectations and needs of all learners can be an effective way to reflect upon various core curricular dimensions and re-consider teachers' attitudes, role and competencies, with a view to democratising learning opportunities. More broadly, it may also help to connect teachers' efforts towards inclusion with those of the entire education system and help teachers to find new ways of working together, across different dimensions, levels and regions. It clearly also has important implications for the current and future direction of teacher education for inclusion.

Changing teacher education is key to laying the foundation for teachers as curriculum co-developers, reflective and accountable professionals as well as lifelong learners. We identify five main issues in restructuring teacher education and its implications:

1. Inclusion and diversity should be crosscutting dimensions of the teacher education curricula, and indeed permeate the syllabus all along its design and development. Issues around inclusion and diversity should not be considered as "thematic units" to add to the curricula. Quite to the contrary, they are crucial to understanding learners in a holistic way and to facilitate for them an effective opportunity to learn. For example, in regards to the ways learners learn, it is important to search for each learner's potential and how they can relate to each other and provide mutual support (i.e. by acting as tutors). Findings from neuroscience and cognitive psychology can progressively inform the teaching and the learning processes, and can lead to a more personalised education based on inclusive principles and orientations.

2. Strengthen training in teacher education curricula and in teacher professional development, with regards to diversity of learning processes and how they can lead to the achievement of pertinent and relevant outcomes. This should include understanding and making available criteria and tools to effectively respond to the wide range of learners' conditions and styles encountered in schools that are increasingly heterogeneous.

3. Assuming the challenges around the development of an inclusive pedagogy in teacher education (Forlin, 2010), institutes must include two key elements: (i) respond to teacher needs and strengthen their self-esteem with regards to working in increasingly diverse multicultural contexts; and (ii) promote to teachers that students come from different ethnic, social and cultural backgrounds and identities.
4. Strengthen institutional, curricular, pedagogical and teacher coordination amongst basic/secondary education and teacher education. The lack of coordination among these levels has constituted a relevant bottleneck in developing processes of education and curricular reform in basic and secondary education. For example, it happens sometimes that at the level of basic education the educational system is leading towards more inclusive approaches, while in teacher education special education remains as a separate track/provision.
5. Teacher education should be seen as the initial stage of permanent teacher professional development, and should provide ample opportunities to reflect and debate around inclusive ideas and approaches, as any change moving towards inclusion entails profound mindset and practice transformations. Inclusive approaches are made up of a combination of values and attitudes as well as knowledge and competencies. It implies working under a long-term vision of educational change.

In summary, teacher education aims to enable the teacher's role and empowerment, enhance their competencies and support customised learning to the specificity of each learner within a diversity of contexts. Rethinking teacher education implies rethinking the education system, and in particular how inclusive or exclusive its visions and practices are. The revision of the teacher education curricula is indeed a societal construction and development, involving key stakeholders from inside and outside the educational system.

Teachers should not be involved in delivering a new paradigm of inclusion without being engaged in building up its rationale, aim, strategies and contents. Empowering teachers to be truly inclusive of all learners requires a foundation of educational systems seen as a wide, strong and flexible range of learning environments and provisions that facilitate personalised learning opportunities, demonstrating respect and care for the diversity of groups and individuals.

References

Blanco. R. (2009) "Conceptual framework of inclusive education", in C. Acedo, M. Amadio and R. Opertti (eds), *Defining an Inclusive Education Agenda: Reflections around the 48th Session of the International Conference on Education*, Geneva, Switzerland: UNESCO-IBE, pp. 11–20.

Braslavsky, C. (1999) "Los conceptos estelares de la agenda educativa en el cambio de siglo [Key concepts on the educational agenda at the turn of the century]", in C. Braslavsky (ed.) *"Re-haciendo escuelas: un nuevo paradigma en la educación latinoamericana [Remaking Schools: Towards a New Paradigm in Latin American Education]"*, Buenos Aires: Santillana.

Florian, L. (2010) "The concept of inclusive pedagogy", in F. Hallett and G. Hallett (eds), *Transforming the Role of the SENCO*, Buckingham: Open University Press, pp. 61–72.

Forlin, C. (2010) "Reframing teacher education for inclusion", in C. Forlin (ed.), *Teacher Education for Inclusion: Changing Paradigms and Innovative Approaches*, New York: Routledge, pp. 3–12.

Halinen, I. (2010) "Developing and implementing inclusive curriculum", *UNESCO Inter-regional and Regional Expert Meeting on Inclusive Education and Curricula*, Beirut, Lebanon, 26–28 May.

Halinen, I. and Savolainen. H. (2009) *E-forum Discussion Paper on Inclusive Education and Inclusive Curriculum*, Geneva: UNESCO-IBE.

Jonnaert, P., Ettayebi, M. and Defise, R. (2009) *Curriculum et compétences: un cadre opérationnel* [*Curriculum and Competencies: An Operational Framework*], Brussels: De Boeck Université.

OECD, Organisation for Economic Co-operation and Development (2005) *Attracting, Developing and Retaining Effective Teachers – Final Report: Teachers Matter*, Paris: OECD.

Opertti, R., Brady, J. and Duncombe, L. (2009) "Moving forward: Inclusive education as the core of education for all", *Prospects, Open file: Inclusive Education*, 151: 205–14.

Roegiers, X. (2010) *Pedagogy of Integration. Education and Training Systems at the Heart of Our Societies*, Brussels: DeBoeck University.

UNESCO, United Nations Educational, Scientific and Cultural Organization (2009a) *Policy Guidelines on Inclusion in Education*, Paris: UNESCO.

UNESCO, United Nations Educational, Scientific and Cultural Organization (2009b) *Education for All: Global Monitoring Report 2010: Reaching the Marginalized*, Paris: UNESCO; Oxford: Oxford University Press.

UNESCO-IBE, United Nations Educational, Scientific and Cultural Organization, International Bureau of Education (2008) *Conclusions and Recommendations of the 48th Session of the International Conference on Education (ED/BIE/CONFINTED 48/5)*, Geneva: UNESCO-IBE.

UNESCO-IBE, United Nations Educational, Scientific and Cultural Organization, International Bureau of Education (2009a) *Training Tools for Curriculum Development: A Worldwide Resource Pack*, Geneva: UNESCO-IBE.

UNESCO-IBE, United Nations Educational, Scientific and Cultural Organization, International Bureau of Education (2009b) *E-forum on "From Inclusive Education to Inclusive Curricula – 26 October–13 November"*, Geneva: UNESCO-IBE.

UNESCO-IBE, United Nations Educational, Scientific and Cultural Organization, International Bureau of Education (2010) "Mission report of presentations", *Chinese–European Conference on Curriculum Development*, Beijing, China, 12–16 April.

World Bank (2008) *The Road Not Traveled: Education Reform in the Middle East and North Africa*, Washington, DC: World Bank.

Chapter 20

Teacher education for inclusion in Europe

Challenges and opportunities

Amanda Watkins and Verity Donnelly

Keywords: Initial Teacher Education (ITE); inclusive education; policy for ITE; models of ITE; European approaches; policy recommendations

Chapter overview

This chapter sets out to discuss the current policy agenda for Teacher Education for Inclusion in Europe and outline how this presents both challenges, but also clear opportunities for development. It presents information from:

- European Union policies for education that impact upon the education of all European teachers;
- The European Agency for Development in Special Needs Education project focussing upon Teacher Education for Inclusion (TE4I) to highlight some of the opportunities and challenges within its member countries in addressing the agenda indicated by European-level policies.

Introduction

Teacher education issues are high on the policy agenda across Europe. The *United Nations Convention on the Rights of People with Disabilities* (United Nations, 2006) is gaining momentum and providing a force for change. Article 24 covers many aspects of education and makes reference to a growing body of evidence that shows that inclusive education not only provides the best educational environment for learners with disabilities, but helps break down barriers and challenge stereotypes relating to all learners who are vulnerable to exclusion. In highlighting steps to be taken in making the transition from a school system relying on special education to an inclusive system, the convention highlights the need to train all teachers to teach in inclusive classrooms and encourage them to support each other. This conclusion is supported by many other communications at the international as well as European level.

The European policy agenda on teacher education for meeting diverse needs

How teachers are prepared to meet the challenges of increasing diversity within education is currently a key area of policy debate at the European level. The Commission communication, *Improving the Quality of Teacher Education (3/08/2007)*, calls for different policy measures on the level of member states in order to adapt the profession to meet the new challenges of the knowledge-based economy. It states:

> Changes in education and in society place new demands on the teaching profession . . . classrooms now contain a more heterogeneous mix of young people from different backgrounds and with different levels of ability and disability . . . These changes require teachers not only to acquire new knowledge and skills but also to develop them continuously.
>
> (Commission of the European Communities, 2007, p. 4)

It also suggests that: "Teachers have a key role to play in preparing students to take their place in society and in the world of work" (Commission of the European Communities, 2007, p. 13) and points out that, in particular, teachers need the skills necessary to:

- Identify the specific needs of each individual learner, and respond to them by deploying a wide range of teaching strategies;
- Support the development of young people into fully autonomous lifelong learners;
- Help young people to acquire the competences listed in the European Reference Framework of Key Competences;
- Work in multicultural settings (including an understanding of the value of diversity, and respect for difference); *and*
- Work in close collaboration with colleagues, parents and the wider community.

Further to this, in the *Conclusions of the European Council of 15 November 2007 on improving the quality of teacher education*, Ministers responsible for education agreed amongst other things, that teachers should:

- Possess pedagogical skills as well as specialist knowledge of their subjects;
- Be able to teach using a competency-based approach and to teach effectively in heterogeneous classes;
- Engage in reflective practice and research;
- Be autonomous learners in their own career-long professional development.

The *Communication from the Commission on Improving Competences for the 21st Century: An agenda for European cooperation in schools (03/07/2008)* also highlights the need for initial teacher training to improve the balance between theory and practice and to present teaching as a problem-solving or research-in-action activity linked more to children's learning and progress. This assertion is developed in the *European Parliament resolution on improving the quality of teacher education (23/09/2008)*, which recognises that:

> the challenges faced by the teaching profession are increasing as educational environments become more complex and heterogeneous; [due to] the increasingly diverse mix of students in many schools . . . and the need to pay more attention to the learning needs of individual pupils.
>
> (European Parliament, 2008, p. 1)

The Council of the European Union conclusions on the professional development of teachers and school leaders (6 November 2009) state that:

> the knowledge, skills and commitment of teachers, as well as the quality of school leadership, are the most important factors in achieving high quality educational outcomes.
>
> (Council of the European Union, 2009, p. 6)

The Council conclusions add that no course of initial teacher education can equip teachers with all the competences they will require during their careers and note that the demands on the teaching profession are evolving rapidly, requiring teachers to reflect on their own learning requirements in the context of their particular school environment, and to take greater responsibility for their own lifelong learning.

In May 2009, the European Council of Education Minsters agreed a strategic framework for European co-operation in education and training for the period after 2010 – the *Education and Training 2020 (ET2020) Agenda*. The conclusions point out that greater efforts are required to implement the Council conclusions of November 2007 in which:

> Member States were invited to ensure a high standard of initial teacher education, to provide early career support and continuing professional development that is coordinated, coherent, adequately resourced and quality assured, to attract into the teaching profession – and endeavour to retain – the most able people, to tackle instances of poor performance, to support all pupils in making full use of their potential and to create school environments in which teachers learn from one another and which focus on improving student learning.
>
> (Council of the European Union, 2007, p. 4)

The various Council conclusions and responses from the European institutions present clear challenges for all EU member states, improving their initial and continuing teacher education systems and aligning them with a competency-based approach in order to ensure all teachers are adequately prepared to work in classrooms where they need to effectively meet a diverse range of students' needs.

The Agency project: TE4I

The European Agency for Development in Special Needs Education (the Agency) was established in 1996 by agreement between the Ministers of Education in member countries. The Agency is a permanent network of Ministerial representatives acting as the member countries' platform for collaboration regarding the promotion of quality and equity in education as a means to achieving social cohesion.

The Agency is maintained by the member countries (Austria, Belgium [Flemish and French speaking communities], Cyprus, Czech Republic, Denmark, Estonia, Finland, France, Germany, Greece, Hungary, Iceland, Ireland, Italy, Latvia, Lithuania, Luxembourg, Malta, Netherlands, Norway, Poland, Portugal, Slovenia, Spain, Sweden, Switzerland, United Kingdom [England, Northern Ireland, Scotland and Wales]) and is supported by the European Union Institutions, although it works independently from these institutions.

The developing co-operation between European policy makers in the area of teacher education is highlighting a range of common concerns and priority areas for future work. These form the basis for the current European Agency for Development in Special Needs Education project on Teacher Education for Inclusion (TE4I) (http://www.european-agency.org/agency-projects/teacher-education-for-inclusion).

The following key challenges were identified by Agency Representative Board members (RBs) and National Co-ordinators (NCs) as being of priority within the Teacher Education for Inclusion project: what kind of teachers do we need for an inclusive society in a twenty-first century school and consequently, what are the essential teacher competences for inclusive education? It was agreed the project would focus upon:

- The training of mainstream, general teachers and how they are prepared to work in inclusive settings; and
- The initial training phase as a priority.

The essential question for consideration is: how are all teachers prepared via their initial training to be 'inclusive'?

The fact that across Agency member countries there is so much agreement on priorities for teacher education presents a major opportunity – shared problems motivate collaborative working at both policy and practice levels. Such a collaborative approach has been the basis for the Agency project.

The project began in early 2009 and, following initial preparatory activities, the project has developed three activity 'tracks' involving 55 experts from 25 European countries. These experts – from policy and teacher education backgrounds – work collaboratively on the overall theme of how mainstream teachers are prepared via their initial training to be 'inclusive'.

International literature review

In order to put the Agency project activities into a wider context, an extensive review of literature has been undertaken and a review of international policy statements and a review of international literature are now available from: http://www. european-agency.org/agency-projects/teacher-education-for-inclusion.

The reviews were developed with input from representatives of the European Commission, DG Education and Culture, UNESCO International Bureau of Education and OECD-CERI. Most importantly, the review of research information covers inputs from experts from 18 countries participating in the Agency project. This research review provides information regarding changing conceptions of inclusion; the European context for teacher education for inclusion; policy frameworks to support teacher education for inclusion and effective practice in initial teacher education for inclusion with a focus on models of training, curriculum, teaching practice and assessment.

Country reports

Country information has been collected via a questionnaire in order to provide a description of the reality of teacher education situations in countries as well as information on practice that indicates ways forward/effective innovations.

All country information has been analysed to identify trends, similarities, challenges and features of innovative practice. This detailed country information is being used in different ways: English and, where available, country language versions of reports are available via the Agency website and the information has been put into a searchable thematic database of key topics. The information has also been used to prepare a project synthesis report (Donnelly, 2011).

Developing a profile of inclusive teachers

The Agency country representatives, via the initial country survey, requested information on the necessary competences, attitudes and standards required of and for all teachers working in inclusive settings in mainstream schools. This is a main concern also identified in the international documents and statements on priorities for teacher education.

A major task of the Agency project is to develop a profile of inclusive mainstream teachers that is based upon national-level information, but is then agreed upon at the European level. This profile being developed considers the following key aspects:

- What attitudes do mainstream teachers working in inclusive settings need?
- What knowledge and skills do they need?
- What initial training to develop both the above do they need?
- What are the implications for training all teacher trainers?

- What systemic changes are needed to allow them to implement their training?
- What policy framework is needed for all of the above to happen?

The *Profile of Inclusive Teachers* developed during the Agency project draws upon all of the information resources collected in the project. Mainly, however, it draws upon the discussions held with project experts that have been used to explore the debates regarding the competences that all teachers need to support their work in inclusive settings (Watkins, in press).

The remainder of this chapter outlines the content agreed upon to spring 2011 with regards to the development of a *Profile of Inclusive Teachers*. During 2011 the profile will be validated during a series of nine country study visits with a range of stakeholders in initial teacher education – students, teacher educators, policy makers, mainstream teachers and school leaders, parents and even learners with disabilities and special needs.

A values-based approach to inclusive education is essential

Inclusive education is an overarching concept impacting on different policies and implementation approaches in compulsory, higher education and teacher education. Inclusive education is concerned with all children and adults and is aimed at increasing individuals' meaningful participation in learning opportunities and reducing their exclusion from education and wider society.

The goals of inclusive education are achieved within settings and systems that value everyone equally and see schools as community resources that promote sustainability.

Inclusive education is essentially a principled, rights-based approach underpinned by a number of central values: equality, participation, developing and sustaining communities and respect for diversity. The values a teacher holds are an essential determinant of their actions.

The necessary starting point for exploring teachers' competences for inclusive education was therefore agreed within the project to be core values. These core values about teaching and learning for all learners are the foundation for acquiring knowledge, developing understanding and implementing skills for all teachers.

Model for *Profile of Inclusive Teachers*

The core values identified as essential for all teachers working in inclusive education are used as the basis for describing the areas of competence. These core values:

- are principles that can be evidenced in a teacher's actions;
- become 'theory enriched practical knowledge' through learning that occurs during teacher education course;
- express and demonstrate 'values in action' through the components of atti-

tudes, knowledge and skills.

Core values identified as essential for all teachers working in inclusive education are used as the basis for describing the areas of competence, which are made up of three elements: attitudes, knowledge and skills. A certain *attitude* or belief demands certain *knowledge* or a level of understanding and then *skills* in order to implement this knowledge in a practical situation.

The goal of the profile document is to outline the essential areas of competence that *all teachers* should acquire within their initial teacher education (ITE) to prepare them to work in inclusive settings.

Rationale for using areas of competence

It can be argued that the *Profile of Inclusive Teachers* document aims for ideals within ITE, but the Agency project experts believe the content is realistic and should be the goal for all ITE if the move towards inclusion is to be achieved across Europe. The following statements outline an agreed rationale for the proposed profile for teachers working in inclusive education.

1. The areas of competence for working in inclusive education are necessary for all teachers, just as inclusive education is the responsibility of all teachers. The areas of competence reinforce this critical message.
2. The areas of competence for inclusive education do not only focus upon meeting the needs of specific groups of learners (e.g. those with special educational needs); they provide all teachers with the foundations they need to work with learners with a diverse range of needs within a mainstream setting. The areas of competence therefore reinforce this critical message – that inclusive education is an approach for all learners, not just an approach for particular groups with additional needs.
3. The areas of competence identified for ITE in this document are the foundation of key attitudes, knowledge and skills that need to be built upon during induction and further teacher education opportunities. Clear progression routes are crucial and areas of competence must be seen as an integral part of a continuum of professional development, including specialist special needs education courses. These areas of competence should be continuously developed during every teacher's professional career.
4. The areas of competence all teachers need to work in inclusive settings are not in contradiction to the specialist education and training for special needs education teachers who may support mainstream teachers in their work. These areas of competence are the foundations for all teachers' work – generalists, specialists and experts.
5. The areas of competence identified in this profile are deliberately broad to support the development of teachers as lifelong learners and reflective practitioners through experiential learning and action-based research. The

model of ITE should focus on the development of learning and competence with a reduced emphasis on a content-based curriculum.

6. The areas of competence can support the professional development of student teachers and be a source of guidance to teacher educators.

7. The integration of the areas of competence for inclusive education within ITE needs to be debated with a wide range of stakeholders within different national situations and contexts. Through such dialogue, the areas of competence can potentially be a mechanism for reducing the disconnection that is thought to exist between classroom teachers and other stakeholders in education.

8. The areas of competence for inclusive education should be seen as one starting point for ITE course design/planning. The principle of inclusive education as a systemic approach should apply to ITE as well as school-based curricula.

Areas of competence for teachers working in inclusive education

Four core values have been identified as essential for all teachers working in inclusive education. These core values are used as the basis for describing the areas of competence all teachers require – the areas of competence linked to each of the four core values are presented in Table 20.1.

Table 20.1 Four core values underpinning areas of competence for inclusive education

Core value	Necessary areas of competence relate to
1. Valuing student diversity – student difference is considered as a resource and an asset to education	• Conceptions of inclusive education • The teacher's view of learner difference
2. Supporting all learners – teachers have high expectations for all learners' achievements	• Effective teaching approaches in heterogeneous classes • Promoting the academic and social learning of all learners
3. Working with others – collaboration and teamwork are essential approaches for all teachers	• Working with parents and families • Working with a range of other educational professionals
4. Continuing personal professional development – teaching is a learning activity and teachers must accept responsibility for their own lifelong learning	• Teachers as reflective practitioners • Initial teacher education as a foundation for ongoing professional learning and development

The possible usefulness of a profile document

During his keynote address at the project meeting in Zürich, Autumn 2011, Professor Tony Booth suggested that: "*The power we have as educators is to engage others in dialogue – that is all*". This insightful assertion essentially encapsulates the intentions of this profile document, i.e. engaging others in debate.

The profile document is not a final product that can be 'transplanted' into country contexts in some way. It has been developed in order to stimulate further debate in a way that may take policy makers and practitioners forward in their thinking.

There are many aspects of teacher education for inclusion highlighted within the document that require further examination:

- There is a developing, but still quite limited research base documenting how teachers working in inclusive settings are being, or should be prepared;
- Many European countries are debating the structure of ITE and considering where and by whom ITE should be delivered (universities and/or schools);
- Course structures and curriculum content are also being debated and revised in many countries.

In summary, what might be meant by effectiveness in ITE is being debated at national and international levels. It is, however, hoped that the *Profile of Inclusive Teachers* will contribute to the necessary discussion and can be used as a means of furthering debate and investigation in countries as well as at the European level.

Conclusion

The following points summarise some initial findings from the project policy and literature reviews, information from Agency member countries, and discussions with country-nominated experts during study visits:

- The reform of teacher education must be part of wider societal reform to support greater inclusion. This requires collaboration between policy makers to ensure a holistic approach and a recognition of the role of inclusive education as one of the main strategies to address the challenges of marginalisation and exclusion, as stated in the Dakar Framework for Action (UNESCO, 2000).
- Reform must include clarification of the language around inclusion and diversity and a clear understanding of the underpinning premises associated with and the implications of using different terminology. This should include a move away from the categorisation and 'labelling' of learners.
- Preparation for teaching must maintain academic rigour, 'educating' rather than 'training' teachers. The status of teachers must be raised and reinforced by the development of training parallel to other professional groups to ensure lifelong learning. In order to select appropriate teacher candidates and reduce drop out from training and teaching, further research is required to look at the

selection process, bearing in mind the need to increase diversity in the teacher workforce.

• There is a need for closer collaboration between training institutions and schools. Teacher educators should 'model' effective practice for student teachers in schools and during teacher education courses and use a wider range of more flexible methods of assessment, such as portfolios. Appropriate induction and training should be developed for teacher educators.

Action on these key points may go some way to addressing the continuing policy and practice priorities in the area. The Council of Europe (Arnesen *et al.*, 2009) states that quality in education implies an active recognition and appreciation of diversity with the process of inclusion transforming communities and schools to become 'diversity sensitive' rather than being seen as an 'add on' to existing structures. They say:

It is urgent that teachers in their classroom practices are able to see the individual behind group labels and to make constructive use of this diversity in developing new ideas and solutions which will increase the opportunities for recognition, equality, achievement and development for all.

(Arnesen *et al.*, 2009, p. 49)

Burns and Shadoian-Gersing (2010) note, "there is a serious challenge involved in changing practices and behaviour since, despite best intentions, the most common form of practice is that which has been observed and experienced personally" (p. 30).

Currently in Europe, however, an opportunity for real developments in the area of teacher education for inclusion can be seen via the fact that the Council of European Ministers for Education recognise the importance of all teachers in taking forward the inclusion agenda; an agenda that must be supported by coherent, long-term policies at the international, European and national levels for the inter-related areas of teacher education, curriculum, assessment and accountability. Such a political-level recognition provides the basis for developments towards teacher education for inclusion that would not otherwise be possible at the European level.

Acknowledgements

For more information on the Teacher Education for Inclusion project, or the work of the European Agency for Development in Special Needs Education, please contact Amanda Watkins: amanda@european-agency.org.

References

Arnesen, A., Allan, J. and Simonsen, E. (2009) *Policies and Practices for Teaching Socio-cultural Diversity – Concepts, Principles and Challenges in Teacher Education*, Paris: Council of Europe.

Burns, T. and Shadoian-Gersing, V. (2010) *Educating Teachers for Diversity: Meeting the Challenge*, Paris: OECD.

Commission of the European Communities (2007) *Communication from the Commission to the Council and the European Parliament: Improving the Quality of Teacher Education*. Online. Available at: http://ec.europa.eu/educatin/com392_en.pdf (accessed 19 August 2011).

Council of the European Union (2007) "Conclusions of the Council and of the Representatives of the Governments of the Member States, meeting within the Council of 15 November 2007, on improving the quality of teacher education", *Official Journal of the European Union* (2007/C 300/07). Online. Available at: http://eur–lex.europa.eu/LexUriServ/LexUriServ.do?uri=OJ:C:2007:300:0006:0009:EN:PDF (accessed 11 October 2011).

Council of the European Union (2009) "Council conclusions on the professional development of teachers and school leaders Brussels", *Official Journal of the European Union*, 302(04). Online. Available at: http://eur–lex.europa.eu/LexUriServ/LexUriServ.do?uri=OJ:C:2009:302:0006:0009:EN:PDF (accessed 19 August 2011).

Donnelly, V.J. (ed.) (2011) *Teacher Education for Inclusion Across Europe – Challenges and Opportunities*, Odense, Denmark: European Agency for Development in Special Needs Education. Online. Available at: http://www.european-agency.org/publications/ereports/teacher-education-for-inclusion-across-europe-challenges-and-opportunities/teacher-education-for-inclusion-across-europe-challenges-and-opportunities (accessed 23 February 2012).

European Parliament (2008) *European Parliament Resolution on Improving the Quality of Teacher Education 23/09/2008*. Online. Available at: http://www.europarl.europa.eu/sides/getDoc.do?type=TA&reference=P6–TA–20080422&language=EN (accessed 11 October 2011).

UNESCO (2000) "The Dakar framework for action: Education for all – Meeting our collective commitments", *World Education Forum*, Paris: UNESCO.

United Nations (2006) *Convention on the Rights of People with Disabilities*, New York: United Nations.

Watkins, A. (ed.) (in press) *Profile of Inclusive Teachers*, Odense, Denmark: European Agency for Development in Special Needs Education.

Chapter 21

The construction of an Institute–School–Community partnership of teacher education for inclusion

Kuen-fung Sin and Sin-yee Law

Keywords: catering for diversity, teacher education for inclusion, tripartite partnership, teacher empowerment, whole school approach, Institute–School–Community

Chapter overview

This chapter proposes an Institute–School–Community partnership of teacher education for addressing the needs of teacher education for inclusion. It is argued that although the Education Bureau (EDB) has organized different kinds of programs involving teacher education institutions and special schools to enhance the professional development of teachers, the lack of coordination among different parties reduces the effectiveness of that training. More importantly, teachers who have taken structured courses in catering for diversity at teacher education institutions still have great difficulty in implementing inclusive education at the school level because of the lack of acceptance of diversity in the schools. In addition to the community effort, it is suggested that collaboration among teacher education institutions, schools and the community is needed to work in the same direction to empower teachers to achieve the crucial mission of inclusive education.

Introduction

Three forms of inclusive education, the assimilation model, the accommodation model and the adaptation model, were identified in the process of development. In the early development of inclusive education in Hong Kong, the assimilation model was adopted in which students with special educational needs (SEN) were required to fit in with the school system. As time went by, schools adopted the accommodation model and the needs of students with SEN were better catered for. Currently, the EDB advocates the adaptation model, with the whole school approach to inclusive education in place. The practice is based on the philosophy of equality amongst all and mutual adaptation. Schools are now expected to cultivate the inclusive culture that takes diversity as a norm. Consequently, traditional models of teacher education that aim at equipping teachers with skills for catering for special needs have become outdated.

Challenges for professional training in catering for diverse learning needs

The challenges of inclusive education have been addressed in many reports and literature (UNESCO, 2005). Previous studies in Hong Kong criticized the sluggish development of inclusive education in Hong Kong (Crawford, 2003). For a long time, the lack of consensus and understanding has been the focus of concern. A recent local study posed a more positive scenario (Sin, 2005). The findings demonstrated that the majority of principals, teachers and parents supported the goals of integration. Over 50 per cent of the principals of inclusive schools and teachers in the study generally agreed to the inclusive education policy. It was also found that even though they endorsed the policy of integration in Hong Kong, they recognized the difficulties of its implementation.

It is well established that teacher preparation is an essential element of any education reform, with no exception for inclusive education. The traditional forms of special needs training are routinely criticized as inappropriate for overcoming classroom challenges and as inadequate in meeting the large demand from regular schools (Sin, 2004). Upon the implementation of the whole school approach to integrated programmes in Hong Kong in 2007, the EDB took the initiative to introduce a three-tier teacher professional development framework to build up teachers' professional capacity in catering for the needs of students with SEN. In addition, workshops, seminars and experience-sharing sessions were frequently organized for principals, teachers and other target groups as appropriate. While the government has great expectations for teacher education institutions to provide professional training for supporting the implementation of the policy, the challenge of teacher education is not to strive forward alone to remove all barriers, but to work collaboratively with relevant parties to develop an inclusive culture in the community. Regarding the paradigm shift, the aim of this chapter is to propose an Institute–School–Community partnership of teacher education for this purpose.

Empowering teachers for inclusive education in Hong Kong

Teachers' willingness to accept diversity and their commitment in effecting change has a decisive effect on the success or failure of special education reform. Teacher empowerment is, therefore, a central issue of concern in the inclusive education movement. A wide range of teacher development activities has been identified.

To enhance the implementation of inclusive education in Hong Kong, the EDB put in place a five-year Professional Development Framework on Integrated Education in 2007. In parallel with the formal teacher education in inclusive education at the teacher education institutions, the framework, initiated by the government, consists of structured courses for teachers on including students with SEN at three levels, namely: a 30-hour Basic Course on Catering for Diverse Learning Needs; a 90-hour Advanced Course on Catering for Diverse Learning Needs with a 30-hour optional School Attachment; and a series of 60-hour Thematic Courses on Specific SEN Types. Through attending the structured courses, teachers learn about the philosophy and concepts of inclusive education as well as adopting the whole school approach to inclusive education (Forlin and Sin, 2010). They gain knowledge about the characteristics of learners with a wide range of special needs and a spectrum of effective strategies to support children with SEN in inclusive settings. It is expected that these teachers will also develop appropriate attitudes to cater for diversity. Such course arrangement offers benefits to teachers in terms of the recognized special education training, in-depth study in the theoretical or controversial issues in inclusion, as well as individual reflections in school-based work.

In addition to the structured courses, the EDB also set up a School Partnership Scheme to empower schools to provide support to students with SEN. Special schools and regular schools with proficient experience in adopting the whole school approach to integration were invited to serve as special-school-cum-resource-centres (SSRC) or resource schools (RS). Teachers of the SSRC and RS share their knowledge and practices of teaching children with SEN with regular school teachers, as well as working collaboratively with them to set up networks of support. The School Partnership Scheme is a form of professional development for regular school teachers to empower them to work in inclusive settings. This goes in line with the recommendation of UNESCO (2005) to provide continuous training to inservice teachers for capacity-building. Teachers of SSRC and RS give direct support to regular school teachers in the field and assist them to acquire the practical knowledge about specific kinds of SEN, and the necessary skills to identify the strengths of children with specific SEN. They advise about planning programs to enhance SEN children's learning and modifying teaching methods to handle diversity in the classroom. Teachers also learn to work collaboratively in inclusive settings. These assist teachers to implement inclusive education successfully (Watson *et al.*, 2003). This mode of partnership emphasizes school-based support, experience sharing and knowledge transfer. However, the scope of expertise and the extent of involvement provided by the teachers of RS and SSRC are limited.

Barriers identified in professional training

A number of areas for upskilling the mainstreaming teachers for inclusion have been addressed in literature (Sin *et al.*, 2010). However, in the review of professional development for catering for diversity in inclusive education, some problems that reduce the effectiveness of teachers' professional training have been identified in the process of teacher education.

The Institute–School Partnership Scheme, in the form of a special school attachment, has been integrated into the courses of the five-year Professional Development Framework on Integrated Education. It signified the joint effort of the institute and special schools to help teachers explore knowledge and pedagogical practices in catering for diversity among regular and special school teachers. In the course evaluations of the structured programs and focus-group discussions with teachers of the Institute–School Partnership Scheme, it is evident that the participating teachers have developed some general understanding about inclusive education through attending the courses and acquired specific professional skills to cater for students' diversified learning needs through the support of the Institute–School Partnership Scheme. Despite the positive impact of exposure and substantial help, the scheme needed to be further improved in relation to the potential limitations. First, teachers attending the structured courses might not come from schools that receive support from SSRC or RS and so might not have benefitted from the accumulative effect of both sources. Second, special education teachers who are supporting the regular schools might not know what regular school teachers have learned from the structured courses and do not have a full understanding about what support they could best give them. Third, the diversified backgrounds of the regular school teachers make teaching the structured courses difficult. Some course participants come from schools that are already adopting the whole school approach to integrated education and have already learned a lot from the support given by SSRC or RS. Other course participants come from schools without SEN children and so have little knowledge at all about SEN. The challenge for the teacher educators to address the diversified background and understanding became a great concern. The joint effort of institute and special schools needs to be further strengthened to overcome these shortcomings.

It is evident that the long-term staff development plan for the implementation of inclusive education may not be appropriately formulated in some schools. Attending the training programs is the only school arrangement for staff development. In order to comply with the training policy, interested teachers may apply for study leave and take the courses. In some cases, if no teachers show interest, the principals will simply appoint those whom they think are available. According to the report of some participants, their schools do not have any plan for developing inclusive education and they do not have any responsibility in supporting other teachers in handling children with SEN after taking the course. Even if they understand the students' special needs better after the training and are prepared to take care of children with SEN, they do not have the required support from the other teachers nor the school administration. Their commitment that was inculcated in the course was then diminished after returning to the schools. Furthermore, instead of recognizing the teacher empowerment for inclusion, some schools still expected more community support and advice from what their teachers had learnt on the courses. Nevertheless, the lack of systematic planning for staff development in schools and the cultivation of their commitment to school practices are the areas to be further addressed in professional training. The mode of Institute–School partnership may not meet the needs of some schools.

Challenges to be overcome in the process of teacher empowerment

Inclusion is an ideal that is not easy to achieve, particularly the change of attitude. Many people think that all problems can be resolved once teachers have acquired the skills to handle children with SEN. This is not the case, though we provide teachers with a number of opportunities for professional development. In reality, committed teachers with proper training and experience in inclusive settings still find it difficult to implement inclusive education in schools. Children with SEN do not live in a vacuum. They do not just stay in the school with teachers and other educators. They interact with peers and with their parents. They may also get in touch with other people in their social circle. Up until now, many schools still find children with SEN a burden to them. Teachers find that their workload is increased if they have to take care of a class with great diversity. Parents of ordinary children complain about the misbehaviour of children with SEN, claiming that their own children have become victims. If they have a choice, many schools prefer not to admit children with SEN. Therefore, attempts to cultivate acceptance of SEN children in regular schools becomes a big challenge.

The concepts of inclusion are also controversial. There can be different forms of inclusive education, and the concepts of inclusive education continue to undergo change. In the early development of inclusive education in Hong Kong, the assimilation model was adopted. They were placed in separate classes in ordinary schools and struggled to meet the school requirements. At a later stage, the accommodation model was adopted. Children with SEN were put in ordinary classrooms. Teachers tried their best to cater for their needs. Currently, the EDB advocates the adaptation model. This goes in line with the international trend as UNESCO (2005) states, "Inclusion is about access to education in a manner that there is no discrimination or exclusion for any individual or group within or outside the school system." The research of Sin (2004) claimed that the school community is more accepting of inclusive education. The core issue is to what form of inclusive education they are referring. The inclusion policy could be operated more smoothly if there were a common agreement on the form of inclusive education.

Individual effort towards inclusion is inadequate for its development. Inclusion is more than just the rhetoric of respect for human rights. It is more than the practice of catering for the needs of children with SEN. It is about quality education for all. It not only benefits the children with SEN, but also children without SEN. The long-term goal is to create an inclusive society. Both teachers of regular and special education schools need professional development in the philosophy and the teaching skills needed for the implementation of inclusive education. Teacher education institutions should play a more proactive role in building a collaborative culture. If different parties work together, the concerted effort will help to achieve the goal more easily.

In short, attitude change, social consensus and collaborative effort are all foci of concern in addressing the barriers in teacher empowerment.

Tripartite Institute–School–Community partnership of inservice teacher education

To promote collaboration among various parties for the development of inclusive education, a tripartite Institute–School–Community partnership of inservice teacher education is required. The most that initial teacher education could provide is an overview of inclusive education to preservice teachers. Even if novice teachers enter the field with enthusiasm to make inclusive education work, their commitment will soon be extinguished by the difficulties they experience in teaching. As a matter of survival, novice teachers often teach according to the set curriculum without much flexibility. Only when their classroom survival is no longer threatened will they start to cater for diversity in the classroom by adapting the curriculum flexibly. Continuous professional development programs are, therefore, of utmost importance to help inservice teachers develop the curriculum adaptations and teaching skills to cater for children's individual differences. To this end, Crawford (2002) cautioned that large audience seminars and lectures are ineffective, and asserted that the best way is to enable practitioners to reflect on their own teaching experiences for evolving means to meet children's diverse learning needs. Along the same line, Vaughn *et al.* (1996) maintained that general and special teachers should be brought together to work collaboratively towards meaningful integration. Furthermore, Moont and Hui (2003) suggested that there is evidence showing that staff development programs conducted through partnerships between schools, communities and teacher education institutions are successful in actually changing classroom practices.

Teacher education institutions must play a significant role in leading the professional development of teachers in implementing inclusive education. In addition to providing structured courses on catering for individual differences, teacher education institutions should conduct research into inclusive education in order to formulate feasible ways of developing more inclusive schools. They should work out a shared vision of inclusive education with regular schools, special schools and the community so that everybody is working in the same direction. They should also help teachers to conduct action research projects to improve their teaching in inclusive classrooms. Not all teachers in regular schools can attend structured courses, hence teacher education institutions should support regular schools in school-based staff development programs as well in order to enable all teachers to implement the whole school approach to inclusive education. Teacher education institutions should also help special school teachers who provide support to regular school teachers to acquire professional skills to carry out that support task properly. Teacher education institutions could also provide project-based support to regular schools and special schools for developing specific teaching strategies to enhance the learning of SEN children. Education of the general public is also crucial for the acceptance of diversity by the community at large. Teacher education institutions might work in partnership with a range of different organizations for promoting this ideal.

At the school level, teachers of regular and special schools have a lot to share: regular school teachers need to know more about children's special needs and special school teachers need to know more about existing practices of regular schools. Curriculum adaptation and teaching strategies developed for children with SEN in inclusive schools could be shared with those in special schools. Regular schools and special schools could work together to develop the best policy for the practice of inclusive education in specific schools for the benefit of all children. Teachers of different regular schools could also share their experiences of successful inclusive education. Furthermore, special school teachers have a lot of knowledge and front line experience on teaching children with SEN. These are valuable resources for regular school teachers. In addition to the existing Institute–School Partnership Scheme, special schools could work with teacher education institutions to provide training in regular schools. In light of their expertise and experience, special school teachers might serve as speakers for seminars, as tutors for tutorial sessions in the structured courses, as practitioners for research-driven implementation projects and as consultants for case interventions. Special schools could be the site for school visits and attachments organized by either teacher education institutions or regular schools.

At the community level, transdisciplinary collaboration is considered the criterion of success in supporting students with SEN. Community resources are the alternative asset for professional development. These include resource materials, training, therapy and consultancy. Many non-government organizations run support groups, care units, training centres, rehabilitation services and parent resource centres for children with special needs. Tertiary institutions and schools will benefit from their support and services too. More importantly, professional dialogue among various parties will further enhance teacher empowerment and boost teachers' confidence in supporting students with SEN in schools. Site visits, centre observations, case conferences and therapeutic training will widen the horizon for school teachers and teacher educators. As a result, team collaboration will further advance the betterment of inclusive education. Under the new funding mode, more professionals, such as psychologists, therapists and counsellers from the community, are working with teachers in school based work for students with SEN.

Conclusion

In the light of the growing recognition of collaboration and support, this chapter proposes the development of a tripartite Institute–School–Community partnership of teacher education for Hong Kong teachers' continuous professional development in inclusive education. Attempts have been observed in projects such as the University–School Partnership Scheme, Institute–School Partnership Scheme, Teacher-in-Training Ambassador of Specific Learning Disabilities (Sin, 2010) and Best Buddies at The Hong Kong Institute of Education. They set up successful examples for teacher empowerment in inclusion by drawing the transdisciplinary effort in a tripartite Institute–School–Community partnership.

Contrary to the popular belief that education reform starts with structural change formulated by the government or the school administration, Hargreaves (1994) points out that if real change is to occur with effect, it involves changing the teachers' work culture. Structural change can easily be effected by the promulgation of government or school policies. However, changing the culture requires collaborative effort from all parties concerned in developing a shared vision that is built upon the tradition. Establishing a genuine collaborative partnership among the three parties – teacher education institutions; special and regular schools; and the community – will best help to prepare teachers for the move.

Not only could a collaborative partnership pool expertise from the three parties, it increases communication and saves a lot of wasted energy because of the lack of direction, duplication of effort, lack of understanding and competence to provide services to meet the actual needs of children with SEN in inclusive schools. More importantly, it helps to develop collaboratively an inclusive culture in the education sector. Partnership does not merely mean that people are working together. Partnership also encourages people to learn from one other. Not only will the system improve through collaboration, individuals as well will be also making progress. The development of genuine inclusion is a process and the road to community-wide inclusion will be both long and difficult. There is no short cut but there is always hope of success through the concerted effort of all who are willing to contribute. The tripartite Institute–School–Community partnership of inservice teacher education for inclusive education is an appropriate starting point.

References

Crawford, N. (2002) "The path to inclusive education for Hong Kong: A personal reflection", *Hong Kong Special Education Forum*, 5(1): 30–45.

Crawford, N. (2003) "Facing the challenges at last: A critical commentary on Hong Kong's approaches to integration and inclusion", in L. H. Hui, C. R. Dowson and M. G. Moont (eds), *Inclusive Education in the New Millennium*, Hong Kong: The Association for Childhood Education International – Hong Kong and Macau and Education Convergence, pp. 278–93.

Forlin, C. and Sin, K. F. (2010) "Developing support for inclusion: A professional learning approach for teachers in Hong Kong", *International Journal of Whole Schooling*, 6(1): 7–26.

Hargreaves, A. (1994) *Changing Teachers, Changing Times: Teachers' Work and Culture in the Postmodern Age*, London: Cassell.

Moont, M. G. and Hui, L. H. (2003) "Hong Kong needs to form its own philosophy for inclusive education", in L. H. Hui, C. R. Dowson and M. G. Moont (eds), *Inclusive Education in the New Millennium*, Hong Kong: The Association for Childhood Education International – Hong Kong and Macau and Education Convergence, pp. 308–22.

Sin, K. F. (2004) "Teacher education on catering for diverse learning needs", *Hong Kong Special Education Forum*, 7(1): 102–9.

Sin, K. F. (2005) "Research report of the inclusive education implementation in Hong Kong primary schools HKSES and HKPERA", *Hong Kong Special Education Forum*, 8, 169–70.

Sin, K. F. (2010) "The practice of inclusive education in an Asian city: Hong Kong SAR", in V. Timmons and P. N. Walsh (eds), *A Long Walk to School: Global Perspectives on Inclusive Education*, The Netherlands: Sense Publisher, pp. 63–82.

Sin, K. F., Tsang, K. W., Poon, C. Y. and Lai, C. L. (2010) "Upskilling all mainstream teachers. What is viable?", in Chris Forlin (ed.), *Teacher Education for Inclusion, Changing Paradigms and Innovative Approaches*, New York: Routledge, pp. 236–45.

UNESCO (2005) *Guidelines for Inclusion: Ensuring Access to Education for All*. Online. Available at: http://unesdoc.unesco.org/images/0014/001402/140224e.pdf (accessed 17 August 2011).

Vaughn, S., Schumm, J., Jallard, B., Slusher, J. and Saumell, L. (1996) "Teachers' views on inclusion", *Learning Disabilities Research and Practice*, 11(2): 96–106.

Watson, S. M. R., Hester, P. P. and Sandler, A. G. (2003) "Reforming teacher preparation programmes to include all students: A look into the future", in L. H. Hui, C. R. Dowson and M. G. Moont (eds), *Inclusive Education in the New Millennium*, Hong Kong: The Association for Childhood Education International – Hong Kong and Macau and Education Convergence, pp. 294–307.

Chapter 22

Teacher education for inclusion

A research agenda for the future

Lani Florian

Keywords: teacher education, inclusive education, professional development, research

Chapter overview

The Global Round Table on Future Directions for Teacher Education for Inclusion, held in Hong Kong in December 2010, provided an opportunity for colleagues in many parts of the world to come together to discuss the challenges and opportunities involved in ensuring that all teachers are prepared for inclusive education. This chapter provides a synthesis of the ideas that were discussed during the meeting and charts a course for researching this important and emerging area of teacher education and teacher professional development.

Teacher education

In today's world, there are many differences within and between countries in the ways in which teachers are prepared. Yet despite these differences there are common questions about how best to prepare teachers to teach all students in an increasingly diverse and global world. That there are common questions despite different approaches to teacher education raises interesting questions about the enterprise of teacher education more broadly. In particular, the field has been subject to increasing scrutiny as some national governments struggle to ensure an adequate supply of qualified teachers, while others question the relevance and adequacy of different forms of professional preparation. At the same time, many stakeholders are looking to the reform of teacher education in an attempt to 'fix' persistent educational problems such as underachievement, and the exclusion of students who experience difficulties in learning.

Inclusive education

The international 'Education for All' (EFA) movement has promoted inclusive education as a strategy to ensure that quality basic education is available to all children, youths and adults (UNESCO, 1990; 2000). Article 24 of the *UN Convention on the Rights of Persons with Disabilities* (CRPD) calls upon States to ensure that persons with disabilities, "can access an inclusive quality and free primary education and secondary education on an equal basis with others in the communities in which they live" (United Nations, 2006, Article 24(2b)). But inclusive education has proved difficult to achieve in practice. Teachers are often blamed for not having the necessary attitudes, knowledge and skills to implement a policy of inclusion and teachers themselves often report feeling unprepared for the challenge of inclusion. There is confusion about whether inclusive education is a school reform strategy that applies to all students or a process that focuses on those who have been previously excluded.

As the international discussion becomes more expansive with regard to diversity issues and the elimination of all forms of discrimination (Opertti and Brady, 2011), many countries continue to view inclusive education as a process of including previously excluded students in regular schools. Since students with disabilities are routinely excluded, inclusive education in many countries has focused on including students with disabilities and those identified as having special educational needs. For example, Smith and Tyler (2011), and Lu *et al.* (2011) provide contemporary examples of how inclusive education is discussed in two very different contexts, the United States (US) and China. These important discussions are necessary but some would argue they provide incomplete responses to the EFA vision of inclusive education as a strategy for achieving education for all as called for by international campaigners.

Given the rights-based imperative of inclusive education and the continued international support for it, it is more important than ever to articulate and clearly address the many broad and complex educational policy debates that surround inclusive education. This was a key task of the 48th International Conference on Education, Inclusive Education: The Way of the Future (UNESCO, 2008), which affirmed Article 26 (the right to education) of the UN Declaration of Human Rights and specified key recommendations in four topical areas: (1) approaches, scope and content; (2) public policies; (3) systems links and transitions; and (4) learners and teachers. Of key interest to the Global Round Table were the six recommendations pertaining specifically to teacher education.

1. Reinforce the role of teachers by working to improve their status and their working conditions, and develop mechanisms for recruiting suitable candidates, and retain qualified teachers who are sensitive to different learning requirements.
2. Train teachers by equipping them with the appropriate skills and materials to teach diverse student populations and meet the diverse learning needs of different categories of learners through methods such as professional development at the school level, preservice training about inclusion, and instruction attentive to the development and strengths of the individual learner.
3. Support the strategic role of tertiary education in the preservice and professional training of teachers on inclusive education practices through, *inter alia*, the provision of adequate resources.

4. Encourage innovative research in teaching and learning processes related to inclusive education.
5. Equip school administrators with the skills to respond effectively to the diverse needs of all learners and promote inclusive education in their schools.
6. Take into consideration the protection of learners, teachers and schools in times of conflict.

(UNESCO, 2008, p. 20)

The Round Table participants agreed that one of the most important aspects of educational policy is how best to prepare teachers to respond to the contested nature of inclusion, its multiple interpretations and the difficult issues associated with its implementation. It was also acknowledged, however, that in many countries a lack of teacher preparedness for the complex and sometimes conflicting demands of inclusive education is cited as a key problem of implementation. As a result, fundamental questions about what teachers need to know and be able to do in order to implement a policy of inclusion are being raised and it has become increasingly clear that very little research has directly addressed these important questions.

While there are many reports in the literature that describe different programs and approaches to preparing teachers for inclusive education, until recently few initiatives have been subject to rigorous evaluation or empirical investigation. With teacher education under scrutiny in many parts of the world, it is more important than ever to specify the professional knowledge and skills that different types of teachers need, as well as being clear about how such skills and knowledge will be acquired. A knowledge base upon which programs of research can be undertaken needs to be established.

Pugach and Blanton (2009) have developed a common framework for researching university-based teacher preparation programs in the US but this framework is not widely applicable outside of the US because many countries use different models of initial teacher education. More work needs to be done to identify the many different models that are in operation around the world and assess the extent to which their features are similar to or different from other teacher education models. Likewise, there is a need to map teacher professional development processes in different regions. Which teachers are afforded which forms of professional development? What are the policy contexts under which professional development opportunities are made available?

A global research agenda

As a first step in developing a global research agenda for teacher education, it is important to recognize the complex terrain that inclusive education occupies and begin to map that terrain. Although inclusive education is widely understood to be underpinned by common values and shared concerns, important differences in national context must be acknowledged. Accordingly there is a need to map national and regional differences in order to identify and better understand some of the complex issues surrounding what it means to prepare teachers to provide a basic education to all. The sections below report the four key issues that were identified at the Global Round Table. These issues form a framework within which future discussions about teacher education and professional learning for inclusion can be located.

Four key issues for teacher education for inclusion

1. The need for clarity about what inclusion means in different contexts and the implications for teacher education

An important common issue with regard to cultural, linguistic and developmental diversity is the recognition that in all countries there are students who are disabled and who are identified as having additional needs. In all countries, the numbers of students whose first language is not the language of instruction in school pose particular challenges. In most countries, there will be immigrant (or internally displaced) groups concentrated mostly (though not exclusively) in urban areas where the proportions of children from these groups within a particular school may be high. As a result of this and other changes, it is common for teachers to encounter a wide range of students in classrooms who have differences in prior experience, languages spoken and other cases. Together such variation may create difficulties in learning for students. Moreover, because teachers themselves tend to be trained locally for jobs in their home countries, they may have little experience of diversity or of the impact of growing up in poverty. There is a growing recognition that learning about and knowing how to respond to issues of diversity is an important part of mainstream teacher education (Blanton *et al.*, 2011).

In addition, in many countries there are children who do not attend school. In some cases this is because there is a shortage of school places, in other areas it is because the schools are not able to provide a meaningful education that is valued by the community. In such cases families may not be prepared to meet the costs of sending their children to school. Even where education is free, there are so-called opportunity costs of attending school, as children are less economically active when in school. Therefore, to achieve universal access to education it is not sufficient only to provide enough school places, but it is necessary to provide a quality education that is valued. Teachers are crucial to providing such a quality education and it is believed that teacher education is a vital component in the process of improving teacher quality.

But what are the elements of teacher education for inclusive education? How do these elements fit in with the national or state standards for acquiring qualified teacher status? The European Agency for Development in Special Needs Education is currently addressing these questions in a 27-country study of teacher education for inclusion in Europe. Of interest here is the extent to which the common values that drive inclusive education manifest themselves differently in terms of how teachers are prepared (Watkins and Donnelly, 2011). As a result, it is important to specify such variables as form, level, content and audience when researching and reporting on questions about teacher education and teacher professional knowledge for inclusion. Each of these variables is considered below.

Form

What form should teacher education for inclusion take? Should issues relating to inclusion be an essential aspect of all parts of the teacher education curriculum in what might be called an infusion model? Should teachers be prepared for inclusive education as part of initial teacher education or is this a topic that is better addressed as part of inservice teacher professional development. Or does it need both? Does it make a difference if the training is based in higher education or the schools, or a combination of both? To what extent is it possible to learn about inclusive education in schools that are not inclusive? Should acquiring the values, knowledge and skills to be an inclusive practitioner be an essential aspect of becoming a qualified teacher and if so how should this be assessed?

Level

In the many discussions about preparing teachers for inclusive education, there is often very little distinction between initial teacher education, continuing professional development, and higher degree work. There is also a wide variation between what it is to be a teacher in different countries. In some countries teachers may only have a brief period of training after completing elementary education. Other countries have an entirely master's level teaching profession. In addition, the status (and pay) of teachers varies hugely between countries. What are the implications of such policies for inclusive education? Do different levels of preparation affect teachers' willingness and/or capacity to teach diverse groups of children?

Content

What is the content of teacher education courses that prepare teachers for inclusive education? Is this content part of special needs education or something else? Curricular coherence has been identified as an important element of teacher education but what forms the basis of curricular coherence for teachers who are being prepared for inclusive education?

Audience

Who is the audience for the training? Regular class teachers or specialists? Are paraprofessionals such as teaching assistants included in the definition of the teacher for professional development purposes or should the training of this group be different? If so, how? Should parents and the voluntary sector have access to this training as providers as well as participants?

2. The need for high quality programs of research designed to help answer questions about what teachers need to know and be able to do to implement a policy of inclusive education

Preparing teachers to respond to diversity in ways that are just and equitable is a goal of teacher education in many countries but little is known about how to achieve this. Teacher education programs with their emphasis on the differences between sectors and different kinds of learners (e.g. early childhood, primary, secondary and special education) have perpetuated the belief that teachers should be prepared to work with particular groups of children on the basis of subject specialism, age and/or some type of special need. In turn this reinforces segregation between different forms of provision. Can teacher education programs prepare teachers to respond to the challenges of diversity without relying on different kinds of programs and services for different types of students? What kinds of studies are needed to answer these questions? How can the political and ethical issues associated with undertaking such research be addressed?

In spite of considerable interest in teacher education for inclusion, there has been little rigorous and systematic research on teacher preparation and continuing professional development, other than course evaluations that largely concentrate on the views of participants. What other kinds of research can be carried out in teacher education? To what extent should teachers be followed into the early years of their professional lives to gauge the impact of their initial teacher education? Is it possible to see benefits for students and developments in inclusion that are linked to particular kinds of teacher education?

3. The need to move away from binary distinctions between special and inclusive education

In recent years, an ongoing debate about what all teachers need to know and be able to do when children experience difficulties in learning has led to different solutions being suggested. In some countries teachers are prepared as specialist special educators in their initial training, in other countries all teachers are trained as regular class teachers, with courses and additional qualifications on special needs being available later in their careers. But what do mainstream teachers need to know and be able to do?

On one hand there is the argument that teachers need to know more about specific types of disabilities and special educational needs, how to identify and assess these, together with the specialist responses associated with addressing those needs. On the other hand, there are those who suggest that additional courses or information on specific difficulties and special education only reinforces the belief that students so identified are the responsibility only of those who have undertaken specialist courses and are appropriately qualified. The current context, however, is one where there is a lack of agreement about the nature and usefulness of specialist knowledge. While some argue that it is key to the success of inclusive education, others maintain that it creates a barrier to achieving inclusion. Nevertheless, the belief that good teaching is sufficient to create inclusive classrooms is too vague and there is a widely held belief that teachers are not being properly prepared to work in schools that are increasingly diverse and are attempting to be more inclusive. At the same time the international policy imperatives of inclusive education as a strategy for achieving EFA and equal educational opportunity under the UNCRPD means that many aspects of cultural, linguistic and developmental diversity are considered as part of the special or additional needs 'mix' in many countries, accounting for much of the variation between jurisdictions in terms of the provision of additional support and how teachers are prepared.

As a result, teacher educators interested in questions of how to prepare teachers to meet the needs of all students have had to be flexible in thinking about developing approaches that link issues of disability and SEN to a broader diversity agenda. And this flexibility has helped in articulating *how we collectively prepare teachers to teach all learners*. The European Agency for Development in Special Needs Education European study on teacher education for inclusion discussed earlier has identified some examples of innovative practice and has been developing quality indicators for teacher education (Watkins and Donnelly, 2011). Despite these innovations, however, it is also true that given the pressures on teacher educators in many countries to prepare teachers to deliver a national curriculum and raise standards, many university schools of education are not very interested in adding much from the diversity agenda to their already overloaded courses. Consequently, many primary and secondary teachers have received very little input on diversity or special education. It is not uncommon for preservice teachers undertaking a one-year full-time postgraduate teacher education diploma course to have as little as a one-hour lecture on special needs.

It is important to move beyond the debate about whether beginning teachers only need to know how to improve teaching and learning or whether they need more specialist knowledge about disability and children's learning needs. In the short time that preservice teachers are in initial training it is impossible to anticipate every type of difficulty they might meet in their professional lives. Further, it is important to bear in mind that there are differences of opinion about the nature of the content of special needs inputs – from calls for more information about disability types to sessions aimed at deconstructing the problematic nature of special needs education and its intersection with issues of race, class, poverty and gender. These debates have occurred while teacher education itself is also undergoing significant reform as preservice teachers spend more time in schools and university courses are more focused on content areas of the school curriculum. A recent report in England, *How Well New Teachers Are Prepared to Teach Pupils with Learning Difficulties and/or Disabilities* carried out by the Office for Standards in Education (Ofsted, 2008) was critical of many aspects of initial teacher education, particularly the quality of the input that student teachers receive while on school placements, because the schools do not have the necessary expertise or a sufficiently wide perspective on this work. Although teacher education programs have an important role in preparing teachers to accept individual and collective responsibility for improving the learning and participation of *all* children, there is little agreement about how it should be achieved. One thing is clear: the adults who work in schools need to be better at sharing their professional knowledge and skills with each other.

4. The need for new forms of professional collaboration

If binary distinctions between special and mainstream teachers are no longer useful, but schools remain staffed by different kinds of teachers because teacher qualification requirements and forms of provision within schools remain unchanged, what can teachers and other adults do to forge new forms of professional collaboration that begin to break down some of the barriers erected by the binary of special and mainstream education? There is a pressing need to develop and research new forms of professional collaboration that are targeted on an inclusive pedagogical approach (Florian, 2010; Florian and Black-Hawkins, 2010), which actively seek to avoid ways of working that mark some students as different. This will require new ways of working with and through others. The skills and knowledge required for working with adults as well as children should form an essential element of all courses.

A particular challenge facing teacher education is that the curriculum is organized around the subjects of the curriculum and phases of education. It may be possible to reform the curriculum of teacher education, but such reform must involve mainstream teacher education colleagues whose professional identity as well as their practice may have to be questioned and changed. If we aspire to train all teachers to be more inclusive in their pedagogy and classroom practice, there will be implications for mainstream teacher educators. How should this sensitive issue be approached and handled?

Conclusion

Despite the diverse challenges faced by countries in different parts of a changing world, there are many common patterns and trends. The Global Round Table participants were united in agreeing a rights-based approach to inclusive education was of fundamental importance. Teacher education and teacher professional development were seen as equally important and it was clear that in countries that do not have well-developed teacher education programs, teacher professional development may offer the most efficient and effective way forward. In countries with well-developed teacher education programs it is time to begin asking questions about the reform of those programs so that they prepare teachers to work in inclusive schools, particularly with regard to curricular issues. In addition, it is essential that programs of research are carried out that can help illuminate the ways in which preservice teacher education and continuing professional development can improve the experiences of children in inclusive schools. In summarizing the discussions of the Global Round Table, this chapter establishes a framework upon which a common foundation for research on teacher education for inclusion may be constructed. It is hoped that individual research interests and national policy contexts will benefit from as well as add to what has been outlined here.

References

Blanton, L. P., Pugach, M. C. and Florian, L. (2011) *Preparing General Educators to Improve Outcomes for Students with Disabilities*, Washington, DC: American Association of Colleges of Teacher Education and National Council for Learning Disabilities.

Florian, L. (2010) "The concept of inclusive pedagogy", in G. Hallett and F. Hallett (eds), *Transforming the Role of the SENCO*, Buckingham: Open University Press, pp. 61–72.

Florian, L. and Black-Hawkins, K. (2010) "Exploring inclusive pedagogy", *British Educational Research Journal*, 37(5): 813–28.

Lu, L., Su, X. and Liu, C. (2011) "Issues of teacher education and inclusion in China", *Prospects*, 41(3): 359–69.

Ofsted (2008) *How Well New Teachers Are Prepared to Teach Pupils with Learning Difficulties and/or Disabilities*, London: Office for Standards in Education (Ofsted).

Opertti, R. and Brady, J. (2011) "Developing inclusive teachers from an inclusive curricula perspective", *Prospects*, 41(3): 459–72.

Pugach, M. C. and Blanton, L, P. (2009) "A framework for conducting research on collaborative teacher education", *Teaching and Teacher Education*, 25(4), 575–82.

Smith, D. D. and Tyler, N. C. (2011) "Effective inclusive education: Equipping education professionals with necessary knowledge and skills", *Prospects*, 41(3): 323–39.

UNESCO (1990) *World Declaration on Education for All*. Online. Available at: http://www.unesco.org/education/efa/ed_for_all/background/jomtien_declaration.shtml (accessed 19 August 2011).

UNESCO (2000) *The Dakar Framework for Action. Education For All: Meeting our Collective Commitments*. Online. Available at: http://unesdoc.unesco.org/images/0012/001202/120240e.pdf (accessed 19 August 2011).

UNESCO (2008) *Inclusive Education: The Way of the Future – Conclusions and Recommendations of the 48th Session of the International Conference on Education (ICE) Geneva 25–28 November 2008*. Online. Available at: www.ibe.unesco.org/.../user.../48th_ICE/ICE_FINAL_REPORT_eng.pdf (accessed 19 August 2011).

United Nations (2006) *Convention on Rights of People with Disabilities*. Online. Available at: http://www.un.org/disabilities/convention/conventionfull.shtml (accessed 19 August 2011).

Watkins, A. and Donnelly, V. (2011) "Teacher education for inclusion in Europe", *Prospects*, 41(3): 341–53.

Index